The International Politics of Whaling

Peter J. Stoett

The International Politics of Whaling

UBCPress / Vancouver

Printed in Canada on acid-free paper ∞

ISBN 0-7748-0605-2 (hardcover)
ISBN 0-7748-0604-4 (paperback)

Canadian Cataloguing in Publication Data

Stoett, Peter John, 1965
  The international politics of whaling

  Includes bibliographical references and index.
  ISBN 0-7748-0605-2 (bound)
  ISBN 0-7748-0604-4 (pbk.)

1. Whaling. 2. Whaling – Political aspects. 3. Environmental
policy. 4. International economic relations. I. Title.
SH381.S82 1997   339.95'9516   C97-910087-9

This book has been published with the help of a grant from the Humanities and Social Sciences Federation of Canada, using funds provided by the Social Sciences and Humanities Research Council of Canada.

UBC Press gratefully acknowledges the ongoing support to its publishing program from the Canada Council, the Province of British Columbia Cultural Services Branch, and the Department of Communications of the Government of Canada.

Set in Stone by Brenda and Neil West, BN Typographics West
Printed and bound in Canada by Friesens
Copy-editor: Maureen Nicholson
Proofreader: Stacy Belden

UBC Press
University of British Columbia
6344 Memorial Road
Vancouver, BC V6T 1Z2
(604) 822-3259
Fax: 1-800-668-0821
E-mail: orders@ubcpress.ubc.ca
http://www.ubcpress.ubc.ca

Contents

Preface

This book adds the chapter of whaling to the expanding literature on global environmental politics, or international ecopolitics. It is by no means a closed chapter, but one that continues to unfold as controversies over whaling and habitat preservation remain unresolved. Nonetheless, a sufficient body of literature dedicated to the cetacean issue-area network has developed, warranting a book that engages in a broad political analysis, looking both to the past and the future.

Over the last few centuries, whales have received extraordinary human attention. Much of this attention, of course, focused on killing them. But the relatively swift ascent of the whale as environmental symbol, combined with the harsh economic realities inherent in hunting a vanishing population, conspired to produce what must be described as one of the more remarkable international regime transitions in ecopolitical history.

The International Politics of Whaling seeks initially to provide an entertaining and informative journey through the intertwined processes that resulted in the present condition of whales and whaling. Ultimately, we explore that condition itself, asking not only what whaling history teaches us about global problems that demand multilateral management, but which challenges face cetacean populations now that the harpoon no longer appears to be the principal threat to their existence. As well, we address the many ethical questions which the whaling story raises. For example, is a global moratorium on commercial whaling an instance of cultural imperialism? Is aboriginal whaling, which is today based on meeting subsistence and cultural needs, still acceptable?

This book grows out of research conducted for an article that appeared in the European journal *Environmental Politics* and my PhD dissertation, written at Queen's University, Canada, from 1992 to 1994. I later devoted a chapter in a book published by Nova Science Publishers of Commack, New York, to the whaling issue.[1] But even while working on the initial article, I realized that the issue was becoming so important to me, in terms of both my appreciation of whales and my fascination with international relations, that a book-length work was inevitable. The whaling issue strongly captures the inherent complexity of the political struggles to control or manage the global commons, especially the human competition and cooperation resulting from the controversy that so often ensues when territorial boundaries are unclear. The issue has brought to the surface stark contrasts between various foreign policy positions and, some claim, deep cultural factors, as well as overt tension between not only an increasing array of involved states, but also state and non-state, or sovereignty-free, actors. In turn, the limited recovery of whale populations presents a challenge to the present anti-whaling regime as the value-split between conservationist and preservationist philosophies becomes axiomatic.[2] Put roughly, conservationists wish to save whales only to the extent that this position facilitates future consumption. Preservationists insist on unwavering opposition to commercial whaling. While this ethical clash reflects orientations towards nature in general, the whaling issue has become especially charged.

The International Politics of Whaling details the historical development of the present anti-whaling regime, asking questions related to the more general themes of global environmental security (GES) and world politics. Within the field of international relations, there is an ongoing debate concerning the analytic primacy of various units of analysis: should we focus on the global, the national, the regional, the local? The introductory chapter explores this debate in relation to ecology, arguing that a multitude of perspectives is necessary to enhance our understanding of contemporary problems. This fact is evident in the field of conservation politics and regime analysis. Thus the framework for this book reflects a preoccupation with a wide lens for viewing world politics.

After these theoretical considerations, we examine, in necessarily limited detail, two endangered species: whales and whalers. The first have biological traits essential to our understanding of the politics that will determine their survival. Their size and intelligence are often cited as the reasons for whales becoming such an important symbol to environmentalists. Yet these factors worked against them in the days of barely regulated whaling, when yearly kills totalled over 50,000 mammals. The whalers themselves emerge from a rich history of human-ocean interaction, and those who remain find themselves displaced from their chief livelihoods. They include the men who laboured, often in dangerous conditions, on whaling vessels; and the capitalists and state managers who decided that excessive whaling made economic sense at the time. We also consider the revolutionary technological developments that permitted large-scale commercial pelagic whaling: the invention of the grenade harpoon, the factory ship, advanced tracking methods, and other qualitative changes that had tragic quantitative results.

We next look at the principal international organization (IO) charged with dealing with the whaling issue, the International Whaling Commission (IWC), the most important link in the issue-area network. As an IO, the IWC is typical: it operates on the basis of behind-the-scenes lobbying from opposing factions, incorporates scientific and economic factors in its decision-making, determines policy with official votes, and has limited power, depending primarily at this point on American influence to enforce IWC regulatory decisions. Its controversial politics are so extraordinary due to the excitement generated by the high-profile issue of cetacean survival, which has become symbolic of environmental health in general, as well as the opposition to this perspective from whaling states, in particular, Japan, Norway, and Iceland.

As mentioned, American policy has been axiomatic in the story I call *cetapolitics*. Yet, with domestic political changes, the seemingly united American foreign policy of opposition to all forms of commercial whaling is becoming an increasingly strained position. We examine that policy as well as the policies of other states instrumental to achieving the 1986 global moratorium on whaling – Australia, the United Kingdom, France, the former USSR (always an intriguing question mark), and several southern nations that joined the organization in the 1980s and began voting consistently with the American position. We also must examine the motives behind the pro-whaling lobby, most notably the highly vocal policy stance of the Japanese delegations to the IWC. Other non-governmental actors, such as the advocacy group Greenpeace and the aboriginal whalers, play significant roles. Together, these actors form the issue-area network under investigation; to focus only on governmental representatives is to exclude a great deal of the scope of contemporary international politics.[3]

This examination of IWC political activity and regulatory policy then leads to a discussion of several important, if insoluble, ethical dilemmas. Has an international regime evolved that has successfully defined the physical act of killing whales as immoral? Though many are inclined to think so, and indeed I once did myself, a closer examination reveals that this is hardly the case. Even Gro Harlem Brundtland, world-renowned environmentalist, supports Norway's whaling community. And there are difficult distinctions to be made between aboriginal or subsistence and small-scale coastal whaling. This issue has led to a serious clash of perspectives between the American and Japanese delegations to the IWC, at a time when US-Japan relations are increasingly strained by trade concerns. As well, a demand recently emerged that the American delegation to the IWC push for acceptance of a renewed gray whale hunt by the Makah people of Washington State. Because the American delegation supports a limited Inuit hunt for bowhead in Alaska, a treaty signed in 1885 with the Makah guarantees whaling rights, and the gray whale is no longer on the endangered species list (having recovered to pre-exploitation levels of roughly 23,000 whales), the demand will most likely be met. That result would upset commercial whalewatchers in the area, would concern environmentalists who fear that a renewed hunt will lead to a commercial hunt (sushi for Tokyo), and might encourage other coastal aboriginals, including those in Canada, to follow suit.[4] The Makah, who haven't hunted since 1926, argue that the traditional hunt is needed to restore a sense of cultural identity to their people. Here, a modern resource-oriented dilemma is taking shape, pitting various conceptions of rights against one another, and the IWC decision will be instrumental in the outcome.

But the most serious threats to long-term cetacean survival are the broader environmental problems that threaten habitat. So it is with many species, including our own. We investigate this theme both empirically – what are the main threats to whale habitat, and what, internationally, has been done about them – and theoretically. There are serious implications for the future of political networks concerned with environmental security, and for our intellectual perceptions of the commons. Though the establishment of non-whaling sanctuaries in the Indian and Antarctic oceans may appear to give geopolitical space to whales, some danger may be associated with this symbolic attention, for it may detract from more holistic thinking about ecosystems.

I should say here with unequivocal insistence that this book is not an effort to demonize whalers or even, for that matter, the commercial forces that made whaling such a short-sighted venture with so little ecological sensitivity. Both agendas have been pursued elsewhere, and a few words at this stage should be said. First, whaling is not by any means a profession that attracted any peculiarly abusive or negligent type of employee. The men (and, in rare cases, women) who worked on whaleships throughout the ages have been sailors and labourers, gathered mainly from lower-income segments of coastal society, short on education and, in many cases, fond of adventure. The work was physically and emotionally demanding. It was not, by any means, a glamorous business, though on occasion the pay was relatively impressive. The business tycoons who paid whalers to continue their profession long after it became evident that several species were on the brink, such as the infamous outlaw whaler Aristotle Onassis, deserve little less than moral condemnation. Similarly, the diplomats who tried to maintain excessive whaling as a way of industrial life, and, even more problematically, cultural life, may warrant moral outrage. But that is not the purpose of this book.

Second, the broad condemnation of societies that whale not only reflects a type of cultural imperialism, but also relies on a seriously flawed set of generalizations, such as the assumption that all citizens in pro-whaling states approve of whaling. Even in Japan, where the whaling-culture link has been made most strongly by the fisheries lobbyists, whalemeat is not considered the delicacy it once was, and whalewatching is slowly becoming a very popular Japanese pastime. Another assumption made by those who would quickly condemn Iceland, or Norway, for their whaling industries, is that governments have an immediate influence on whaling policies. This may not always be so, and it may not be the case that whaling policies can be used as some sort of barometer of the environmental sensitivity of governments. For example, the firm American position against even limited commercial whaling was a source of great pride to consecutive American administrations, yet it would take a rather supple imagination to consider the United States a stalwart leader on most other global environmental issues. Similarly, France pushed very hard for the Southern Ocean sanctuary, established in 1994, yet that same year, it began highly controversial shipments of plutonium to Japan by the way of the Indian Ocean, and the year before had conducted widely condemned nuclear weapons tests in the Pacific. There are no absolutes in world affairs and certainly no absolute angels. In the end, we must be aware of the complexity involved in any issue-area network, including its connections with others. *The International Politics of Whaling* captures this complexity for the benefit of students of international affairs and wildlife conservation and anyone else interested in planetary futures.

I would like to thank all those who helped me reach the final product. At UBC Press, I am very grateful to two excellent editors, Laura Macleod and Camilla Jenkins, as well as an extraordinary copy-editor, Maureen Nicholson. The secretarial staff at the Department of Political Science, University of British Columbia, deserves special mention; as does Don Blake, chair at the time, who helped me settle in. I thank several scholars for helpful discussion and advice, including Ellen Chu, Fred Knelman, Bill Graf, Mark Zacher, Eric Laferriere, Oran Young, Don Munton, Charles Pentland, Robert Boardman, and many others. A special debt of gratitude exists to the many people involved in the cetacean issue-area network who answered my questions, especially the IWC commissioners from various member-states (please see the list at the end of the bibliography), and in particular IWC secretary Ray Gambell. Thanks also to two anonymous reviewers, and to Megan Brodie for last-minute word processing. Naturally, any errors that appear in this book are the sole responsibility of the author.

For the essential support any writer needs, I thank family and friends. These are turbulent times for young academics, and one would be lost without the comfort and guidance those close to us provide. Most of all, for both inspiration and companionship, I thank my daughter Alexandra, otherwise known as my little dolphin.

This book is dedicated to the oceans, source of past and future human inspiration, exploration, and sustenance.

The International Politics of Whaling

1
Ecopolitics: The International Dimension

> The whole point of being a doomsayer is to agitate the world into proving you wrong or into doing something about it if you are right.
> – Les Kaufman, 1993[1]

Has any mammal inspired such romantic images of the sea and love for nature as much as the whale? The days of large-scale whaling, when men would stand ankle-deep in blood as they flensed the blubber from a slain leviathan, are behind us. Yet whaling remains a way of life for many small communities and, in others, would resume as such if not for distant political forces. Those forces are international in scope; they involve not only an international organization, the International Whaling Commission, but the foreign policies of states, and the actions of transnational activists. The whaling story is that of the science, actors, institutions, and normative context of what this book terms the *cetacean issue-area network,* and it is necessarily located within the broader sphere of international relations.

The International Politics of Whaling adds to an increasing number of texts that ask questions related to international affairs and environmental issue-areas, or what is often termed *global ecopolitics.* Contrary to popular belief, the majority of researchers interested in environmental problems, even those problems big and frightening enough to qualify as global, are not doomsayers. Their work is often inspired by previous efforts to instil a sense of urgency. However, most of the literature emerging today is much less dedicated to doomsaying than to evaluating policy options and/or producing critical reflections that can help us move beyond the present situation.[2]

It was not always this way. In the early 1970s, doom appeared to many to be just a question of time, and not necessarily a long time. The Cold War, despite episodes of detente, threatened us with nuclear annihilation. The population explosion was becoming a common theme, provoking fears of global collapse and mass migration. We were becoming aware of the rapid loss of soil in some areas and tropical rainforest in others. Oil spills were front page news. And the whales were dying.

This book details the political processes that reversed that last trend, and the controversies that continue to make cetacean survival a fascinating case study of international organization and ethical confrontation. If, as many people both in and out of the marine ecology field insist, the state of whale populations can represent a barometer for planetary health, then the earth's condition would appear to have improved as several species have made their trip back from the brink of extinction. Further, if this improvement is an indication of the state of human-nature relations, all is not doom and gloom. Some species, such as the gray and minke whales, have completely recovered from the ravages of full-scale commercial whaling. Others, such as the blue, right, and humpback whales, are much less in the clear or remain highly endangered. We simply don't know enough about whales, a point that inevitably surfaces in any cetacean-related study, to determine the health of entire species. But if there is reason for guarded optimism, much of this is due to the political evolution of the cetacean issue-area network.

The IWC has, as we will see, changed remarkably over the years: its orientation has been transformed from pro- to anti-commercial whaling. In 1982, enough anti-whaling votes were registered to pass an amendment to the Schedule of the International Convention for the Regulation of Whaling (1946), which, in effect, placed a moratorium on all commercial whaling.[3] The moratorium went into effect for the 1985-6 whaling season and remains in force to this day, more than ten years later. It was hailed by many as a substantial victory for the environmental cause. But this transformation has occurred under great stress, and today the IWC is the formal location of an ongoing battle between those who would resume commercial whaling if stocks were adequate (and some probably are), led by the Japanese; and those who would ban commercial whaling outright and forever, led – indisputably and continuously since the early 1970s – by the Americans. A Japan-US clash of values has rarely been so vividly dramatic. Both camps eye the other with suspicion. In effect, a Cold War over whale utilization has developed, and the long-term effect upon the IWC itself could well be disastrous.

Meanwhile, a heavily contested Revised Management Procedure (RMP), which would allow a rather conservative regulatory regime to monitor renewed whaling, is being delayed by an ostensible debate over its costs. The Norwegians continue a small (and perfectly legal) hunt of minke whales, the Japanese continue to hunt minkes under highly controversial 'scientific whaling' permits, and aboriginal groups from Alaska, Russia, and Greenland take a small subsistence catch. The anti-whalers' fear, however, is not that these extant fisheries will get out of hand, though many challenge their legitimacy. Rather, anti-whalers generally feel that, should the official IWC moratorium be lifted, in addition to the loss of a symbolic milestone, we might see the resumption of profit-motivated overhunting as in earlier, darker decades.[4] Yet if the safety of whales is at all contingent upon the strength and, even, survival of the IWC, they are already in trouble. Put simply, the moratorium is slowly rendering the IWC a less effective body, which Iceland has recently left, and Norway or Japan may also leave in frustration.

In the awkward context of international relations, if we link the long-term survival of cetaceans to the control of whaling, we arrive at the reluctant conclusion that the IWC should allow some whaling to take place lest it become a useless international body. For example, the moratorium, as a result of the many factors detailed in this book, penalizes certain small-scale whalers while others are allowed to continue. The arguments to justify this discrimination are not by any means decisive ones. And fears that lifting the moratorium will result in a return to carnage are not well founded. Due to a normative shift that has taken place in many states in the last few decades, a large market for whale products is unlikely. Again, put simply, the IWC offers an opportunity for a global dialogue on cetacean survival that could be lost if uncompromising ideological divisions persist.

Further, the greatest threat to today's whales is not the resumption of large-scale whaling. In fact, given the adherence to the partly negotiated RMP, resumed whaling will probably not threaten the species themselves. Arguably, the greatest threats to cetacean survival are the problems associated with industrial, agricultural, and marine activities that impinge on the ecological health of the oceans themselves. Avoiding the destruction of the oceans is perhaps the greatest institutional challenge faced by the international community, which remains locked in patterns of competitive economic and resource conflict. We might not be able to meet this challenge, of which the cetacean issue-area network is but a small part. This point needs mentioning at the outset lest anyone suspects I am incapable of a bit of doomsaying myself.

To contextualize the dilemmas presented by contemporary whaling questions, we will first deal with the special question of the commons within the field of global ecopolitics. Since whales are generally highly migratory and live in the open seas, whaling has always been an international question. Thus, we address below the international dimension of environmental regulation, in particular, the formation of regimes designed to manage the commons. This discussion leads to the framework for the rest of this book.

The International System: The Special Issue of the Commons

Whaling is a primary example of the difficulties involved in the global management of the commons. Whales are viewed as common property resources by regime theorists interested in the question of interstate cooperation. Wilfred Beckerman has summarized this viewpoint well. Referring to emissions of greenhouse gases, he notes the classic tragedy of the commons 'refers to situations in which nobody can be excluded from the use of an asset – such as common grazing land, or fishing grounds, or the atmosphere [but] one person's use of the asset reduces the amount available to other potential users ... Unrestricted use of the asset can easily lead to over-use, so that only if some voluntary or enforcement mechanism is introduced can the supply be matched to the demand.'[5] In a world of competitive states, the pure market fails us, and some form of multilateral state intervention becomes vital.

The essential economic problem, then, is that everyone has an incentive to conserve the commons together, but an incentive individually to exploit them. This problem becomes a political issue when cooperation is necessary to balance these counter-incentives. Or, as Stephen Krasner puts it, what he terms liberal cooperation theory holds that 'the basic challenge for states is to overcome market failure, the situation in which individual rational self-interested policies produce outcomes that leave each state worse off than it might otherwise have been.'[6] The added dimension of environmental concern, therefore, demands that we move beyond asking how states can share resources, towards how they can simultaneously conserve or preserve them.

Solutions to typical problems of the commons are elusive. Many have argued that the privatization of land or other resources will foster a sense of environmental responsibility in those entitled to the property. This proposition is debatable within national confines, but it is even less clear in the international arena, where privatization is akin to territorialization. The 1982 Law of the Sea Convention (LOSC) designated new 200-nautical-mile Exclusive Economic Zones, where coastal states would have not only resource rights but also inherent environmental responsibilities. The hope was that, inside the 200-mile limit, increased coastal authority by individual states would lead to better management. Instead, 'coastal countries such as Canada and the United States displaced overseas fleets from Europe and Japan with new programs and subsidies to build up their domestic fleets [then] scooped up cod and salmon on both coasts with alarming speed, and disastrous results.'[7] Further, areas of the commons, such as the open seas and atmosphere, are not amenable to the expansion of national territories.

Some proposed solutions to problems of the commons do not necessarily reflect the political complexities involved. Norman Myers, taking a cue from the editorial position of the *Economist*, believes the question of whale preservation 'could be resolved at a stroke' if all whales were declared the property of humankind with property rights vested in a United Nations body, 'whereafter anyone wishing to exploit a whale, whether consumptively or not, would have to purchase an exploitation permit at the latest market price. In turn, market price would be determined by all consumers in the marketplace, including conservationists who wish to outbid Japanese whalers for a whale permit and then sit on it (or ceremoniously burn it in the global village square).'[8] Those who want to kill whales would have to outbid those wishing to preserve them, and the force of the United Nations would be behind the result.

Not only would it be a difficult task to set a 'market price' as Myers suggests, but we could anticipate rather stiff opposition from those dependent on whaling, including the aboriginal peoples represented by the biggest non-whaling country, the United States. In fact, the adoption of this proposal could lead to disaster. Its success is contingent on the assumption that anti-whalers will have the financial means to 'buy' enough whales to put whaling out of business for good. This proposal is not only uncertain at best, but fails to mention the vital necessity for a strict regulatory regime should whaling resume. Finally, limiting such a system to whales seems arbitrary. What about smaller cetaceans and fish, atmospheric and marine pollution, and all the other aspects of the commons? Would not an entirely new and authoritative United Nations be necessary for such a task? And is such an institution likely to evolve from the present one?

Such market-based approaches put the onus on environmentalists to find economic values for these perceived 'goods,' and this tactic presumes the acceptability of a certain utilitarian perspective on natural resources and wildlife. In this perspective, without some economic value the commons become irrelevant. Thus we have attempts to measure, for example, the aesthetic value of sunsets in monetary terms or the dollar value of species preservation.[9] Though assessing the natural world adds an environmental spark to the dismal science of economics, it is not always helpful to reduce questions of cooperation and the divergence of interests to an economic equation when attempting to institutionalize agreements. For now, we seem destined to muddle through with more conventional modes of diplomatic interaction and regulation. That is, unless that mode breaks down altogether, which is a very real possibility in the case of the troubled IWC.

A central question for scholars is the issue of national sovereignty, the cardinal principle of the Charter of the United Nations. Does the increase in transboundary pollution problems justify infringements on the sovereignty of states? Does the need to regulate the commons, or at least to avoid the tragedy of the commons, demand a pooling of sovereignty in certain issue-areas? Have some issue-area networks served, through the creation of institutions designed to mitigate environmental damage or improve telecommunications (to use but two examples), to provide 'governance without government'[10] in the international arena, or even to threaten the long-term future of the nation-state as predicted by the functionalist[11] school? It is clear, in the legal sense, that the principle of national sovereignty remains sacrosanct. In 1962, the UN General Assembly adopted a resolution that referred to the 'inalienable right' of all states to freely 'dispose of their natural wealth and resources.'[12] Malaysia made particular reference to this precept during the forestry negotiations leading up to the United Nations Conference on Environment and Development (UNCED) in 1992. Moreover, the resolution relates to a common North-South sticking point as southern elites claim any global environmental agenda infringes on their sovereignty.[13] Principle Two of the Rio Declaration asserts that 'states have ... the sovereign right to exploit their own resources pursuant to their own environmental and developmental policies.' The international politics of whaling suggests that, ultimately, sovereignty remains a vital concern for decisionmakers, even when dealing with non-sovereign mammals that travel widely in the global commons, in this case the high seas.

Japan, by staying in the IWC, has effectively surrendered the right to decide what its coastal whaling communities can do. While the central Japanese government takes extraordinary measures to protest this imposition, it has so far complied, though a black market trade in whale products exists in Japan. Norway rejected the imposition and insists on registering an objection to the 1982 moratorium, which legally allows it to hunt minke whales today. Canada resigned from the IWC in 1982, at least partly because the federal government at the time rejected the idea that an international body should make decisions affecting remaining whaling communities in the Canadian North.[14] The issue is tricky, because it relates to actions taken not only by nationals within their territories (including the 200-mile exclusive economic zone established by the Law of the Sea), but also by individuals in areas where no one has territorial jurisdiction.

Another question is cost allocation, or who should pay for international efforts to save the commons. With issues such as ozone-layer depletion and global warming, an obvious and potentially decisive North-South split looms. The agreements reached today, such as the Montreal Protocol to the ozone-layer agreement and the Convention on Global Warming, will set important precedents for cost-sharing and the question of sovereignty. R.E. Benedick concludes: 'As a consequence of the ozone issue, the richer nations for the first time acknowledged a responsibility to help developing countries to implement needed environmental policies without sacrificing aspirations for improved standards of living.'[15] Similar debate clouded the negotiations for a Biodiversity Treaty where, 'even before the negotiation began, there was a history of disagreement about the allocation of the economic benefits and technological advances derived from Southern biodiversity.'[16] Principle Seven of the Rio Declaration makes note of the 'different contributions to global degradation' and resulting 'common but differentiated responsibilities.'[17] The basic argument is that, because the South has suffered from the North's indulgence in industrialism and, even more directly, in colonialism, future resource-sharing agreements must reflect this principle.

Though it is not well known, southern hemispheric, or 'developing'[18] nations, did play a large role in transforming the IWC. But the North-South split has been less axiomatic than the split between the United States plus the 'like-minded states,' which reject commercial whaling outright, and Japan and Norway (and, until its resignation, Iceland), which would resume limited commercial whaling. However,

the question of cost certainly is pivotal here: the main formal obsta-
cle keeping the IWC from adopting the RMP is the question of who
should pay for its implementation. Some argue that this cost should
be the responsibility of the whaling nations, which derive direct
benefit from killing whales. Others propose that the cost is an obligation of the entire IWC membership, which would gain from a strict
management of the commons that avoids the overhunting of the past.

These are just a few of the inevitably thorny questions that surface
when multilateral regimes are formed. We turn now to a brief overview of these admittedly fuzzy conceptions, including how they have
been categorized in the literature.

Multilateral Regimes

Robert Keohane defines institutions as 'persistent and connected sets
of rules, formal and informal, that prescribe behavioral roles, con-
strain activity, and shape expectations.'[19] In the environmental field,
the rise in scholarly concern with international institutions reflects
the vast increases in multilateral contractual arrangements in the last
three decades, and a willingness by states to accept some (though
exactly how much is contestable) limits to their sovereignty. Already
it is obvious that 'United Nations policymaking in ecosystem issue
areas [has] focused primarily on the creation of international regimes
[which] frequently required new institutions for implementation and
monitoring.'[20] In 1992, Hillary French found 'more than 170 environmental treaties concerning subjects of shared concern: acid rain, ocean
pollution, endangered species protection, hazardous wastes export,
and the preservation of Antarctica, as well as ozone depletion.'[21] Jim
MacNeill acknowledges that 'extensive institutional structures' exist,
but reminds us they lack 'political strength, cohesion, depth, and
financial capacity.'[22]

The subfield within the discipline of international relations known
as *regime analysis* stems from mainstream (and mainly American) academia's mid-1970s preoccupation with the concept of interdependence
in world politics. Regimes have been defined, succinctly and now
famously, by Krasner as sets of principles, norms, rules, and decision-
making procedures around which actors' expectations converge.
Regimes are often regarded as 'intervening variables': they do not
change the fundamental structures of political power, but they may
influence the ultimate outcome of behaviour emanating from the
international system.[23] Of course, we may be more or less enthusiastic

about just how 'intervening' these variables are. This point doesn't always seem to matter: in its current usage, the term regime has acquired fantastic flexibility. A loose definition of what exactly constitutes a regime – and a tight definition is unnecessarily constraining – leads to the conclusion that most areas of international collaboration can be so described, whether or not some hegemonic leader provides the 'public good' of leadership. What were once functionalist projects in political integration, for example, have become regimes.[24]

Oran Young has identified three categories of regime formation: self-generation, negotiation, and imposition.[25] The first process involves little, if any, active diplomacy: a convergence of interests makes a regime spontaneously emerge. We might argue that the IWC, formed in 1946, was initially an instrument that helped cement such a regime. All of the original members were united in the fundamental principle that commercial whaling was not only acceptable behaviour but quite necessary following the hardships caused by the Second World War. The regime also served to relieve potential strains among members regarding access to the resource. As we see in ensuing chapters, the present political configuration is quite different. Because the IWC engages in a continuous process of bargaining, we may be looking at a negotiated regime as well. For example, any major changes in the regime's approach to its particular problem-set requires a large majority. Furthermore, the IWC ultimately demands consensus, given that members always have the option of filing a formal objection and opting out, as the Norwegians have done with regard to the minke whale hunt. However, because of the priority the American government has given this issue-area, and its (rather uneven) readiness to engage in economic sanctions against detractors, we might even have an imposed regime here, one that since 1982 has been foisted upon whaling states.

Another key question in the regime literature asks if regimes are in fact effective in achieving their initial purposes. One way to approach this question is to ask if regimes make a difference. Do they influence the outcomes of events, or are they mere epiphenomena? The issue has been put many ways, but all the empirically oriented formulations hinge on effectiveness as a dependent variable. That is, if we can discover which factors lead to effective regimes, then we can in future strive to reproduce those conditions and thus establish the context for successful environmental problem-solving at the international level.

Naturally, this strategy raises many problems regarding the external validity of such generalizations.

At its heart, then, the common resource regime literature is most focused on changing the *behaviour* of selected groups, and is characterized by the systemic study of the behavioural impact of extant regimes. Thomas Bernauer expresses a cautious optimism in a recent essay published in *International Organization:* 'If the degree of success in international collaboration can be influenced by the institutions we establish and operate, we can be more successful if we know how to design institutions that produce the desired effect.'[26] An effective regime or institution – the terms are different, but they are commonly used interchangeably – 'channels behaviour in such a way as to eliminate or substantially to ameliorate the problem that led to its creation.'[27]

Two issues that generate particular concern are those of leadership and compliance. Do regimes need strong leaders, especially those states that are involved in international relations and commit ample resources to maintaining related institutions? And, how can states be induced to comply with the political outcomes, or decisions, taken at the institutional level? Andrew Moravcsik notes that regimes 'foster compliance with international norms not by altering the external incentives facing a unitary state, but by altering the domestic incentives facing societal groups and politicians, thereby shifting the domestic coalitions that define state preferences.'[28] We return to these important questions in our concluding chapter, after our analysis.

Several behavioural models of regimes are put forward by Levy, Osherenko, and Young. Regimes can be viewed as *bestowers of authority;* adherence to the rules set out by the relevant international institution is related to the legitimacy of that institution as seen by its members. No doubt, the IWC manages to maintain a certain legitimacy, because the work of the Scientific Committee, though politically troubled, is generally well respected.[29] Also, we have Japan's continued, if openly reluctant, adherence to the outcome of official IWC votes. However, so many exogenous factors are involved that it is difficult to say if the rules established by the International Convention for the Regulation of Whaling and the process of cooperation within the IWC is responsible. When Iceland pulled out in 1992, it clearly did not feel constrained to stay within the IWC, and Norway has flagrantly countered the total moratorium with its restricted minke hunt. However, since Norway launched formal objections, it is not in truth violating the rules, even if many would claim it is violating the present spirit, of the convention. In turn, Norway and Japan argue that the moratorium violates the spirit of the convention. A more important concern, perhaps, relates to the future legitimacy of the IWC, which is indeed in jeopardy.

Regimes can also be seen as *utility modifiers,* altering the cost-benefit analysis prognosis of actors. In other words, joining an institution changes the international landscape for decisionmakers. States like the US will have a large impact on other actors in the system. We might also argue that even American behaviour is at least partly modified and influenced by the institutions to which it belongs. The United States is hardly known for a strong environmentalist ethic in world affairs, though the current Clinton administration usually fares better than the Bush-Reagan era in most evaluations. Yet at the IWC, the US is a vociferous defender of the anti-whaling position. It is also, however, just as vociferous a defender of the aboriginal whale hunt. The establishment of the Convention on International Trade in Endangered Species of Wild Fauna and Flora (CITES) is often regarded as an international development that contributed to changing perceptions as well. For example, during the heated debate in 1989 over including the African elephant in Appendix A of CITES, the initial Japanese reluctance was overcome. This change resulted from the desire, in the words of the head of the Japanese Environment Agency, to 'avoid isolation in the international community.'[30] It is clear that, through American influence, membership in the IWC has modified the behaviour of the major whaling states, though other variables are involved, including the drastic fall in whale stocks and reduced demand for whale products.

Regimes are, with little doubt, *enhancers of cooperation,* to varying degrees. International institutions can act as *confidence-building measures,* an old term invented for the purpose of reducing East-West military tensions during the Cold War. They can, for example, increase transparency, giving all participants a better view of what others are doing. This function will be vital if the RMP is ever put into effect; it is also important in regimes designed to alleviate conflict over other fisheries and natural resources in general.

Further, and returning to a question raised earlier, regimes can also be considered *learning facilitators*. International organizations in particular can 'initiate processes of social learning in which actors alter their behaviour.'[31] For example, and this point reiterates an old liberal theme expounded by writers such as Immanuel Kant, new ideas are generated by cross-national exchanges of information, helping to form a voluntarily rational global society.[32] The IWC produces a great deal of information related to whale survival, but the learning process is more complicated than data compilation. When the movement towards a complete moratorium gathered steam in the early 1970s, many nations did not have a large, if any, stake in cetaceans as a resource. But in 1972, the publicity surrounding the United Nations Conference on the Human Environment, in Stockholm, helped change attitudes, as did intense anti-whaling campaigns by western NGOs. Learning, in the sense of becoming aware of an issue, takes place on a number of levels. (This fact is one reason for preferring the inclusive term *issue-area network* to describe the set of multi-levelled actors involved in any case study.)

Granting institutions an even stronger role in causal significance, a perspective largely rejected by the *realist* school in international relations theory, we might argue that participation in institutions actually *modifies the roles* played by various actors, state and non-state alike. This approach can, of course, lead to tautology. For example, the United States is clearly the leading anti-commercial whaling nation within the IWC. American delegates are simply adamant about their position. As the IWC has developed, especially since the political achievement of the moratorium, the Americans have become even more attached to this role. Put simply, IWC annual meetings are fully expected, by participants and the media, to be showdowns between the American and Japanese delegations, the two largest and most powerful participants with quite opposing perspectives. But which came first: a role as defined by interaction within the institution, or the individual foreign policies, decided in Washington or Tokyo, then pursued at the meeting? Thus, as suggested by Moravcsik, regimes might be seen as *agents of internal realignments* in the domestic politics of the involved nation-states.

It is difficult to isolate the factors that affect a regime's ability to regulate an area of activity. Instead, we might ask whether the environmental impact of that activity would have been worse had the regime not existed. This strategy is the general *counter-factual* approach taken by Ronald Mitchell in his prize-winning analysis of the shipping sector, which concludes that regimes do indeed matter, though which regulatory tactics they employ is fundamentally important.[33] The essential question then becomes: would improvements (or, on the other hand, worsening conditions) have been possible in the absence of a regulatory network? If the regime is viewed as a variable, can we discount the effect of possible intervening variables? Indeed, this determination might not be possible in a social science field, where replicable experiments are often not an option.

Without the IWC, the whaling industry may well have followed the 'bioeconomic logic' explained by George Small and presented in Chapter 2, and we might not have any great whales left. Then again, we might argue instead that it is more likely that the whaling industry shut down because not enough whales were left to justify continued operations, and the initial costs of whaling fleets had been recovered. Fred Pearce writes that hunting blue whales declined in the 1960s as the Japanese simply couldn't find any more whales to kill. 'Slowly and painfully, the hunt subsided, as much due to financial realities as to either the rapidly advancing science of estimating whale numbers or the concerns of environmentalists.'[34] At one point, the Soviet Union was one of the primary pelagic whaling nations and, in the late 1950s, constructed 'the two largest factory fishing ships in history: the *Sovetskaya Ukrania* (launched in 1959) and the *Sovetskaya Rossiya* (launched in 1961).' These ships, roughly the size of aircraft carriers, represented a huge investment. The result, writes cetologist and anti-whaler Robert Payne, was that those like him who attended IWC meetings 'had to sit and listen to the delegation from the Soviet Union use every trick, every scam, every absurd argument possible to keep their whaling industry alive long enough so that the cost of these two fuel-guzzling white elephants could be amortized ... [Eventually] the ships were finally and mercifully too dilapidated to continue operating in such a remote area as the Antarctic without a major refit.'[35] Indeed, the present state of the Russian whaling fleet remains a primary reason experts doubt the Russians will resume whaling.[36] In short, a plethora of factors was involved in the cessation of commercial whaling: the reduced market, changes in perception in the West, increased costs of whaling, and political events within the IWC. To ignore any one of these interrelated variables would produce an incomplete analysis.

Indeed, analyses that rely solely on the study of regimes may be incomplete in many ways. Though liberal assumptions permeate the regime literature, it is quite desirable to put some of the more optimistic aside.[37] Regimes, if we view them as causal agents in the international system, cause problems as well as provide possible solutions.

For instance, while regimes articulate agendas for action, they may restrict actions as well, by defining unacceptable and acceptable behaviour and discourse. Restrictions may amount to delegitimization, involving labelling a certain type of behaviour as illegitimate and proscribing it. Such regimes have been specifically referred to as *global prohibition regimes:* they are guided by norms that 'strictly circumscribe the conditions under which states can participate in and authorize these activities and proscribe all involvement by nonstate actors.'[38] The international condemnation and eventual formal abolition of the slave trade is often used as an example of these norms in action. At the same time, regimes have a corresponding positive function of legitimizing behaviour, and what is considered acceptable behaviour changes over time. Thus, the IWC was originally viewed as a whalers club that clearly served to promote the interests of whalers. Many argue the IWC should retain this initial function, while others insist the institution has changed so fundamentally that it has become another regime altogether.

More generally, the tendency to equate regime formation with a progressive evolution in world affairs overlooks the dual nature and, at a policy level, the possible manipulation of such institutions. In a reflective essay, one of the leading proponents of the regime perspective is quick to point out that 'not all cooperation has worthy purposes – governments often cooperate to make war, to exploit others, and to conceal the effects of their depredations.'[39]

As importantly, the role non-governmental actors play in international organizations is essential and often overlooked by the regime literature. One of the greatest challenges to conventional international political theory made by ecological crises stems from the need to consider non-governmental participants in any evaluation of the situation. As Simon Dalby writes: 'Focusing on states as the [sole] providers of security limits the possibilities of active intervention by NGOs (nongovernmental organizations), social movements, and individuals in the process of international politics.'[40] Some scholars even suggest we adopt the term 'world civic politics' to describe what the latter actors are doing.[41] James Rosenau has referred to them as 'sovereignty-free actors'[42] organized in complex groups such as Friends of the Earth.[43] They are often strategic political actors: the use of the media, as we will see in Chapter 3, was an important strategy for NGOs involved in the whaling issue.[44] Here we often find the most vocal proponents of the need for a new ethics related to the environment, and for fundamental changes in human-nature relations.[45] The case of whaling offers some inspiration, since we have largely stopped killing them. But a look at the IWC shows the divisive outcome of institutional and foreign policy decisions based on calculations of national interest. And the ethical questions that the whaling case raises are very tough indeed.

Three Analytical Components

The International Politics of Whaling focuses on the questions raised above by introducing three essential components in the study of global environmental problems. As mentioned in the preface, this book is about whales, whalers, and anti-whalers, but it is also an attempt to understand the political context in which these actors operate. There is no single perspective on world affairs that, by itself, allows us such a view. In an unabashedly eclectic spirit, therefore, we offer the framework for analysis used for this study, though it is not a key that can unlock the universe, or a shovel to unearth the roots of world politics.[46] This framework seeks to carry on the tradition Dennis Pirages introduced in his 1978 textbook, which asked critical questions concerning the agenda, actors, and power relations that constitute global ecopolitics. Pirages writes, '[Ecopolitics] presents the emergence of broader ecological, ethical, and economic issues and conflicts in international politics as a partial substitute for the narrower military power issues typical of the international politics of the industrial era.'[47]

Again, there are three essential analytical components to global ecopolitical issues as conceived here: environmental problems, political developments, and normative considerations. Though they are presented as separate components, they are all interrelated. The word 'global' is used specifically to connote the international character of problems such as ozone-layer depletion, soil erosion, atmospheric warming, ocean pollution, and transborder pollution flows. The chief point is that these issues cannot be solved by any single individual or nation-state. They demand at least collaboration, if not an ever more inspired cooperation. They need not be issues related to the theme of the global commons, but these points obviously qualify. This book proceeds to deal with global problems, political developments, and normative considerations, chapter by chapter, as they pertain to the cetacean issue-area network. First, we must study the environmental concern itself: in this case, the biology of cetaceans, and the objective identification of threats to environmental health, here the recognition that whales were nearing the point of extinction. Put briefly, the environmental entity – be it whale, fish, river, marsh, ozone layer, even outer space – must be identified, and the impact of human activity upon it must be explored. Second, we must look at the actions of state and non-state actors and the formation or transformation of international institutions and social movements. In the cetacean issue-area, I have labelled this process *cetapolitical analysis*. Third, we must examine and ponder the normative or ethical background for issue-areas. So much social science deliberately tries to avoid this step that it is often charged with chasing the impossible dreams offered by positivist inquiry. The obvious corrective is to deal explicitly with the tough ethical questions about rights and obligations and their distribution.

This framework may seem inductive. We begin with the nature of the problem. We next look closer at political processes that have evolved, and the ethical dilemmas evident in attempts to deal with the problem. We then ask what implications can be derived for the larger questions affecting, and affected by, our issue-area. While this sequence may be advantageous for investigation, it does not imply a linear causation. We could reverse the sequence and argue that the special place of marine issues in the global commons affects international regime politics, which affect normative thinking, which affects human-nature interaction and thus the environment itself. Put another way, normative thinking creates possibilities for regime formation or transformation, which leads to gradual changes in the broader international system, which ultimately affects individual species that are threatened with extinction. Here, I make no necessarily futile attempt to decide where this chain of events begins or ends, or which component, if any, in a given situation exerts the strongest influence. In other words, all three of the analytical components are interdependent and essential.

We return to these methodological themes in the conclusion of the book. For now, I present a brief elaboration of the framework.

Science and Knowledge
Within the environmental field, a dominant paradigm – ecology – has emerged, through which scientists see the world's problems. This development does not mean scientists belong to a sect that demands orthodoxy, but some practices are common. For example, established

techniques of measurement determine what environmental problems exist and what alternative responses are explored. Naturally, none of this activity takes place within a political vacuum, and, in fact, the whaling issue demonstrates the important link between science and politics. Many cetologists emerge from their studies with very strong anti-whaling perspectives (Robert Payne, quoted earlier, being the most notable), while others argue that the IWC anti-whaling agenda is unscientific, neglecting the significance of whale stock recovery. Indeed, the chairman of the IWC Scientific Committee recently resigned over this contentious matter.[48] In the words of one observer, the plight of the whale generated 'strong public attention [that] seems to have muddied the waters between science and politics.' Based on interviews with Norwegian representatives in the Scientific Committee, the same observer concludes that 'scientific discussions ... on politically sensitive issues are often characterized by *mutual distrust, tactics and communication difficulties'*[49] (italics in original).

What most ecologists have in common is a desire to identify threats to environmental security, though the task of defining environmental security is not simple. Barry Buzan defines it as a concern with 'the maintenance of the local and planetary biosphere as the essential support system on which all other human enterprises depend.'[50] This is indeed a rather tall order. At its broadest conception, the Gaia hypothesis suggested that the entire ecosphere is analogous to a single living organism.[51] As Lynton Caldwell writes in his extensive survey of international environmental policy:

> Once the biosphere concept was accepted, human impact upon the environment took on a new significance. Whereas an earlier generation had worried about the health effects of coal smoke in the air over London and Pittsburgh, informed people in the 1960's became concerned about burning coal for energy and the resulting carbon dioxide balance in the earth's atmosphere.[52]

Yet the global-warming debate, based on projections about the impact of that imbalance, suggests a pattern similar to that which developed in whaling issues: some scientists support the general idea that increases in temperatures will lead to disaster, and others consider this concern unfounded. We can argue, however, for some shared perspectives among the scientific communities and networks that have sprung up in the last few decades around environmental concerns.

Without question, the earth needs certain things to survive: intact nutrient cycles; an absence of atmosphere-transforming polluting gases or particles; an intact ozone layer in the stratosphere that protects from the sun's ultraviolet radiation; relatively clean oceans, lakes, rivers, and streams; a level of ionizing radiation that does not interfere with the normal processes of life and bioreproduction; and biological diversity. It is the latter need – that of a varied natural world – where we find a focus. In the Western world, concerns over threats to biodiversity have been popularized by Norman Myers, other authors, and television programs.[53] At the height of great whale exploitation, many scientists, including those in the IWC Scientific Committee, called for drastic reductions in kills, because they were concerned that individual species, such as the right, blue, and humpback, were heading directly towards extinction. Now that road appears averted, and we are left with the fundamental ethical question of whether whales should be killed at all.

Chapter 2 begins with a description of the whales themselves, with reference to their biological and social characteristics. We also briefly recall the whalers, the rise of whaling as a commercial activity, and the eventual recognition that both hunter and prey were in big trouble.

Actors and Institutions

The second integral component of global environmental problems is more directly political: after risks to environmental health are discovered or redefined as problems, we must look at the decision-making process that led to that risk and at the possible political developments that could reduce it. In other words, we must identify the chief actors and their interests, and the institutions in which they interact.[54] This is no small task, since decision-making takes place on many levels, and we deal with the aggregate effects. For example, it is often argued that global warming is in part the result of increased carbon dioxide emissions in the atmosphere. This increase is the result of millions of minor decisions, such as driving or walking to work, yet the cumulative effect can present a global political problem, one demanding an institutional response at a global level. Also, we must avoid adopting any single concept of rationality to characterize decision-making processes. Instead of generalizing these cognitive events, we must look at trends in behaviour and patterns of decision-making. In our case, we focus on the politics of the IWC itself, an evolving international institution many people have heard of but not examined. As such, it is a centre where individual foreign policy decisions coalesce. It is also a place where non-state actors have played an increasingly visible and controversial role.

Decision-making theory has evolved on its own in the often overlooked field of foreign policy analysis. This rich body of work borrows from social psychology (especially group dynamics), bureaucratic-organizational models, and models of individual behaviour and perception (or cognitive psychology).[55] This book does not attempt to add to the literature of those fields. We can say, however, that all the commonly used models must somehow take account of the political context of decision-making, both internal and external to the nation-state, the governmental department, or the bureaucratic office. (Again, the 'political context' is also determined by our other two analytic components.) With the IWC, we have an example of a historical transformation of a decision-making body in crisis, and a demonstration of how international organizations remain pivotal 'fora for choosing innovations,' where the 're-examination of purposes is brought about by knowledge-mediated decision-making dynamics.'[56]

At the international level, as we have seen, it is not unusual to address problems of the commons in terms of the formation and maintenance of regimes or multilateral institutions, but this approach retains a very state-centric orientation that is hardly ever appropriate in global ecopolitics. Rarely are states, or more precisely governments of states, the only significant actors involved. Mostly for this reason, I prefer to use the term issue-area network when referring to the actors involved. The term has been used before in several contexts. Political scientist Hugh Meclo has examined the American political system by identifying political alliances among departmental officials, interest groups, politicians, experts, and even foreign governments, who share similar views on certain political issues.[57] This conception of an issue-area network captures the many actors involved and draws us immediately to the links among them. Stressing the role of NGOs, Kathryn Sikkink writes of networks of organizations 'working together on behalf of human rights, a network that also included parts of global and regional intergovernmental organizations (IGOs) and private foundations.' She refers to this 'broader set of organizations as an international issue-network.'[58] However, there is no need to assume a consensus. Networks are simply chains of interconnected persons/ groups.[59] The Japan Whaling Association is attached to the same issue-area network as Greenpeace; they even confront each other directly in the IWC, and in fact they influence the governmental representatives from the US and Japan, respectively. Their ethical positions are virtually diametrically opposed, but what brings them together is their mutual concern for the environmental issue of cetacean survival and whaling.

We will define networks simply as *identifiable groups of participants, usually divided into perspective-sharing coalitions.* Coalitions are vital in our understanding of networks. Barbara Crane, for example, refers to the concept of a 'transnational policy coalition ... coalitions whose memberships transcend national and institutional boundaries. Such coalitions, based on common policy preferences, draw members and supporters from national governments, international organizations, academia, and private associations.'[60] As such, our choice of participants is hardly bound by the 'conceptual jail' of state-centricity.[61] As for the theme that unites participants, I have employed the slightly more cumbersome term issue-area network because it demands greater specificity. For example, there is no 'single human rights issue,' there is a variety of issues (torture, imprisonment, voting rights, environmental security, racial equality, gender equality, child rights, and many others) that can be considered issue-areas in themselves. Similarly, there is certainly no single, cohesive, wildlife conservation issue, but there is a broad and heavily interlinked issue-area that involves concern for many threatened species, biodiversity, habitat protection, poaching, hunters' rights, and so on. Indeed, the concept of eco-holism suggests we need a more inclusive approach (and we must always try to account for the context in which actors operate), but, for the purpose of historical narrative, we must draw limits somewhere.

Transnational wildlife conservation issue-area networks are nothing new, though they have become increasingly visible.[62] Both intergovernmental and transnational conservationist organizations, usually European and more often than not concerned primarily with economic factors, have been with us throughout this century. Early organizations included the International Council for Bird Preservation, established in 1909, and the International Congress for the Protection of Nature, established in 1913. The latter organization had planned to discuss the whaling issue in 1914, but European nations became justifiably preoccupied with more urgent matters in that historic year. As early as 1886, the Treaty Concerning the Regulation of Salmon Fishing in the Rhine River Basin was signed by Germany, Luxembourg, the

Netherlands, and Switzerland. In all likelihood, the first international agreement to conserve a marine mammal was the Fur Seal Convention of 1911, signed by Japan, Russia, Great Britain (for pre-independence Canada), and the United States. Unfortunately, this agreement, which banned all pelagic commercial seal hunting in the North Pacific, prompted renewed interest in whaling in that area.[63] Another ground-breaking agreement was the US-Great Britain Migratory Birds Convention, signed in 1916. Today, what Robert Boardman has called the 'linchpin of the system'[64] of international conservationist organization is the International Union for the Conservation of Nature and Natural Resources (IUCNNR), formed in 1948 in conjunction with the United Nations Educational, Scientific and Cultural Organisation (UNESCO). The IUCNNR is a unique umbrella organization that covers intergovernmental and transnational conservation activity, often working laterally with a plethora of other organizations – both state multilateral and non-governmental in composition – which have achieved global significance. At the state level, the Convention on International Trade in Endangered Species of Wild Fauna and Flora is often heralded as a diplomatic success; it resulted in the current – and controversial – international ivory trade ban of 1989.[65]

Many international treaties are concerned with cetaceans in one form or another. We touch on these in Chapter 3, which chronicles the shift of the IWC from a pro- to an anti-whaling body.[66] For now, we need mention but a few to indicate the extensiveness of contemporary international treaties. The Convention for the Regulation of Whaling was signed in 1931; and an International Agreement for the Regulation of Whaling was signed in 1937, then amended in 1938. The IWC itself was established with the International Convention for the Regulation of Whaling (ICRW), arguably the most important treaty affecting cetacean survival in the century, signed soon after the Second World War. These treaties may be seen as formal articulations of certain regimes, but to examine the political processes that breathe life into them, we must look into the issue-area networks themselves.

Chapter 3 provides a political history of the IWC that outlines the performance of the main actors, which we choose according to their relative importance in that arena.

The Normative Dimension
Political history, however, takes place within a normative context. This fact influences the ethical perspectives of the actors involved in

political developments, moving those perspectives towards ultimately tough and divisive issues, in particular, questions of rights and obligations. What are the obligations of present populations to future ones? What are our obligations towards non-humans? Are there different rights for different animals? Most troublesome, is it ethically legitimate to argue that conceptions of rights and obligations, towards each other and towards other forms of life, should be or even can be universalized – that is, held in common by all governments and people? We have, for example, a Universal Declaration of Human Rights, but no one would argue that everyone enjoys the same rights or has the same obligations. Of course, these questions are not raised here because they can be definitively answered. Rather, it is important from an analytical perspective to identify the central ethical issues related to any aspect of a political issue, and to offer some conclusions regarding the comparative influence of these different lines of thought. To quote Robert Cox: 'A valid paradigm for the investigation of global change would need to include the historical interaction of human organization with the other elements in nature.'[67]

This strategy makes it possible to speak in terms of normative transitions, stages in which dominant thinking about norms and values changes or at least begins to change. In keeping with the note of caution that should accompany any optimism in the field of international affairs, we should not exaggerate the potential of organizations, such as the IWC, to act as conduits for the transmission of values. It is indeed difficult to speculate, as Robert Boardman once did, that global conservationist organizations may be unwitting 'embryonic institutions of representative government for [non-human] species of the planet.'[68] This outcome would require a remarkable transformation in our collective anthropomorphic conception of democracy, as well as near-consensus on such matters, which clearly eludes our current grasp. Nonetheless, if a discernible normative transition has taken place, this development might give even the more cynical of international relations scholars reason for optimism.[69] Before the late 1960s, few people were concerned with whales, and fewer still held firm beliefs concerning the validity of killing them. But those attitudes and beliefs have been changed by the rise of the issue-area network in the international arena, the participation of various members of the network, and, in particular, the influence of non-governmental organizations. This development must be weighed against the claim that the spread of such values, accompanied by the power of their chief promoter, is a form of cultural imperialism, be it of the older expansionist variety or at the more subtle level of the ideational.

To return to an issue raised earlier, if environmental security is to be seen as a right, what about the security of future generations? This question is complicated by present inequalities, which suggest that progress must be about improvement, and not simple conservation, for most of the human race. Perhaps we are so caught up in a race driven by what has been termed *diachronic competition* ('a relationship whereby contemporary well-being is achieved at the expense of our descendants')[70] that viewing the well-being of future humans as a policy priority is beyond our decision-making mechanisms. Nonetheless, this goal remains logical, both for organizational objectives and for the articulation in international law of such principles.[71] As well, as mentioned in our discussion of the global commons, the idea that northern industrialized countries have an obligation to aid southern nations in their pursuit of sustainable development has gained formal articulation. Principle Six of the Rio Declaration[72] refers to the 'special priority' that should be given to the needs of the 'most environmentally vulnerable nations.' Similarly important, Principle Three declares: 'The right to development must be fulfilled so as to equitably meet the developmental and environmental needs of present and future generations.' On this distributive question, Henry Shue argues that, even 'in an emergency one pawns the jewellery before selling the blankets ... whatever justice may positively require, it does not permit that poor nations be told to sell *their* blankets in order that rich nations may keep *their* jewellery.' The Montreal Protocol on Substances that Deplete the Ozone Layer recognizes this position by establishing a mechanism for technology transfer from North to South.[73]

The cetacean issue-area network invariably brings ethical positions to the forefront, and the clash between conservationists, who wish to conserve whale stocks but allow strictly controlled whaling, and preservationists, who deny the ethical validity of whaling altogether, is severe. The intergenerational issue is important, however, since it provides an opportunity for at least limited agreement between conservationists and preservationists. Either way, whaling or not whaling, we may argue that whale species must be preserved for the enjoyment or utilization of future generations. If commercial whaling were to resume, many unscrupulous whalers might emerge, reminiscent of the so-called pirate whalers who hunted outside the IWC regulatory framework with impunity in the 1960s and 1970s. Fears that such unthinking brutes would come to dominate the industry are perhaps based on the greater fear that we, as a species, have yet to come to terms with the intergenerational issue and the concern that human cruelty knows no bounds.

Chapter 4 discusses this clash of values and the debate over the imposition of values through multilateral institutions as a form of cultural imperialism.

The Broader Context

Finally, we must remove ourselves from the exigencies and related issues of the issue-area network and look at the bigger picture. No one would argue that resumed whaling could not possibly lead to resumed disaster. The whaling issue is, with important differences, similar to the nuclear weapons question: after something negative has happened, we know it can happen again and must strive to avoid it. Whaling, however, is not the biggest survival threat to cetaceans today, that is, to all cetaceans, including porpoises, dolphins, and great whales.

James McNeely, writing for the IUCNNR, asserts that the three major threats to biological diversity as a whole are habitat alteration (usually by highly diverse natural ecosystems affecting less diverse agrosystems), overharvesting, and climate change.[74] If the gravest danger to wildlife is human encroachment upon and alteration of habitat, any attempt to preserve cetaceans must involve a parallel effort at preserving their fragile environments – the oceans. We must mention, therefore, the importance of these related issue-areas, including the fishing industry, ocean pollution, and ultraviolet radiation and climate change.

The pollution issue is perhaps the most ominous. A recent report to the IWC by Theo Colburn of the World Wildlife Fund suggests that the dumping of chlorine-based chemicals into rivers and oceans is probably affecting dolphin, porpoise, and whale fertility. Kevin Brown of Durham University in England, meanwhile, has estimated that at least 150,000 anthropogenic or human-made chemicals, a total that increases by 2,000 each year, end up in the oceans. And Mark Simmonds of the University of Greenwich in London reports that six mass deaths of seals and dolphins have been recorded since 1987, 'all in highly contaminated waters such as the North Sea, compared with only four over the previous 80 years.'[75]

What the oceans present is a complex challenge of multilateral organization. It is premature to proclaim the preservation of the oceans as an impossible feat. Indeed, much progress has been made on the diplomatic front and significant agreements already exist. D.M. Johnston categorizes these agreements in six broad families: general law-making conventions, such as the Law of the Sea, which is constantly evolving; global marine pollution conventions, such as the London Dumping Convention; regional arrangements, which are usually but not always associated with UNEP's Regional Seas Programme; intergovernmental liability and compensation schemes; industrial liability and compensation schemes; and, finally, general maritime safety conventions. Johnston, borrowing from the neofunctionalist literature that helped give rise to the liberal institutionalism we have already discussed, argues that the *'primary* emphasis in the field of marine pollution diplomacy should now be placed on the *integration* of existing treaty-based arrangements at the regional level, rather than on the resort to new global treaties'[76] (italics in original).

In many respects, this task will be the greatest challenge of all, and the IWC, troubled as it may be, has a vital role to play. (It does have an official mandate to look into environmental questions.) We can argue further that the contemporary symbolic power of the whale will play a role as well. However, it may be a strategic mistake to focus attention on a single species if what we need is an ecosystem-based approach. Rather than as an inspiration for environmentalists, whales might instead be seen as a distraction from the most important issues facing ocean life and oceans management.

It is fitting that we end on a discussion of whales themselves, and our understanding of them, for this point is where we begin our story of cetacean survival and international politics.

2
The Whale and the Whaler

> Beyond the image of the planet earth itself, the most poignant
> symbol of the world environmental movement has been the
> whale ... The survival of whales continues to be an object of
> international anxiety ... and perhaps better than any other issue
> illustrates the difficulty of reconciling the multiple conflicting
> interests and values of nations in the management and protection
> of the biosphere.
>
> – Lynton Caldwell, 1990[1]

In many coastal communities around the world, whales have played a direct role in subsistence hunting, and this role has been reflected in various rituals and cultural artifacts. But the whale has also become a symbolic fixture in contemporary western society, representing both natural magnificence and human folly. As even a brief look at the history of human-cetacean relations indicates, western cultures have always been fascinated with the majesty of whales; they have been perceived as kings of the sea and sources of bounty, and perhaps they were once even considered a threat to human domination of the land. Now, whales are viewed largely as benevolent monarchs, but in the past they were seen as monsters whose blood boiled with the strength of waves, often bringing out the best and (as famous tales such as *Moby Dick* suggest) the worst in those attempting to pursue them. To the emergent western industrial culture of the 1800s, conquering the whale made certain linear historical sense. Whaling also made for an unparalleled source of industrial supplies, from oil for lamps and machine lubrication to baleen for umbrellas and corsets. In short, whales have contributed materials instrumental both to the upheavals of the industrial revolution and to the more ephemeral fashions spotted on London and New York streets.

A nostalgic romance coloured the early days of commercial whaling, a romance put to rest by close studies of the industry. The latter days of whaling, however, assume a very different aura; they are known by photographs of the blood-drenched decks of huge factory ships, by the whaler's near-realization of cetacean extinction, and by the whale's symbolic attachment to (or, as others would insist, totemization by) the environmental movement. Whaling has followed a discernible pattern of overexploitation: stocks are reduced to the point where they no longer offer feasible targets, and the industry has then turned to other stocks, either in different locations or different species.

That whales have come to occupy a special place in the public mind in such bastions of industrialization and commercialization as the United States is in itself an interesting phenomenon. However, three factors in particular make whales different from most species and have converged to challenge the conventional notion that whales should be seen as simply resources for human utilization. First, and most obviously, the sheer size of the great whales, especially the blue whale, the largest mammal to have lived on earth, is hard to overlook. In terms of wildlife conservation, size and public curiosity (and empathy) seem to be positively correlated. Elephants, rhinoceroses, gorillas, polar bears, and other large mammals, which have been quaintly labelled 'charismatic megavertebrates,' capture our imagination perhaps because they make us, unaccustomed to humility as we are, seem small.[2] The whale is supported and protected by its immense quantity of blubber; blood vessels within the blubber open (vasodilate) and close (vasoconstrict), and thus cool and warm the mammals who often travel from the tropics to the poles and back within the course of a year. Blubber was the source of whale oil (with the single but important exception of the sperm whale, which has *spermaceti*, the finest of oils, in its skull). As a result, the whale's size has historically worked against it, since its bulk presented to enterprising whalers a virtual bounty of natural resources. This fact also made whaling profitable long after a whaleboat returned with its load of whale oil or, in this century, meat. A relatively small catch could still bring with it a large profit.

Second, the intriguing and still rather controversial question of cetacean intelligence, which was popularized when large aquatic exhibits began training killer whales to jump through the hoops of commercial displays, has concerned an entire generation of scientists. Whales have more neocortex than any other mammal, that is, they have bigger brains, especially the sperm whale.[3] The varying anthropocentric verdicts on this point are based inevitably on comparisons with human intelligence and reflect differing perspectives on whaling. For example, the Japan Whaling Association is prepared to equate whales with domesticated cows. While cetologists quibble, the consensus is that whales have extraordinary communication skills. Some claim that whales, who have lived in relative harmony with their environment for ages, may even be wiser than humans.[4] Those who argue that this perspective is romanticized may be right, but that is not the point: many people have formed a mental bond with the whale, as a symbol, precisely because it is perceived as highly intelligent. Such bonding, which has occurred within the non-conducive social context of western scientific and industrial civilization, is significant in terms of human-nature interaction.[5] It is indeed ironic that attempts to somehow measure whale intelligence in the tradition of positivist science have led to changes in the normative understanding of the effects of our own.

Most importantly from the perspective of international relations, whales are migratory mammals: the great whales escape the jealous confines of sovereignty that have been imposed upon the planet with the advent of human organization.[6] If the interdependence of environmental problems in general challenges the logic of the nation-state system, this point is especially challenging for questions of the global commons, where the risk-oriented decision-making process cannot be a unilateral affair. Moreover, the sovereignty issue becomes even more significant, with concerns over cultural and political sovereignty continuing to be major and divisive issues within the IWC. But this 'common' character of whales remains another aspect of the charged symbolism of the whale as species.[7] In a famous statement made in 1946, US secretary of state Dean Acheson waxed poetically about whales: 'The world's whale stocks are a truly international resource in that they belong to no one single nation, nor to a group of nations, but rather they are wards of the entire world.'[8]

Species Impoverishment

As a problem of global proportions, the whale issue, and the political network that developed alongside it, fit into several larger issue-areas, including the question of human-nature relations and the cultural differences that it raises. From an ecological viewpoint, the crisis presented by dwindling whale populations and current attempts to save them is an issue of biodiversity, or, put more emphatically, what M. Brock Fenton and others term *species impoverishment.*[9] Though there is nothing unnatural and certainly nothing new about extinction, this century has seen an unprecedented number of extinctions in the wild.[10] During the height of whaling, many feared that the great whales would go the way of the dodo, not because of any natural catastrophe, but because of human misunderstanding and, worse, greed. Today, a similar fear underlies attempts to save what is left of the tropical rainforests.

Scientists are still debating the causes of the large dinosaur extinction during the late Cretaceous period, about sixty-five million years ago. As David Jablonski notes in a fascinating essay, the late Cretaceous extinction is a very complex phenomenon, especially in terms of its varying impacts: 'Tropical marine groups were more severely affected than temperate or polar ones; open-ocean plankton and larger swimmers, such as the mosasaurs, were affected more than bottom dwellers; and large land dwellers more affected than small ones, even though some larger forms survived as well.'[11] Speculation about the cause of the extinction includes a meteorite or some other extraterrestrial body that scattered dust around the globe. Whatever the cause, it did not kill off all species, nor even came close to doing so. And here rests a key difference from the whaling issue: the Cretaceous extinction was not preventable through human effort. (In fact, there were no humans around.) On the other hand, humans are believed to be at least partly responsible for the extinction of land animals in the Pleistocene period. That is, the development of agriculture has so fundamentally changed the human-nature relationship that we have been able to affect the ecosystem, even the biosphere, with our economic activities.

The human tendency to overhunt constitutes a principal threat to biodiversity. In what was called the New World, Columbus discovered the Caribbean monk seal, the single tropical pinniped. It has not been seen since 1922. In the Aleutians, a Russian hunting expedition in 1741 spotted the Stellar's sea-cow. It was regarded as extinct by the late 1700s. More recently, in Lake Victoria in Africa, we have witnessed massive fish extinctions – more than 200 species. There were many causes for this loss, including overfishing, pollution, and alien species, such as the Nile perch. (Les Kaufman has referred to Lake Victoria as the 'Hiroshima of the biological apocalypse.')[12] Eastern Canadian and European commercial fishers know all too well the economic effects of the rapid reduction of fish species such as cod and turbot; the role played by overfishing was at least significant.

A smaller population may have a severe impact on the reproductive health of a species. While some individuals may have better access to limited resources and therefore increased likelihood of survival, the group as a whole may have reduced chances. The important element here is the gene pool, which itself must be sufficiently diverse for healthy populations: 'Gene pools are being converted into gene puddles ... vulnerable to evaporation in a ecological and evolutionary sense.'[13] The loss of genetic diversity may well be the most serious long-term threat to our environment. As James Scarff notes, the

> elimination of a species reduces the genetic capacity of the ecosystem to respond to perturbations or long-term changes in the environment. Such a loss may also initiate irreversible ecological adjustments which destabilize the ecosystem leading to further extinctions. Economically, the extinction of a species represents the permanent loss of a renewable resource of unknown value ... [as well as] potential uses for medicine, scientific research, human food, education, and recreation.[14]

Within this context of biodiversity and potential species impoverishment, then, the whaling story takes place, though we must add that this century has seen the evolution of the commercial extinction of whalers as well.

Cetacea

The three major orders of sea mammals are Cetacea, Pinnipedia, and Sirenia. Cetacea include whales, dolphins, and porpoises. Pinnipedia are in fact a suborder of Carnivora and include the seals and walruses, which live both on land and in sea. Sirenia are otherwise known as sea-cows, or manatees and dugongs. (The Stellar's sea-cow, as mentioned, was exterminated by hunters at Bering Island in the North Pacific about 1768.) Sirenia share a common ancestry with Proboscidea, whose modern order is represented by the African and Asian elephants. They bear a superficial resemblance to Cetacea in body shape, lack of hind limbs, transverse tail flukes (unlike fish), flippers instead of forelimbs, and lack of hair. And, like all of these mammals, they breathe fresh air and are warm-blooded. But the resemblance ends there.[15]

Several blanket caveats may precede this quick survey.[16] First, I only deal with the more popular whales, those whose images are familiar to readers and those which have been involved in the whaling story. Second, several biological and social characteristics are universal. For example, all the whales discussed here migrate, following prey to warmer waters in winter, although migratory patterns vary widely. Third, while we are constantly reminded of how little we know about whales, scientific advances are slowly increasing our knowledge base. For example, recent advances in molecular genetics have made it possible to identify different whale species from meat samples alone.[17] Interested readers should consult more detailed texts should they wish to pursue the many biological mysteries of cetacean research.

Another major caveat must be thrust upon the reader: although we can speak with some confidence about the size of existing whale populations, we must note that cetacean demographics is at best an imprecise science. The most authoritative text on the topic identifies serious problems (that is, sources of possible error) in the estimation of whale populations.[18] The estimation technique involves using an index of abundance based on 'sightings [or pre-moratorium catches] per unit effort' (CPUE). If the CPUE fell by 50 per cent, stocks were assumed to have fallen by 50 per cent. Though this approach is a common strategy in fisheries management (which does not have an impressive record), it has two obvious problems: errors in estimated numbers sighted and errors in the measure of 'effort.' The first problem is more easily explained: with few exceptions, such as the coast-hugging gray whale, the large deep-sea whales do not present themselves every year for a quick roll-call. Another important component of population estimation is the age distribution of a group, which is not always discernible from mere sightings. However, marking whales has long been a practice of cetologists, if a very labour-intensive one, and it has met with some success in determining characteristics of the whale population.

The second problem is not easily rectified. The effort index was based on whaling activity: the relation between the catch per searching hour and the catch per day provided a measure of the availability of stocks. As K. Radway Allen notes, this method was flawed in several respects.[19] And, for most individuals involved with the cetacean-issue network today, it is unthinkable, since the index relies on a fully functional whaling industry. The scientific whaling program can be justified on these grounds, to the staunch protests of anti-whalers. However, the method can be adapted to reflect whale sightings rather than hourly or daily catch. In other words, the relation between the distance or area that an aircraft travels and the number of whales sighted can provide an alternative measure of effort. At this time, however, the resources needed for this approach are not available. Another option involves the use of echo-location equipment, known as ASDIC. Initially, this underwater sound monitoring led to an increase in the efficiency of whaling operations; it has been used by Japanese whalers since about 1960. In fact, ASDIC has the effect, in the baleen whaling industry, of 'frightening whales, so that they remain on the surface and follow a straight course, and thus become easier to catch.'[20]

There are additional problems with measuring any of the vital parameters of a population, including the mortality rate, recruitment rate, age at sexual maturity, pregnancy rate, and sex ratio in the breeding population. And there are large variations in knowledge of different whale species. While we know a great deal about killer whales, whose numbers and behaviour can be closely observed in places like British Columbia, the deep-diving sperm whale and the rare blue whale are comparatively mysterious. Demographic models can't account for rapid changes in habitat, under-reporting (which, unfortunately enough, is encouraged in loose common-resource regimes), and other unpredictables. The Revised Management Procedure, however, which is currently accepted by the IWC Scientific Committee, offers a model that demands uncertainty be at least acknowledged in any study of whales.

Some disagreement remains over the evolution of whales, though most people assume the whales emerged from the sea some thirty million years ago, then returned to what presumably had become a more hospitable sea. It is generally thought that whales are ancestors of modern ungulates, which evolved in order to maximize their survivability in an aquatic environment. This process resulted in the development of blubber, and the ability to grow very large, an outcome at least partly resulting from an abundance of marine food.[21]

Within the order Cetacea, there are two main suborders: baleen whales are of the suborder Mysticeti, and toothed whales are of the suborder Odontoceti. The ten known species of Mysticeti are all whales. Of the sixty-seven known species of Odontoceti, most are dolphins and porpoises. Mortality rates are difficult to determine. With baleen whales, age can be determined by counting the ridges formed on baleen plates, much like one would count the rings seen on the top of a tree stump. However, as these ridges get worn down in time, they are only really effective in determining the age of younger whales. A more common practice is to count the pairs of waxy plugs that form in the ear plugs. This technique began in the mid-1950s and requires a dead (or an extraordinarily cooperative) whale. For toothed whales, it is believed that a pair of laminar structures in the teeth are formed annually.

We discuss the Odontoceti or toothed whales first.

Table 1

Selected hunted great whales

Species	Characteristics	Status
Sperm	Temperate/polar regions; 60-70 feet; 15-70 tons; life span, 70 years; gestation, 14-16 months; valued for spermaceti and meat	Slow recovery
Blue	Polar/tropical regions; 80-110 feet; up to 190 tons; life span, 80 years; close to extinction, valued for oil and meat	Endangered
Fin	Polar to tropical; over 80 feet; 70-80 tons	Vulnerable
Sei	Polar to tropical; 59 feet; 30 tons	Not endangered
Bryde's	Tropical and subtropical seas; 43 feet; 26 tons	Not endangered
Minke	Polar to tropical; 36 feet; 10 tons; strong demands for a resumption of hunt for this species, for meat only	Good recovery
Gray	Pacific coastal waters; 39-50 feet; 16-34 tons; gestation, 13 months; life span, over 70 years	Slow recovery
Right	Temperate, both hemispheres; 16-60 feet; 50-6 tons; gestation, 10-11 months; life span, 30 years; heavily hunted because they were slow and floated when dead	Endangered
Bowhead	Arctic basin; 11-66 feet; 60-80 tons; gestation, 10-11 months; life span, over 30 years	Endangered
Humpback	Polar to tropical; 50-60 feet; 40-65 tons; life span, 95 years	Endangered

Sources: S. Savage, *Endangered Species: Dolphins and Whales* (Hong Kong: New Burlington Books 1991); various IWC documents.

Odontoceti

One of the most popular cetaceans is not in fact a whale at all but a member of the ocean dolphin and porpoise family (Delphinidae). The killer whale (*Orcinus orca*) is frequently associated with the whale family because of extensive media coverage, including popular family films and well-rehearsed aquarium showings. It is by far the largest of the dolphins, and is perhaps the mightiest carnivore on earth (although the even larger sperm whale could be classified as such). Adults are typically twenty to thirty feet in length. The distinguishing characteristics of the killer whale are well known: the black-and-white body (though completely white and completely black species have been spotted); the tall dorsal fin (up to six feet in adult males); and, thanks to Marineland and SeaWorld, the popular image of the killer's formidable teeth, juxtaposed against its playful (albeit captive) nature. The killer has been described as 'the most widely distributed mammal on earth'[22] because it inhabits polar, temperate, and tropical seas, although it is most frequently sighted in the eastern and western Pacific, the northeastern Atlantic, and the Antarctic seas.

Compared to most cetaceans, the killer is a shore-dweller, swimming at up to 25 knots (28.8 miles per hour) and usually staying within 800 kilometres of shore. This proximity has led to inevitable confrontation with human fishers. The killer has two basic social arrangements: 'residential' whales that have fixed feeding and breeding grounds and subsist by eating fish; and 'transient' whales that travel up and down coastlines in search of large prey.[23] The latter will eat – put bluntly – whatever they want, including other whales, sea lions, and sharks. (In the Arctic, rumour has it that even polar bears avoid lengthy dips because of their fear of killer whales.) Killers are born at over 350 pounds, after a year-long gestation, and spend their first two years close to their mothers. Killer pods are matriarchal societies, rooted in the leadership of mothers and grandmothers.

The killer has not been a frequent target of whalers. It is relatively small and (perhaps as important) relatively fast. This makes for a hard catch with little bounty. Though killers have been hunted by Norwegians and Japanese in the past, their most common human use today is in oceanaria. Their intelligence and adaptability make them crowd favourites; and a tame killer whale (not a contradiction in terms) is indeed a fascinating creature. While births in captivity are troublesome, they have occurred successfully. At one time, the killer was feared as a supreme menace by fishers. Of course, they do consume great quantities of food, and if they get stuck in fishing nets and panic as they are drowning, they can do great harm to the nets. In the relatively recent past, the US Air Force used orca pods as target practice, shooting at them from planes. But the killer has undergone a drastic image reconstruction in the last quarter-century.

Pilot whales are also famous, but for a different reason. The two types of pilot whales are long-finned (*Globicephala melaena*) and short-finned (*Globicephala macrorhynchus*). The former can be found in cool waters, the latter in warm waters. Both are fairly deep divers for their size and eat mainly fish and squid. Indeed, the name pilot whale derives from an ancient practice of following these whales to locate schools of herring. They can grow to twenty feet and live up to fifty years. Their social habits remain a bit of a mystery; for example, post-reproductive females have been noted to nurse calves until the latter reach adulthood, which is highly unusual and has given rise to theories about 'cultural transmission.'[24] They are easily recognized by their bulbous head and have been known by a panoply of names: Atlantic pilot, northern pilot, blackfish, pothead, and piloto. The females are capable of reproduction at around six years and generally produce a calf every three years, following gestation periods of some fifteen to sixteen months. The pilot whale is highly social, demonstrating what many call a 'herding' mentality.

Their fear of killer whales often drives them ashore. They also have a fear of motorboats, which enables what many regard as the worst case of whaling occurring today, the Faroe Islands' annual slaughter of pilot whales. Though the Faroe Island drivery (as it has been called) is the last remnant of its type, it also occurred in Newfoundland, Greenland, Iceland, the Shetland Islands, and Orkney Islands. While each pilot whale can yield around forty gallons of blubber oil and two gallons of head-and-jaw oil, the Faroe drivery is today basically a meat-oriented hunt. The whales are easily herded together and driven ashore with sharp-pointed gaffs, where they are killed with spears. Though this tradition dates back to the 1500s, many animal rights activists regard it as an extreme example of brutality, one that encourages children to stab small and defenceless whales. The drivery raises particularly acute ethical questions for anti-whaling crusaders, especially concerning the obstinate persistence of the Islanders in conducting the hunt. The Faroe Islands insist on the sovereign right to continue the annual slaughter and the IWC cannot challenge this position. In fact, Denmark, which protects aboriginal whaling rights on its other island territory, Greenland, does not question this right either.[25]

The beaked whale family (Ziphiidae), hunted on a smaller scale due to their smaller bulk, includes some rare whales. Beaked whales are named for their peculiar snout, which, juxtaposed against their especially bulbous heads, has the appearance of a beak. Some of these whales are too rare to have been hunted in great numbers. For example, the Indo-Pacific beaked whale (*Indopacetus pacificus*) is known only through two skeletal findings: a skull found on a beach in Australia, and another found on the eastern coast of Somalia. To the best of my knowledge, a live Indo-Pacific beaked whale has never been seen, much less killed, though this claim is impossible to verify because so many whalers have not kept adequate records. The most common beaked whales are the bottlenose whales (*Hyperoodon*), which are split into the North Atlantic (*Hyperoodon ampullatus*) and southern (*Hyperoodon planifrons*) varieties. The latter is a rare species, but the former has been hunted fairly heavily, especially in the Arctic during the nineteenth century. Their popularity is related to the spermaceti-like oil found in the whales' heads. The bottlenose whale can reach over ten metres (thirty-two feet) in length and can be identified by its 'projecting, almost hemispherical melon and pronounced beak.'[26]

Bottlenose whales swim in small pods, though large ones of up to 100 have been spotted. It is difficult to estimate past numbers, since the bottlenose was hunted so long ago. It was an easy catch: smaller and more manageable than the great whales, the species attempted to help wounded members of the social group, thus harpooning one whale would draw others. At the 1995 IWC Meeting, Denmark was asked if it intended to seek a quota for bottlenose whales, which are currently a protected species under the ICRW Schedule. The North Atlantic Marine Mammal Commission (NAMMCO), which has been set up by Iceland and Norway, had apparently concluded that the whales were no longer endangered. And this conclusion raised concern that Denmark, a member of NAMMCO, might attempt to resume commercial whaling of the bottlenose. Denmark declined to discuss the issue at the meeting.

Another small whale family that has received attention over the years is the narwhal and white whale (Monodontidae). These whales, unique in several respects, have been hunted mainly by the North American Inuit. Both species in this family, belugas and narwhals, have a skeletal structure in which the bones of the neck are not fused;

in other words, they can turn their heads, unlike other species. This characteristic makes the beluga (*Delphinapterus leucas*) a delightful whale to watch, even if it is usually seen in captivity, such as at the Vancouver Aquarium. Belugas, a circumpolar species that grows whiter with age, can reach twenty feet in length and are bottom feeders who eat squid, flounder, herring, smelt, eels, and crustacea. They inhabit northern areas in winter but go south in summer and have a natural life span of around twenty-five years. They are known for their strong calling abilities and their smile-like lips.

Aboriginal peoples have hunted the beluga for skin, flesh, and oil, but a commercial beluga fishery has never been established.[27] A small take continues in the Mackenzie River Estuary in the Northwest Territories.[28] Belugas have few natural enemies, save the killer whale and the polar bear. The largest threat they face, without question, is related to habitat degradation: toxic wastes in the St. Lawrence River, pollution in the Baltic Sea, and offshore oil exploration and extraction in Arctic waters. Cetologists are increasingly concerned with how the immune systems of whales can adapt to their modified and fragile aquatic environment. As many Canadians know, corpses of the St. Lawrence beluga are now classified as toxic waste. In March 1994, the Canadian government announced the appointment of an eight-member recovery team of scientists to focus on these whales, whose population declined from 5,000 at the turn of this century to less than 500.[29]

The narwhal (*Monodon monoceros*) is similar to the beluga in shape and size, with two very noticeable differences. It is a bluish grey colour on top and nearly white on its bottom. The males sport an elongated, single, left canine tooth that develops into a horizontal tusk, slowly spiraling in a counter-clockwise direction as it grows, pushing through the upper lip and reaching lengths of eight to ten feet. With what is undoubtedly the largest tooth on earth, the narwhal has been known as the tusked whale or even the unicorn whale. Despite its prominence, the tusk has an unknown purpose. Perhaps, it is a defensive structure, used to scare off killer whales or other possible predators. It could be used in the perennial battle to win mating rights. It might be used to poke airholes in ice, because the narwhal, like the beluga, is primarily an arctic species (which has been spotted off England's coast in the past), and ice cover always presents a great danger. Or the tusk could have had some former purpose and evolution somehow overlooked its vestigial presence.

The narwhal, hunted as much as the beluga, remains fairly common.[30] A difference is that the odd tusk, considered at one time by many to be the distinguishing feature of the unicorn of the sea, has always attracted hunters – much as elephant and rhinoceros tusks and horns encouraged poaching in this century. In its powdered form, narwhal tusk was believed by some practitioners of oriental medicine to reduce fever. (Because the Chinese felt a bowl made of unicorn horn could actually absorb poison, such dishes became valuable to leaders fearing assassination attempts.) The magnificent sceptre of the Hapsburgs was made of a narwhal's tusk and now sits on display in Kunsthistorisches Museum in Vienna. The throne of Denmark was built of narwhal and walrus tusks (no doubt obtained in Greenland) in the mid-1600s for King Christian V. Today, the Inuit still use both types of tusks for their beautiful carvings; the use of narwhal tusks was discussed in general at the September 1995 CITES Animals Committee Meeting.[31]

The final toothed whale that demands introduction is by far the most famous, the most widely hunted, and the largest. This is the great sperm whale (*Physeter macrocephalus*), also known as the cachalot.[32] Early drawings of whales featured images of the sperm, and indeed the logo of the IWC includes a small (and less than accurate) outline of the cachalot. A third of the sperm's body is its head: a massive, straight-edged head full of spermaceti, the most coveted of whale oils. A full-grown adult female can reach 11 metres and a male 20 metres (up to 65 feet), and each can weigh over 90,000 pounds. The sperm whale is widely distributed, preferring warmer tropical seas but migrating towards cooler water in the summer. Much like the narwhal, older males (known as bulls) migrate first, followed by females and calves. The whales prefer deep water (at least 600 feet) but seem to keep closer to shore when heading north rather than south. Sperm whale dives are exceptionally deep, well over 1,000 metres (3,270 feet), and can last over an hour.[33] When they surface, they can make up to 50 blows, giving off a 10- to 13-foot spout. Mating occurs in warmer waters in what is known as 'harem style': two or three males will mate with up to forty females, with the males often fighting among themselves during this season of arousal. In 1912-13, a group of between 3,000 and 4,000 adult sperm whales was reported off Patagonia; such large groups are unheard of today. Solitary 'polar bulls' are often sighted in northern latitudes. But the highly polygamous social structure of the sperm is unmistakable, and many experts believe this fact accounts for the marked discrepancy in size between males and females.[34]

Sperm females will give birth on average every three to four years, with gestation periods as long as seventeen months. Perhaps the most noticeable feature of the sperm, besides the giant head (which contains a twenty-pound brain), is its huge teeth: eight inches long and four inches wide. The teeth don't even pass the gums until the whale is ten years old. They are indeed the most formidable set of teeth in the world, facilitating the sperm's diet of large squid, skates, other fish, and sharks. And in a full-grown bull, the throat is big enough to swallow a large man whole, thus the association of the sperm with the tale of Jonah. In this century, the sperm was immortalized by the sailor and author Herman Melville, whose Captain Ahab engaged in a relentless pursuit of the rather unreceptive sperm albino Moby Dick. Indeed, irate bulls were often known to ram whaleships when a harem was under attack.

Sperms have been one of the most heavily hunted of all whales. This hunting took place in two periods, from 1720 to 1860 and from 1946 to the early 1980s.[35] Spermaceti, from which the whale's name is derived, was initially the most valued whale product; however, the postwar hunting period was more concerned with oil applications, such as extreme pressure lubrication and industrial waxes, than with meat products for both humans and so-called fur farms. The exact biological function of this liquid wax is still a puzzle, though it may contribute to a hydrostatic system that controls buoyancy for deep-diving purposes.[36] The spermaceti may also be used as some sort of acoustic lens, which allows the whale to stun prey with a short burst of high-intensity sound. Regardless of its natural use, spermaceti was used by humans for purposes as diverse as candle-making and military aircraft lubrication. Gradually, however, all these needs have been met with substitutes, though their commercial viability was always a question. The use of jojoba shrub oil (*Simmondsia chinensis*) is an example; found in the arid Sonoran Desert (located in California, Arizona, and Mexico), the shrub's acorn-like fruits produce oil for use in gearboxes or in machine tools. In its hydrogenated form, the oil can act as an industrial wax. In fact, the Israelis developed jojoba plantations in order to export the liquid.

The sperm whale also supplied regular blubber oil, ivory (from its huge teeth), bones, and meat. Another product was ambergris, a fixing agent for perfumes. Generated in the alimentary tract, ambergris would be extracted during processing. (Understandably, the perfume industry was not inclined to reveal the origins of one of its most important ingredients!) Ambergris is rarely found in caught whales and is as likely to wash ashore. The ancient Greeks and Romans ascribed healing powers to the balls of ambergris that did so. In the Middle and Far East, where it was considered an 'antispasmodic' drug, the Turks used it as an aphrodisiac. And, apparently, 'seamen used it as a laxative.'[37]

Today, the sperm remains a protected species and shows some evidence of recovery.

Mysticeti

The Mysticeti are quite different from toothed whales. Most noticeably, they tend to be bigger (with the obvious exception of the sperm), and have baleen, or large plates of elastic substance that filter out food from water, instead of teeth. The skeletal 'hand' concealed within the flippers (with one exception) has four fingers instead of five. The blow-hole has a double nostril, while toothed whales have only one. The three main families of baleen whales are the gray, rorquals (including the humpbacks), and right whales.

The first family contains but a single species, *Eschrichtius robustus* – the gray whale or, more commonly in North America, the California gray whale. The species is found only in the North Pacific, usually along the coastlines where it makes an epic annual migration. The gray was previously known in the North Atlantic, but it was hunted out of existence as early as 1725. It is often considered the most primitive of baleen whales, with no dorsal fins and medium-long tail flukes. The females are larger than the males and can grow to 50 feet and 35 tons. (This weight can increase by 25 per cent during the 12- to 13-month gestation period.) Most grays are found in the western Pacific. The eastern Pacific grays, which travel between the Sea of Okhotsk, the Kamchatka Peninsula, and the Aleutian Islands, then southwards to Korea and Japan, are scarce. In a remarkable procession, which attracts tourists from around the world, the west Pacific grays migrate up the coastlines of California (where they were hunted until the early 1970s), Oregon, Washington, and Vancouver Island, to the Aleutians.

At the turn of the century, the gray was hunted heavily, for a female can yield twenty-five to forty barrels of oil. Calving lagoons in Baja California, Mexico, were very heavily hunted, despite the gray's initial reputation as a 'devilfish' that would ram whalers. Today, population estimates are over 20,000, which is probably close to what is termed the pre-exploitation level and represents one of the all-time best recovery stories in the annals of conservation. Indeed, in 1994, the gray was actually taken off the United States endangered species list. The gray is not without problems, of course. Since it is a bottom feeder, it likes to stay in shallow lagoons for rest periods during the trips south and north, and these lagoons are increasingly being diminished by human shoreline development. Overzealous whalewatchers can often be obtrusive. On occasion, killer whales will take calves. And, in an interesting development, which we treat in greater length in Chapter 4, the Makah aboriginals in Neah Bay, Washington (just south of Vancouver Island), have decided they want to resume subsistence whaling at the rate of five whales per year.[38] Overall, the gray whale clearly demonstrates the resiliency of a rugged marine mammal, contributing greatly to a North American West Coast appreciation of whales.

Of the rorquals, the humpbacks (*Megaptera novaeangliae*), so named because of their distinctive hump and arcuate dorsal fin, may be most popular to whalewatchers because of their playful social habits. Humpbacks are often curious when boats approach, and their haunting underwater songs are famous. Nigel Bonner informs us that whales 'do not have vocal cords and, as they sing while submerged, they cannot afford to release large amounts of air to the exterior. Nevertheless, it seems likely that the songs are produced by the movement of air setting in vibration some specialised tissue, perhaps part of the larynx.'[39] Sounds have now been recorded from all Mysticeti, except the rare pygmy right whale, and cetologists have learned to distinguish songs from calls. Songs occur when a noticeable pattern is repeated, that is, a regular sequence and patterned time. Three general types of calls are used: simple (often described as moans, usually frequency-modulated and low-frequency signals); complex (broadband and more like screams, roars, or growls); and a final category variously labelled as clicks, pulses, knocks, and grunts (all short duration signals).[40]

While songs have been reported for blue, bowhead, fin, and humpback whales,[41] the humpback remains the most famous singer, given the popularity of its recordings and the easy access for recording this coastal species. Little is known about the social function of singing, though it seems to have some connection with mating. In addition, humpbacks seem to enjoy breaching, finning, and lob-tailing, proving quite agile despite their tremendous bulk. (Many are over fifty feet and forty tons).[42] Some controversy persists about whether these whales might not constitute a separate genus, since they have relatively enormous flippers. (In fact, *megaptera* means 'great wing,' a reference to these flippers.) Humpbacks can be found in all the seas; they migrate north and south, escaping cold in winter and heat in summer. With a natural life span of forty-five to fifty years, after years of protection some of them in fact are living that long.

The hunt for the humpback was substantial, even though the whales sink when they are killed. Before a technical modification was introduced, this fact made them difficult to retrieve. Humpbacks often come into shallow water to rub barnacles off their skin along the rocky bottom, making them easy targets for shore whalers, who operated out of a shore-based factory, hauling each catch back for processing.[43] The days of pelagic whaling were little different. Perhaps more than any other whale species, the humpback became symbolic of the overhunting that followed the Second World War. Humpbacks were killed in Atlantic and Pacific waters alike. Since they were relatively easy to study, they became the banner whale for cetacean research. And since they were rather personable, they became a favourite among environmental activists from the late 1960s onwards.

Two rorquals are very similar: the sei whale (*Balaenoptera borealis*) and the Bryde's whale (*Balaenoptera edeni*). These are moderate-sized whales, which means they are rarely over fifty feet. They are widely distributed, though the Bryde's prefer warmer water, venturing into tropical areas, while the sei do not. The sei are known for their huge eyeballs – twelve inches in circumference – and they are the fastest swimmers among the rorquals. Bryde's are named after Johann Bryde, a Norwegian consul in South Africa. The sei were named by the Norwegians after a fish by the same name, because both whale and fish migrate into Norwegian waters at the same time of year. Though few sei were taken in the Southern Hemisphere before the 1960s, both species were eventually and ambitiously hunted, especially the sei, which is supposed to have the best-tasting flesh of all the whales. A peak kill of the species was recorded in 1964-5, at about 20,000. The IWC eventually restricted sei catch levels in the Southern Ocean, which led to newfound interest in the much smaller minke whale. The Bryde's whale was not harvested commercially in the Southern Hemisphere.

The fin whale (*Balaenoptera physalus*), also known as the razor-back whale, is the second-largest living mammal and was at one time the most abundant whale in the Southern Ocean. Most adults are over sixty feet, and many have been recorded at over eighty feet. The fin whale, not surprisingly, has a rather distinct fin, easily discernible when surfacing. The species is distributed globally, though rarely found in extreme cold or heat. Its life span has been estimated by some as 90 to 100 years, though this point remains controversial. Northern fins would yield five or six tons of oil; southern fins over nine. Though this amount is under half the yield of a blue whale, it was certainly sufficient to excite the whaling interests: at one stage, a single fin catch could justify an entire whaling expedition.

The largest rorqual is the blue (*Balaeoptera musculus*), a species driven to the brink of extinction by overhunting made possible with the technological introduction of the huge factory ships in the 1930s. The blue is widely distributed but primarily frequents the Antarctic, feeding off the krill in the local plankton. Its size is legendary: no other whale could match its yield of up to eighty barrels of oil. The spout from a blue's blow-hole can reach forty feet, and a male blue's penis can be ten feet in length. Blues occasionally give birth to twins, which is rare in the cetacean world. There are three sub-species of blues: the northern blue, the Antarctic blue, and the much smaller pygmy blue, found mainly in the southern Indian Ocean.

As the blue provided a virtual bounty of commodity goods for its takers, and the species was not effectively protected by the IWC until 1965, its numbers were decimated in short time. Estimates vary, but most experts fear that fewer than 1,000 blue whales exist today. This low population raises fears about the gene pool dynamics discussed earlier.[44] However, recent reports from Russian delegates to the IWC indicate that many more blues were taken after they were given protection than was originally known. Therefore, the lack of recovery of blue whales may be due to sheer loss of numbers rather than any current inability to reproduce.

The minke whale, or lesser rorqual (*Balaenoptera acutorostrata*), is a much smaller species, which escaped large-scale hunting campaigns until fairly recently. Few minkes were taken at all before the 1970s. They became a target species as a direct consequence of the stock exhaustion of the larger whales. The minke is the smallest of the rorquals at twenty-three to thirty-three feet in length, and rarely weighs over eleven tons. Norway and Iceland both insist on their right to hunt the minke, arguing that the species is not near extinction. Minke whalemeat is sold in Japan, despite the IWC prohibition of its sale. This species has thus become the last of the hunted, largely valued for meat. The minke has also been hunted for 'scientific research,' with Japan continuing this practice.

Finally, there are two species of right whales, one of which is somewhat confusingly also called the right whale (*Balaena glacialis*). This whale was perhaps the most heavily hunted of all, and it remains a very endangered species. Its name derives from early whalers' conviction that it was the 'right whale' to kill: it floated when dead, yielded substantial oil and whalebone, and swam slowly. As Charles Boardman Hawes wrote in 1924, this whale was perceived as right 'since his "bone" was finer and longer and his oil more abundant than that of other whales.'[45] Right whales grow up to sixty feet and female adults can weigh as much as 100 tons; they have no dorsal fin and a characteristic v-shaped double spout. The right is known by its characteristic 'bonnet' head, which is in fact a patch of thickened white skin known as a callosity. Each whale has a peculiar arrangement of callosities, making it easy for observers to identify individual whales in photographs. Callosities have scattered hair growing from them, including facial hair that grows in patterns similar to human hair.

Blubber insulates whales from cold, but it must also allow heat to escape, or it would in fact be lethal. When a whale engages in sudden jolts of action, the energy released must be allowed to escape through the blubber.[46] The right whale is known to have blubber that is twice as thick as other baleen whales, perhaps because it does not engage in much quick-action behaviour. This factor made the right irresistible to early whalers, who hunted them in the North Pacific, although they also found them fairly widely distributed in the South. In fact, the right was hunted by Europeans in Spain's Bay of Biscay as early as 1100. At present, the North Atlantic right whale is by most estimates the most endangered of all whales, numbering fewer than 400, despite a 100-year reprieve from hunting.[47] Canadian Inuit take the occasional right whale, and the whales are studied in breeding grounds off Argentina.

The other species of right whale, the bowhead (*Balaena mysticetus*), has an even more unusual head shape. Also known as the Greenland right whale, the Arctic right whale, and the great polar whale, the bowhead could reach sixty feet and was found in Arctic waters across the northern coasts of North America, Europe, and Asia, although it has also been observed near California. The bowhead, like the right, was important in early whaling efforts, since it shared the latter's physical traits and yielded seventy to ninety barrels of oil. In fact, the rapid depletion of the bowhead and the right turned the whaling industry towards the Pacific and its humpbacks and sperms. One group of bowhead, which spent the winter along the eastern coast of Greenland and the summer in the seas near Spitzbergen, Franz Josef Land, and Novaya Zemlya, was exterminated entirely. At various points from 1600 onwards, the bowhead was hunted by the Danes, the British, the Dutch, the Germans, the French, and the Basques. Davis Strait would become a busy whaling area until the reduced numbers of the bowhead made its hunt unprofitable.[48] Today, bowheads remain the targets of occasional aboriginal whaling, which we will discuss later.

The remaining type of whale, the pygmy right whale (*Caperea marginata*), is very rare and not known to be hunted.

Whalers

A wooden fort bristling with cannon stood sentinel at one end of town. For sailors with a few hours of leisure there was a church and a tavern, but leisure was in short supply at Smeerenburg, a town that never slept. Night and day crews stoked the blazing furnaces, boiling up the oil, filling the casks, then laying them down in the ships' holds. The season was short; not a minute could be wasted if the whalers hoped to make a profit.

– Daniel Francis, 1990[49]

We turn our attention now to another endangered species, the whaler. Whaling has gone through so many boom-and-bust periods over the last 500 years that no attempt will be made to chronicle them here. In the 1800s, whaling was a major industry, and in the era following the Second World War, it again played a large role in the economies of several nations. Currently, however, commercial whaling is limited to the few Norwegian and Japanese whalers who continue to take minkes and to very few other whalers scattered across the globe. Aboriginal whalers have also shifted from their traditional roles in many areas, though subsistence whaling does continue in the Arctic and around some Pacific and Atlantic islands.

It is a popular error to consider the near-extinction of the great whales as a true 'tragedy of the commons.' No doubt, whales are part of what the sovereignty-dominated world political system has seen fit to declare is the commons. But the basic idea behind the tragedy of the commons is that, in order to pursue what on an individual level is self-interest, economic actors, such as medieval farmers or contemporary fishers, would allow their livestock to graze on as much fallow common land or would take as much common fish as possible. The tale of whaling may more properly be viewed as one of barely mitigated greed on the part of several actors, which, supported by the state apparatus of the sovereign nations where they chiefly operated, went about whaling with little if any regard for the future of whales or, for that matter, whaling. As the market dwindled over time and whale stocks diminished, whaling becomes less a tragedy of the commons and more a race for survival among whaling operations.

That description applies particularly well to whaling in the present century. As G. Kent writes, 'Excessive whaling by Japan and the Soviet Union ... represents the exercise of oligopolistic power more than it represents a tragedy of unlimited access by large numbers of equal competitors.'[50] However, the tradition of excess within the whaling industry in fact began in the 1800s. Even at that time, and though whalers may have mistakenly believed that whales were capable of rapid reproduction, even those with little experience could not help but know better. As Robert Webb writes, 'It is a parable of the whale fishery, now well understood, that each new whaling area yields up the bulk of its harvest in the first few years of whaling. Increased use only depletes the natural resources and leads to a failure of the ground. This proved to be as true in the western Arctic as it had been on the [Pacific] Northwest Coast. The Arctic whalemen hunted further and longer and, eventually, the bowheads were extirpated like their more southerly cousins.'[51] It is not difficult to identify or recognize near-extinction from overhunting of most species, and the depletion of large cetaceans – which must be caught individually – is particularly visible.[52]

The larger paradigm of frontier economics permitted this approach to resource management to define the industry for so long. Francisco Sagasti and Michael Colby, who argue this paradigm is now being eclipsed by others, define it as 'characterized by the view that the environment consists of limitless resources and that economic growth may be disembodied from nature.'[53] Whalers probably had a better empirical grasp of the finiteness of nature than most economic actors in the seventeenth to twentieth centuries. As with any fishery, overinvestment played a crucial role: investments had to be recovered, which often took an intolerable toll on whale stocks. That mammals larger than dinosaurs and roamers of the seas for millions of years were threatened with extinction by something as transitory as the sunk costs for a whaling fleet says much about human economics, consumption, and technological power.

Whaling seems inextricably linked to the early histories of most naval powers. The Basques apparently were whaling before the tenth century. The Norwegians, who are generally quite proud of this tradition, were whaling as early as 1250. The Dutch had major whaling operations in effect by 1500, joined soon after by the French and English. And the early American whaling trade is well popularized by literary classics such as *Moby Dick*. Historical accounts of early commercial whaling are proliferating, revealing much about the relationships between industrial expansion, human-nature interaction, and international relations.[54] As whaling became a more institutionalized industry, complete with technological innovations and legal arrangements, the industry increased its range, most notably into Arctic, and then Antarctic, waters, which were less accessible before the days of modern naval vessels.

In effect, whaling was one of the economic activities that helped spread European civilization into previously uncharted waters and areas. It drove exploration by sea, and, simultaneously, its products helped drive industrialization on land. Indeed, whaling has evolved a unique folklore and mythology. Whale products have contributed a good deal to the development of industrial society: whale blubber, once burned on whaling vessels themselves, provided oil for lubrication, candles, and reading lamps, until America's early interest in whaling began to wane with the 1859 discovery of petroleum in Pennsylvania. Blubber was also used to make soap; the explosive nitroglycerine was made from one of the by-products of the soap production process. The list of whale products, extended into the current century, is truly amazing; and, so long as whales (and whalers) were perceived as abundant, humankind was slow to develop substitutes. A partial list includes flexible baleen filaments for watch-springs and umbrellas, oils for purposes including illumination, plastics, margarine, lipsticks, detergents, brushes, engineering coolants, fertilizers, medicines, gelatine, and corsets. Hawes writes that whalebone was once 'shredded into plumes for the helmets of noble knights in tourney. The vertebrae were made into chair seats, and the entire skeleton into garden fences.'[55] Spermaceti oil, obtained from the sperm whale's head, has been used in space research; and ambergris has been used as a fixative in the perfume and cosmetic industries. Today – and this point deserves stressing – the only really valuable whale product is meat for limited human consumption and animal feed.

But oil was once the staple whale product, and spermaceti the most prized of all, yielding up to forty pounds per ton. The American whaling industry discovered the sperm whale in the mid-1700s and exported the oil to Great Britain. As Ommanney writes:

> By 1755 Joseph Russell, a farmer, had built the first Sperm oil factory at Bedford, Massachusetts, later called New Bedford. It was supplied by a fleet of 50-ton sloops which made voyages of two or three months as far as Newfoundland and Virginia. These were comparatively short trips, known as 'plum-pudding voyages' presumably because the ships were home for Christmas, but by 1775 some 60 sloops were sailing from New Bedford each year as far afield as the Falkland Islands.[56]

Governments have a long history of benefits from the whaling industry, since, as an economic activity, it was certainly taxable. In fact, Charles Boardman Hawes has written on what may well be the earliest example of taxation on whaling:

> In the 12th Century (1197) King John of England, acting as Duke of Guyenne, laid the first tax on whaling when he assigned to Vital de Biole a certain sum to be levied on the first two whales of the year captured at Biarritz. In 1261, all whales landed at Bayonne were tithed, which tithing undoubtedly had its origin in the earlier custom of giving the whales' tongues to the Church.[57]

Several centuries later, whaling would be involved in another taxation incident, though this one would have much more serious implications for the history of the United States. In what many at the time viewed as yet another imposition from Britain upon North American settlers, the infamous Stamp Act was passed by the British Parliament on 22 March 1765; all vessels clearing port were supposed have their papers stamped after paying a tax. This requirement bothered the whaling Nantucketers, adding fuel to the fire of American independence. However, 'public pressure combined with bodily threats led to the resignation of the stamp collectors at Boston and Newport,' with the act being repealed in 1766.[58] Indeed, one of the whaling interests affected by the Stamp Act was the House of Rotch. Though this powerful whaling family was not revolutionary, Rotch vessels were involved in the famous Boston Tea Party. The vessels went to London initially 'with cargoes of whale and sperm oil,' returning loaded with tea, and the rest is American history.[59]

Whaling history is replete with tales of conflict on the high seas and not just between the hunter and hunted. The British Muscovy Company, protected with a twenty-year monopoly granted by the queen, did most of the Arctic whaling in the early 1600s. At Cherrie Island, in 1612, the Muscovy Company arrived to hunt and was shocked to find a Dutch whaling vessel, another from San Sebastian, and two other English vessels not attached to the Muscovy Company. The Dutch had apparently been led to these whaling grounds by an Englishman who had once worked for Muscovy but had been 'obliged to leave his own country for debt.' This man's actions appeared 'to have been little short of treason, in the eyes of the Muscovy Company's men, and they made the most of it.'[60] Both the British, on the strength of Sir Hugh Willoughby's 1553 voyage to Northern Russia, and the Dutch, on the strength of Jacob van Hemmskerk's May 1596 sail, claimed the discovery of Spitzbergen. By 1613, ships from England, the Netherlands, Flanders, and France made their way there. In 1615, Denmark tried and failed to hold back all except the English. The Dutch then established the first permanent Arctic whaling station: Smeerenburg, which by 1619 had 1,000 citizens every summer.

The Dutch would temporarily win the battle for prominence. In 1698, according to Hawes's records, of the 189 vessels in the North Atlantic, 129 were Dutch. They also took 1,255 of the 1,968 whales captured, and made £250,000 of the £380,000 that constituted the aggregate proceeds of Arctic whaling.[61] Whaling prowess thus coincided with the Dutch naval prominence at the time. As well, violence was a factor here. In 1617, five Dutch ships, in reprisal for similar attacks, took two English ships and a pinnace, rifled them, and burned their casks of whale oil. The Muscovy Company ran aground soon thereafter and was sold at auction in 1622.

Before the invention and deployment of the submarine, war was generally good to whales. Dutch whalers, who had enjoyed unparalleled success on the high seas, including the bowhead hunt in Davis

Strait, were practically put out of commission when, from 1795 to 1813, Dutch ports were blockaded by the British navy.[62] Earlier, the American War of Independence temporarily stopped American whaling, resulting in much confusion and anger over the duties imposed on American whale oil exports to Britain. For example, writes Ommanney, 'in 1775 the American War of Independence began and [this] temporarily ruined the young American whaling industry because the ships could not go to sea for fear of capture by the British. Whaling ports were raised [burned] and the warehouses were choked with unsold oil. Nantucket almost starved.'[63] Whaleships were relatively defenceless targets, and, in times of war, whalemen might be called on for navy duty. The sperm whale hunt from Nantucket, New England, which began in earnest around 1815, had expanded rapidly after 1750 when Davis Strait bowhead whaling became financially all but impossible and American settlers' demand for candles increased. Even this expansion, however, 'suffered a severe setback at the advent of the American War of Independence in 1775. Very little whaling occurred thereafter until 1783 due to the loss of any vessels and the restriction of movement of others.'[64] The Second World War severely affected whaling, stopping it across the globe. Despite this hiatus, whale stocks did not rejuvenate as some might have expected. Then, ironically, the United States encouraged Japan to resume whaling to supply much-needed protein and oil to a then impoverished nation.

Whaling remained at best a challenging financial enterprise, prone to boom-and-bust cycles. These cycles partly reflected broader currents in the economies of whaling nations, but also reflected the human drive to see a quick return on initial investment, and the biological inability of sixty-ton creatures to reproduce as quickly as fish. As a result, whales faced extinction even during the age of wind, before the quicker and more mobile steamships prowled the seas. In the sixth century, the Atlantic gray was wiped out along the European coast; in the early eighteenth century, its North American counterpart met the same fate. By the thirteenth century, right whales were overexploited by Basque whalers in the Bay of Biscay.[65] In the sixteenth century, the Basques had also hunted bowhead and right whales in the waters off Eastern Canada.[66] Whaling has always been a bloody and dangerous business, a prime example of the risks of the maritime life and industry. But whaling by wind and sail and whaling by modern commercial technologies differ quantitatively and qualitatively.

The evolution of modern pelagic whaling has been spurred by technological improvements in nautical prowess as well as more efficient
means of killing and flensing. These improvements include the introduction of sail-based whaling in the early 1800s, the harnessing of
steam, shore-based whaling stations, grenade harpoons, and inflation
devices that allowed carcasses to float. With the single exception of
the right whale, whales sink when killed. Inflation devices, shot into
a whale's rib cage, literally inflate the whale and float the carcass. A
distinctive flag is then attached to the device, other ships recognize to
whom the whale belongs, and the catcher ship carries on with the
hunt. This means of identification was apparently well respected
among whalers. Other significant technological developments were
made by the Norwegian Svend Foyn, who in the mid-to-late 1800s
developed the exploding grenade harpoon, the first modern whaling
station, a steam-winch for hauling carcasses, and a system for making
fertilizer or 'guano' from leftover bones. The exploding harpoon, aimed
at the whale's head, kills the whale as soon as possible and allowed
for the taking of blue, fin, and other large whales. It also reduced the
time spent chasing struck whales. Writes historian Robert Webb: 'The
efforts of the mythic Svend Foyn became the earliest legends of modern whaling as advancing industry resolved the herculean joust
between man and whale into a unilateral cannon-bombardment.'[67]

Another particularly significant invention was the factory ship,
whose introduction in the mid-1920s doubled the global kill. Factory
ships were the biggest fishing boats ever made, with large slipways at
the stern so that an entire whale carcass could be hauled on deck for
assembly-line processing. Previously, the dead whale had to be taken
to a shore station or, much more dangerously, flensed of its blubber
and other valuables while floating tied to the ship.[68] One of these
gigantic vessels, which made even the mammoth blue whale look
small, would be serviced by several much smaller catcher boats. The
Japanese and Soviets would base their emerging whaling industries
on these vessels. A symbolic progression is discernible: once a great
struggle with nature, whaling became a methodical commercial function of hugely expensive applied technology.

With these leaps in killing technologies, any pretensions about the
romance of whaling were banished to the realm of fiction. However,
the changes benefited whalemen, who contrary to public perception
never enjoyed lives of glamour at sea. The physical act of whaling was
dangerous, and many whalers were killed throughout the industry. The

great respect accorded to whalemen by various aboriginal groups reflects the intense dangers of the early whaling hunt, which initially involved throwing a hand-harpoon from a small boat, and then repeated and close-range thrusts of a hand-lance. The explosive lance was not used until the mid-1800s.[69] Early Japanese whalers used large nets to catch whales, ending again with stabbing. This work is not easy. As well, the process of flensing was filthy, as was running the tryworks, in which blubber was burned to oil. Further, whaling voyages were infamously long, with friction among crew members often resulting in violence.

We have referred to whalemen, rather than whalepersons, not to be provocative but to reflect the fact that this industry was highly male-dominated. Though captains' wives occasionally joined extended whaling voyages, such companionship was rare. Most contact between men and women in the whaling industry involved prostitution. This is certainly the impression gathered from reading of the antics of American whalemen in the eighteenth century: companionship was sought in many foreign ports. Of course, the impression relates to a broader perception of sailors, but the whaleman's life seemed particularly harsh. Commenting on early American whalemen, Reverend Sheldon Dribble wrote in 1839: 'Let us never name the ungodly conduct of seamen without deep self-reproach for our neglect of them. *Why are they, as a class, wicked and degraded?* Who of us would have possessed a better character if we had been left to grow up under the same neglect and abuse?'(italics in original).[70]

Whaling expeditions could last weeks, months, or over a year. The Nantucket sperm whaling ship *Mariner,* for example, sailed from 14 September 1836 to 20 June 1840. It traveled from the American east coast across the Atlantic to the Azores, down to Cape Verde (off Senegal), through Drake Passage below South America, and then halfway up the Pacific for a three-year stay before turning home. In the Pacific, the *Mariner* followed a basic 'itinerary, repeated for three years, [which] included Summer hunting on the Japan Ground and Autumn on the Hawaiian Ground, with Winter and Spring either at the On The Line Ground or in the Tuamotu Archipelago.'[71] Young men seeking their dreams by sea were in many cases soon disappointed.

When the whales were sparse, life aboard a whaleship was an interminable experience of sea and ennui. Captains had unusual authority on these lengthy journeys, often resorting to physical punishment of non-compliant sailors, including flogging and using the dreaded cat-o'-nine-tails. According to Briton Cooper Busch, who has produced a most comprehensive and insightful treatment of the social life of eighteenth-century whalers: 'Occasionally the punishment was extraordinarily severe. On the ship *Canada*, the steward was not only flogged but subsequently confined for six weeks, until the vessel made port, in a closed cask in the hold. The [ship's] log notes he was sometimes taken out for an "airing."'[72] Crew members would generally sign a contract with the ship's captain promising servitude; fear of mutiny was high owing to the conditions of work. Hawes reproduces a Contract Between the Commander and Crew of a German Whaler Sailing to Greenland in 1671. Among other things, the crew had to 'promise to be content with the food which shall be given us by order of the commander'; and 'whosoever shall learn or discover any evil design against the vessel, etc., shall be bound to denounce it, and shall be recompensed for his fidelity.'[73] Indeed, food was a major problem in this age before refrigeration, as an amusing excerpt from Busch's excellent study suggests:

> [In 1857] fresh meat was a rare treat for any long-voyage whaleman, enough so, for example, to inspire the master of the bark Richmond of Providence to haul his mainsail aback and order two boats lowered in midpassage, all to rescue a single chicken that had accidentally gone overboard (the result was not logged).[74]

Contrary to image, then, whalers had difficult, and often short, lives. Wages were low, and, as most whalers borrowed funds for various reasons, pay was weighed against any debt accrued to the ship's owners. Whalers were paid according to the number of whales taken. This procedure both encouraged overexploitation and ensured that whalers suffered severe economic hardship after the whale stocks diminished. Desertion was common and mutinies occurred. Whalers must be seen as labourers in the larger field of seafarers, an occupation that even today remains hazardous.[75] But whaling was a particularly dirty business. A sense of the dark industry, which no doubt also has its tales of heroism, bright moments, and inspiration, is captured well by Nigel Bonner:

> Antarctic whaling was a bloody business. I spent ten years living next to a whaling station in the Antarctic. I grew accustomed, but never indifferent, to their great carcases lying on the flensing deck as, amid the roar

of the steam winches, their oleaginous blubber was ripped off. The method of killing – the internal explosion of a cast-iron grenade packed with 400 g (14 oz) of black powder – was undeniably cruel (although most of the whales died quickly). The philosophy of the industry was deplorable. The whalers were aware that they were destroying their own livelihood, but for the most part they had no other trade to turn to.[76]

One last point about whalers no doubt flows from the migratory pattern of the whales themselves. Whaling crews were always international in composition and perhaps more so as time passed. Though certain nations, notably Norway and Japan, have produced most of the whalers in this century, these men have found employment in diverse areas, including pirate whaling, which really has no official nationality. There is nothing new in this form of industrial cosmopolitanism. Hawes reports that in a German whaleboat off Greenland in 1800, all but five of the forty-two men were Danes, Dutch, or Jutlanders.[77] Additional crew members were picked up as the whaleboat made its longer journeys, replacing those who had deserted or died. The American *Minerva* of 1859 had thirty-three foremast hands; three Cape Verdans, two Azoreans, three Chamorros from Guam, three East Indians, two Malays, one Bengali, thirteen Hawaiians, one Tahitian, and another from Wellington Island.[78] In the early 1900s, British companies employed Norwegian whalemen exclusively, and 'even in Japan the personnel of the modern steam whaler is Norwegian, although there all the shore operations are done by Japanese labour.'[79]

Commercial whaling was clearly an international affair.

Whaling Management

Whaling management has gone through distinct phases; however, most of the management has been directed at distributing a common property-resource rather than preserving it. This goal is no longer the case, but could be expected in earlier years: any common resource that attracts consumers worldwide is bound to be the focus of international conflict. For example, a treaty between Russia and the United States, prompted by a dispute over whalers' access to the Russian Pacific, was signed as early as 1824. But the present institutional arrangement was not realized until 1946.

Early international attempts at formally regulating the whaling industry were characterized by a lack of initiative and commitment, though obvious economic incentives encouraged establishing a whaling regime. For example, in the early 1930s, the killing of many blue whales flooded the market with whale oil, quickly driving down prices. As Daniel Francis writes, 'It was evident to the whalers that national controls were not enough. Some kind of international regulation was necessary to stabilize the wild price fluctuations afflicting the industry.'[80] In 1931, the Convention for the Regulation of Whaling was signed in Geneva and, in 1937, was amended as the International Agreement for the Regulation of Whaling. This agreement did establish certain guidelines: right whales and bowheads, virtually extinct by this time, were exempted from further killing; prohibitions were placed on killing pregnant or lactating whales or calves; and paying whaleboat crews per whale taken was outlawed. But the very nations that were expanding whaling operations (Japan, Germany, Chile, Argentina, and the USSR) refused to sign. Negotiations throughout the 1930s, when modern whaling technology was employed at a frightening pace, resulted in little more than almost 'doubling of the kill [from 30,000 to 55,000 whales per year] and an intensification of the hunt.'[81] Regulation within the League of Nations framework amounted to 'regulated recklessness.'[82]

It was not until 1946 that the International Convention for the Regulation of Whaling, which legally created the IWC, was signed.[83] (Japan would sign once it resumed whaling in 1951.) As this step occurred in the immediate postwar international climate, it was unsurprisingly the result primarily of American initiative. The American government wanted to encourage some order in the global private investment in whaling and in whale-product trade. This approach would contribute to bringing Japan into the larger economic system 'while also exercising some control over the activities of the newest whaling nation, the USSR.'[84] There is what Jeremy Cherfas calls a 'fine irony' in America's original insistence that the 1946 convention not be a binding instrument: Article V allows states to escape from IWC decisions, provided notice of any objection is given within ninety days. Only two decades later, the US would begin to lead the anti-whaling coalition. The American insistence, however, is not surprising, because sovereignty was (and remains) the core formal principle upon which the United Nations system was (and is) based.[85]

The IWC includes one representative from each state that is party to the ICRW. It has a small administrative secretariat, a technical committee that eventually recommends policy (and which operates more like a forum for pre-voting consultation among appointed commissioners), and a scientific committee of cetologists and other marine mammal experts. Members of the latter committee, somewhat divorced from industrial interests, have played a limited yet important role in the evolution of the whaling regime.[86] Most significantly, in 1974, the committee was able to persuade members to discontinue the devastatingly shortsighted 'Blue Whale Unit' (BWU) system of quotas. Previously, and with the exception of fully protected species, individual species were not protected by quotas designed to reflect concerns about their populations. The BWU system, established in 1939 by the Bureau of International Whaling Statistics, measured whale populations and allocated quotas based on the expected oil yield in comparison to that produced by the blue whale, regardless of the state of particular populations.[87] This system was replaced by the more specific 'maximum sustainable yield' (MSY), which has since been further modified.[88] (During the reign of the BWU in the 1960s, the whales diminished so rapidly that the number of kills could not even keep up to the absurdly high quotas set by the IWC.) The Scientific Committee was to become an increasingly important component of the IWC after 1975, when what was then termed the New Management Procedure (NMP) was established. The NMP ordered the world of Cetacea in three categories: initial management stocks, which could, in the committee's opinion, be reduced to MSY without damaging future population levels; sustained management stocks, which could be hunted only with great care, since they were already at MSY levels; and, finally, protected stocks, which were already below the MSY and needed full protection from hunting. K.R. Allen, commenting upon the weight placed on the committee's attempts to regulate whaling through scientific management, notes:

> Even the decision as to whether or not a stock should be protected may require its level to be assessed to the nearest 1% of its current position in relation to the MSY level. Similarly the Committee has to recommend to the Commission a precise figure for the quota calculated as 90% of MSY. It is obvious that none of the analyses can provide estimates which approach this level of accuracy.[89]

Before the number of whaling nations was diminished, members would negotiate the allocation of quotas outside the IWC. According to the Frost Inquiry report: 'Sales of pelagic operations by various companies had as their main purpose the transfer of quota shares between companies.'[90] This strategy enabled the withdrawal of British and Dutch whalers from pelagic whaling; quota rights were sold to the Japanese and ex-whalers were paid in turn.

The Whaling Market

The Japanese and the Norwegian coastal whalers argue no contemporary equivalent means of compensation is available for those displaced by the present moratorium.[91] They are right, of course, but critics argue that this fact results from the nature of business and cannot be avoided in a declining marketplace. Although the whaling issue has been politicized to an extent rarely seen in any field of economic activity, we would be remiss to neglect the central importance of supply and demand relationships. As Daniel Francis writes in his epic history of whaling, the IWC 'and conservation groups administered the death blow to commercial whaling, but it was already seriously wounded by declining profits, rising costs and a depleted stock of animals.'[92] No attempt is made here to gloss over this central point in the name of political science; in fact, the preceding argument should also list the crucial economic factor of declining demand. For example, by the late 1800s in the United States, whale oil was replaced by relatively clean-burning kerosene:

> In Vermont in 1858 ... kerosene, at $1.24 per gallon, outpriced whale oil at $1.12; thus the inconvenience of added smoke and smell saved twelve cents. A dozen years later, kerosene was forty cents, and whale oil, though its price had fallen by half, could not compete. In 1880, a gallon of whale oil still cost fifty-one cents, but kerosene a mere eighteen cents.[93]

Thus, whaling became prohibitively expensive in many areas and remains so today. Though there is a market (and, many would insist, a thriving black market as well) for whale products, it is very limited. Both the United States and the European Union reject whale products entirely. This position is perhaps the best guarantee we have that the days of mass consumption of cetaceans are well behind us.

The depletion of whale stocks has attracted great attention. The field of mathematical bioeconomics, for example, was founded by Colin Clark in the early 1970s, and he used open-access fisheries, and in particular the whaling issue, to discuss whaling's logical, mathematical implications. Clark argued that we should consider resource stocks as capital assets of stakeholders in order to understand the economic imperatives driving fisheries towards self-extinction. In his now-famous model based on the blue whale, Clark offered an illustration:

> Imagine that through past operations the industry has reduced the original 150,000 whales to the MSY level of 75,000. If $10,000 represents the market value of the products obtained from an average blue whale, then an MSY policy will result in an annual revenue of 20 million at 2000 whales caught per year. On the other hand, the industry might decide to capture the remaining 75,000 whales immediately, overlooking the possibility of sustained production altogether. Assuming that this could be accomplished in one season and neglecting the problem of [demand elasticity], the industry would obtain a lump-sum revenue of 750 million. Invested at [even] 5% per annum, this sum would yield an annual return of 37.5 million ... extermination of the blue-whale population appears to constitute a considerably more profitable policy than MSY.[94]

I hasten to add that Clark was not advocating such madness; he was trying to understand some of the economic forces involved in open-access fisheries. By the time he had written about mathematical bio-economics, the blue whale population numbered less than 8,000 and the species was no longer commercially viable. Even today, the blue remains one of the most endangered species, with an estimated fewer than 1,000 individuals remaining.

In the next chapter, we examine the political context in which this tragedy occurred and upon which any future conservation will at least depend. We should, however, keep the economic considerations in sight. They are important as we enter the stage of post-scarcity common resources, as indicated by the recovery of minke whale stocks in particular.

3
Cetapolitics: The IWC, Foreign Policies, and NGOs

It is really deplorable that the IWC has become an organization to protect the rights of whales.

– Kazuo Shima, Japanese commissioner to the IWC, 1993[1]

The International Whaling Commission is located in Cambridge, England. As international organizations go, the IWC is as modest as its home is British. It is not the United Nations, or even a program or agency of the United Nations. It is not a large multinational corporation with global reach, or even a popular non-governmental organization with widespread public support, like Greenpeace or Amnesty International. It is, by most accounts, a small and moderate operation that exists primarily to facilitate discussion among states that have a stake in the cetacean issue-area, though it is also capable of exerting limited influence in this capacity through its scientific committee. And it is in trouble.

The trouble stems from the contemporary dilemma of post-scarcity cetapolitics. The IWC has shifted dramatically over the years, from its beginning in 1946 as a pro-whaling industrial club, through many years of virtual ineffectiveness, to its current status as what many view to be – with markedly varying levels of approval – an anti-whaling establishment. However, with the limited increase in whale stocks, in particular minke stocks, whaling states still participating in the IWC process, especially Japan and Norway (Iceland has left the organization at present), see no need for the 1986 global moratorium on whaling. The voting structure of the IWC, and American influence within it, has made the moratorium a seemingly permanent feature of IWC decision-making, and this perception delegitimizes the entire organization for those who support some commercial whaling. This chapter traces the evolution of the IWC, looks at the related foreign policies of some of the key states involved, and examines the contribution of non-governmental organizations.

By defining the IWC as a troubled institution, we might be imposing

an early bias. Many would argue it offers a model worthy of emula-
tion. In one sense, with the normative transition of the IWC from a
'whalers club'[2] to an official agent of conservation, the whale slowly
begins to symbolize not humanity's inability to respect the beauty of
nature, but our ability to cooperate to preserve nature. This transition
is of interest not only to ecologists and wildlife conservationists, but
to scholars of world politics concerned with international cooperation
and change. However, the IWC by no means enjoys solidarity on this
issue; in fact, the organization is in great conflict, with two seemingly
irreconcilable philosophies clashing in a political maelstrom. The
future of the IWC will hinge on the outcome.

An Institutional History

In the whaling season of 1961-2, a peak kill of 66,900 large whales
was registered with the IWC.[3] By 1982, the IWC had accepted a global
moratorium (effective in 1986) banning all commercial whaling by
all of its members, then numbering thirty-two. Fewer whales were
available for the hunt, of course, and the whaling industry had died
out in many states on its own. But the 1980s saw a new IWC, where
the majority of members – many had joined for this very purpose –
saw fit to censure continued whaling by Japan and the Soviet Union.

The moratorium seems even more remarkable when we review the
initial goals of the IWC. The organization was part of the broader
global order set up by American foreign policy at the end of the
Second World War. The International Convention for the Regulation
of Whaling (included here as Appendix B) was signed in 1946 in
Washington, creating the legal entity we know today as the IWC. As
mentioned, the Americans wanted the Japanese to whale, because
postwar Japan, under American occupation, needed protein. The long
history of whaling and a skilled workforce lent itself naturally to using
the industry to meet this need. At the time, the longevity of the IWC
was unknown; the hope was that it would facilitate pelagic whaling,
helping to avoid a return to tensions among whaling states.[4]

The IWC was as weak as any other international organization, lack-
ing effective mechanisms for policy enforcement and even observation of whaling activities. However, it has a fairly wide mandate for
regulatory action, as outlined in Article V of the ICRW:

1. The Commission may amend from time to time the provisions of
the Schedule by adopting regulations with respect to the conserva-

tion and utilization of whale resources, fixing (a) protected and unprotected species; (b) open and closed seasons; (c) open and closed waters, including the designation of sanctuary areas; (d) size limits for each species; (e) time, methods, and intensity of whaling (including the maximum catch of whales to be taken in any one season); (f) types and specifications of gear and apparatus and appliances which may be used; (g) methods of measurement; and (h) catch returns and other statistical and biological records.

The broader question was whether this mandate could be carried out when the IWC was composed of states with direct stakes in the whaling industry itself, an industry that did not traditionally lend itself well to conservation of species. And, importantly, in the immediate postwar period, few nations other than the United States had a stable infrastructure; all products were scarce, including oil and meat. This fact made the scientific recognition of whale stock depletion even less likely. As J.L. McHugh has written:

> In the IWC, as in all international fishery agreements, an inverse correlation can be recognized between the economic importance and political strength of that segment of the national fishing industry and the ability of the national delegation to give priority to scientific objectivity in reaching policy decisions. Coming into existence shortly after the end of a major world war, when the world faced a serious shortage of fats and oils, the Commission was influenced from the start by short-term economic considerations.[5]

In retrospect, it would have been fanciful to expect anything other than the continuation of large-scale whaling following the creation of the IWC. It was, after all, set up in a postwar context of widespread scarcity with the mandate 'to provide for the proper conservation of whale stocks and the orderly development of the whaling industry.'[6] Today, this point is made over and over again by pro-whalers: the IWC is not mandated to stop whaling that does not interfere with the conservation of whale stocks (i.e., if the species are abundant); and, arguably, a total moratorium is hardly conducive to the 'orderly development' of the whaling industry.

To criticize the industrial collusion between the IWC and the whaling consortium is thus rather unfair, since this relationship was perceived as perfectly legitimate. In short, the IWC was administered by the whaling industry itself and its voting structure demanded a three-quarter majority vote to change the convention. So long as the majority of members were whaling nations and government delegates to the IWC were prepared to represent domestic whaling interests, the IWC would remain an instrument with which the whaling industry legitimized and, to some degree, regulated itself. Appropriate governmental representation was assured not only in the case of the Soviet Union, where civil society had little say in the matter regardless, but also in polities where such interests were powerful economic actors. This situation is particularly apparent in Japan, where the whaling industry, as a subsector of the immensely powerful fishing industry, has received inordinate promotion and protection from the central government.[7] Thus, Japan's IWC commissioner from 1951 to 1965 was K. Nakabe of Taiyo Fishery Co. Ltd., arguably one of the most powerful Japanese companies even today, with direct links to the giant conglomerate Mitsubishi.

As in many other international organizations, voluntary membership has always instilled a sense of pragmatism in the IWC proceedings, though this attitude was more evident before the adoption of pro-moratorium policies by the majority of members. In terms of binding agreements, the fear that extremism will spell the ruin of voluntary organizations is common and logical. J.L. McHugh, a former American IWC commissioner, said in 1978 that 'blind insistence on a total moratorium can be counter productive by destroying a viable international mechanism of control achieved after long and hard bargaining.'[8] Provided they give sufficient warning, members are entitled to opt out of a particular decision. Another structural feature of the IWC, however, would facilitate its transformation: any state that is willing to pay dues (and it doesn't matter who in reality is paying those dues) may join. This feature allows for the de facto sponsorship of one state's membership by another state, a point of some contention. By 1982, enough non-whaling nations had joined to make a majority decision imposing a complete ban on whaling. Voluntarism, which most diplomats consider an evil necessity, thus also creates the possibility of change. More to the point, the alternative to voluntary participation is coercion, an infringement on the principle of sovereignty. The IWC may have somewhat coercive origins, as the Japanese, for example, had no real choice but to participate when it was created.

The process of the physical growth and normative transition of the

IWC began in earnest outside the IWC arena itself, at Stockholm in 1972, during the first United Nations Conference on the Human Environment (UNCHE).[9] Activists were able to use the image of the threatened whale as a 'representation of the nonhuman living world,' and this image made an impression upon the attending army of diplomats and media. More specifically, a huge inflatable whale was paraded through Stockholm during the proceedings, a spectacle to be repeated at future IWC annual meetings.[10] What came out of that conference, personally delivered by Secretary General Maurice Strong at the next annual meeting of the IWC, was Resolution 33, a call for a ten-year moratorium on commercial whaling, which was proposed by the United States and adopted almost unanimously.[11] Japan voted against this resolution and the Soviet Union was not present in protest of East Germany's exclusion from certain panels. Resolution 33 was subsequently rejected as extreme by the whaling nations in the IWC. Ten years (and thousands of whales) later, however, the moratorium would be accepted by the necessary majority of IWC members.

Stockholm would change things forever. The 1972 conference generated more action and global increases in environmental awareness than the more recent UNCED could ever hope to. More than half of the 140 multilateral environmental treaties that were negotiated and adopted since 1921, and are extant in the early 1990s, were instituted after this conference.[12] Certainly, it had an impact on the IWC, not only in pushing members towards the eventual adoption of the commercial whaling moratorium, but also in establishing the organization's importance and some administrative stability. Prior to 1972, the IWC had only a part-time secretary and part-time office staff provided by the United Kingdom's Ministry of Agriculture, Fisheries and Food. After UNCHE, and finally materializing in 1976, the IWC obtained a full-time staff, with headquarters in Cambridge, and a full-time secretary, the outstanding international civil servant and cetologist, Ray Gambell.[13]

As important, the post-UNCHE period saw the rise in the United States of environmental awareness and, indeed, activism. As the American whaling industry had long been eclipsed, it was not a domestically problematic policy shift for the American delegation to the IWC to begin pushing very hard for a ban on all whaling and, in particular, on certain highly endangered species. But changes in the IWC cannot be solely attributed to American initiative. In the late 1970s and 1980s, many nations joined the IWC after lobbying from

the Japanese and from the anti-whaling coalitions, including persua-
sive NGOs. Again, given the potentially universal membership structure of the IWC, non-whaling nations are free to join and, regardless
of their international stature, have a full vote. Thus, even the small
Seychelles delegation, funded largely by the British conservationist
Threshold Foundation, was able to play a significant role after joining in 1979, proposing bans on sperm whale hunting and a moratorium on Indian Ocean whaling (renewed at the 1992 Glasgow meeting).[14] Patricia Birnie feels the 'strong environmental policies the
Seychelles brought to the IWC emerged as a forceful counterweight
to the traditional attitudes of the developing member states that were
dominated by economic and sovereignty considerations.'[15]

The impact of the new members (see Table 2) cannot be underestimated. The fact that they were largely southern or 'less-developed'
nations, such as Uruguay, Senegal, Monaco, Kenya, Egypt, and Costa
Rica, is of analytical interest. As Birnie reports, many southern nations
entered the IWC for seemingly ulterior purposes, such as public relations, and keep their participation to a bare minimum. (Many of them
joined during negotiations for the United Nations Conference on the
Law of the Sea – UNCLOS III – in the early 1980s.) Birnie elaborates:
'Dominica never even appointed a Commissioner; Jamaica did so for
only one year; Egypt and several other countries merely sent a delegate from their local embassy for a single day to cast a crucial vote;
and many countries still have not paid their contributions.'[16] These
points hardly matter to the whales whose lives were saved, but they
do suggest that we should avoid interpreting the actions of these
nations as motivated solely by altruism or idealism. Indeed, some
claim that other nations are joining the IWC to vote against the moratorium in their efforts to obtain Japanese development assistance.[17]
This issue will dog the IWC since voluntary membership leads inex-
orably to influence-peddling on both sides of the debate. But, up to
this point, the anti-whaling forces have been the victors in the complex North-South arena of the cetacean issue-area network.

Other long-standing members contributed to the changed attitude
of the IWC. Australia's delegation, pushed by domestic opposition,
slowly turned to oppose commercial whaling. Indeed, the whaling
question generated quite a stir in Australia at this time. The inquiry
by Sir Sydney Frost, MP, into the whaling question, which was presented to then prime minister Malcolm Fraser on 1 December 1978,
is viewed by many as a landmark document in the anti-whaling

Table 2

Membership in the International Whaling Commission, 1972-92

Year	IWC quota	No.	Members
1972-3	42,500	14	USA, Britain, Mexico, France, Argentina, Australia, Canada, Panama, Denmark, Japan, USSR, Norway, Iceland, South Africa
1973-4	40,979		
1974-5	39,864	15	Brazil joins
1975-6	32,578		
1976-7	28,050	16	New Zealand joins
1977-8	23,520	17	Netherlands joins
1978-9	20,428		
1979-80	15,653	23	Seychelles, Sweden, Chile, Peru, Spain, Korea join
1980-1	14,523	24	Switzerland and Oman join; Panama withdraws
1981-2	14,233	32	Jamaica, St. Lucia, Dominica, Costa Rica, Uruguay, China, St. Vincent, India, Philippines join; Canada withdraws
1982-3	12,263	37	Egypt, Kenya, Senegal, Belize, Antigua, Monaco, Germany join; Jamaica, Dominica withdraw
1983-4	9,393	39	Finland, Mauritius join
1984-5	6,623		
1985-6	0*	41	Ireland, Solomon Islands join
1986-92	0	36	Ecuador, Venezuela join; Solomon Islands, Mauritius, Belize, Egypt, Philippines, Uruguay, Dominica, Jamaica, Iceland withdraw
1994	0	35	Seychelles withdraws

* discounting aboriginal and scientific whaling quotas (see Appendix C).
Source: D. Day, *The Whale War* (Vancouver: Douglas and McIntyre 1987), 97; and documentation from the IWC main office in the UK.

movement. It was an explicit recommendation, by a former coastal whaling nation, for an end to all whaling.[18] (It is also a very well written and concise document – an exceptional example of what a governmental inquiry can produce if the right people are involved.) Mexico also added impetus to conservation efforts by declaring Scammon's Lagoon – a tourist attraction that benefits from an annual gray whale migration – a whale sanctuary in 1972. Observers of the Law of the Sea deliberations will recall Mexico's enthusiasm for the principle of the common heritage of mankind; whales would seem to fit in with this theme. So many members, both new and old, supporting within a legal framework a moratorium on the consumptive use of whales, presents a strong image of a 'normative snowball.' At present, the IWC has some thirty-eight members, including China, Ecuador, France, Germany, Oman, the United Kingdom, and many others. Canada, which banned commercial whaling in 1972, dropped out of the IWC in 1982, disappointing many whale enthusiasts. It maintains observer status and contributes to the work of the IWC Scientific Committee. Canadian officials saw the moratorium as an excessively intrusive step, and Canadian Inuit whalers have resented the IWC for some time.

The IWC was only one of a number of international organizations that played a role in its own normative transition. In 1981, the General Assembly of the IUCN declared that 'the view is now held by the people of the majority of nations of the world that for scientific, ecological and aesthetic reasons whales should no longer be killed for industry.'[19] In fact, the IWC is strengthened by a network of other international institutions, primarily by the environmentalist agenda of several United Nations agreements and bodies, such as the United Nations Law of the Sea Convention. Article 65 stipulates: 'States must abide by the regulations of the IWC, whether or not they are Parties to the Whaling Convention, except where they adopt stricter measures for the conservation of whales.' This point is particularly significant for states that do not belong to the IWC but ratify LOSC and that have allowed 'pirate' whalers to fly their national flag in order to escape IWC restrictions.[20] Several other agreements and alliances play a role in the IWC's normative transition: CITES, since all cetaceans whose catch is regulated by the IWC are listed in Appendix One of the LOSC; the European Union, which in 1981 banned the import of whale products for commercial purposes; the important 1982 Convention on the Conservation of Antarctic Marine

Living Resources (CCAMLR), which regulates the exploitation of relevant mammals and krill; and, even more recently, the United Nations Conference on Environment and Development (UNCED).[21] Agenda 21, the lengthy framework that emerged from UNCED, makes explicit mention of the importance of whale conservation and the role of the IWC and the IWC Scientific Committee. Nevertheless, the IWC itself is recognized as the central institution in the cetacean issue-area network. During negotiations for what was originally to be named the Earth Charter but ended up being called the Rio Declaration, one attendee reported: 'New Zealand tried to raise the issue of whaling and had to be reminded (following the unfortunate Stockholm precedent) that this was a subject for the IWC.'[22]

Before looking at some of the motives and actions of key participants in the cetacean issue-area network, two points deserve attention. These sub-issues are aboriginal whaling, which has been allowed despite the global moratorium on commercial whaling; and the establishment of whaling sanctuaries, which has occurred despite the strong reservations of the Japanese and Norwegian delegations.

Aboriginal Whaling

Coastal whaling operations date back thousands of years in many areas. Though aboriginal or subsistence whaling has died out in many places, often due to lack of whale stocks after European exploitation, the practice continues in several isolated communities. The IWC itself exerts influence only in areas where aboriginal communities belong to member nations. Aboriginal whaling thus includes the Alaskan Inuit bowhead hunt in the Bering-Chukchi-Beaufort seas; the Russian Aleut Chukotka gray whale hunt; the Greenland minke hunt; and a very limited humpback hunt in St. Vincent and the Grenadines. Of course, the role of whaling for aboriginal communities has changed over time, but many insist they need to whale to retain cultural integrity.[23] The Portuguese, still whaling in the Azores region, claim this whaling is also subsistence, though Portugal is not a current member of the IWC.[24]

The 1931 International Convention for the Regulation of Whaling, predecessor to the final 1946 version, enshrined the rights of aboriginal or subsistence whalers. The key difference between commercial and subsistence hunts is that the former is conducted for profit, involving commercial transactions and payment of whalers; subsistence hunting, however, is for survival – or was at one time in history – and involves a very strong cultural attachment. The IWC determines whether aboriginal hunts are justified largely on its appraisal of these two points. This approach raises immediate controversy because the Japanese and Norwegians claim that their small whaling coastal communities have equally significant historical ties to whaling and thus should be permitted to resume the minke hunt with IWC approval. The United States, which allows the Inuit to take an obviously endangered whale (bowheads remain near extinction), insists that the renewed Japanese coastal hunt would be commercial, not subsistence, whaling.

The history of aboriginal whaling has always been controversial. During the 1980s, when the Americans were leading a fervent campaign to stop Japanese and Russian whaling, they were reduced to bargaining with the Japanese to obtain permission for the Alaskan hunt. As Day puts it, the administration was caught 'between the Save the Whale lobby and the Save a Vote in Alaska lobby,' and the general trade-off seemed to be one bowhead for 200 sperm whales.[25] Proving the validity of subsistence whaling also has its problems. For example, one group of Siberian operations was exposed as nothing more than operations to provide food for Soviet mink or fur farms.[26] The demands by the Makah of Washington State has been met with fears of Japanese connections – and I have seen little ground for such fears, incidentally. The aboriginal whaling issue thus raises serious ethical concerns and creates a crisis of legitimacy for not only American foreign policy but the IWC itself.[27]

Non-Whaling Sanctuaries

Another important sub-issue concerns 'non-whaling sanctuaries' – areas that the IWC has made off-limits to whalers, although scientific whaling and reservation-based whaling can still legally continue. This move is seen as largely symbolic, but nonetheless it has divided the IWC further. Many countries have now established national whale sanctuaries: Mexico has several gray whale sanctuaries; Canada has Pacific Rim National Park (at Wickannish Bay and set up under the National Parks Act of 1930), Telegraph Cove, and Robson Bight (Michael Bigg) Ecological Reserve; and Japan has Seto-naikai (Inland Sea) National Park (set up in 1934 under the National Parks Law).

Some misunderstanding has arisen over the most recent initiative, which has been commonly reported as the establishment of an Antarctic sanctuary.[28] In fact, an Antarctic sanctuary was designated in the first Schedule to the 1946 ICRW, though the area was again opened up for whaling in 1955. The establishment of the Indian Ocean sanctuary north of 55 degrees occurred in 1979 and was celebrated by whale enthusiasts at the time. This sanctuary comprises the waters of the Northern Hemisphere from the African coast at 100 degrees, including the Red and Arabian seas and the Gulf of Oman; and the waters of the Southern Hemisphere in the sector from 20 degrees east to 130 degrees east, with the southern boundary set at 55 degrees south. The IWC will decide in 2002 whether to renew the status of the Indian sanctuary. One observer, however, dismissed its significance as 'somewhat of a token gesture since minke whales are only taken south of 55 degrees, and sperm, blue, fin, humpback, sei, right, and Bryde's whales were already protected in this area.'[29] Regardless, the symbolic importance of the Indian sanctuary should not be overlooked.

Of much greater import was the 1994 decision at the 46th Annual Meeting of the IWC (held in Puerto Vallarta, Mexico) to proclaim the Antarctic Ocean (south of 40 degrees latitude) as a sanctuary. This idea was first proposed by France in 1992, but it was put off until two years later. And the decision generated the expected controversy, innately political but shrouded in science. For example, delegates to a preparatory conference on Norfolk Island in the South Pacific (20-24 February 1994) argued about whether the slow recovery of the blue whale was related to the rise of minke whale stocks (the Japanese and Norwegians want to resume large-scale hunting of these stocks), or if Soviet disclosures of false catch reports in the past explained the lack of recovery. The Japanese have been direct in their assertions, found wanting by some marine biologists, that establishing a sanctuary would harm the marine ecosystem. This position is explained in a pamphlet produced by the Beneficiaries of the Riches of the Sea and the Institute of Cetacean Research, both from Tokyo, which was distributed before the 1993 IWC Meeting held in Kyoto, Japan:

> The large species in the Antarctic were depleted from the first decade of this century as a result of the loose control exercised over whaling operations by fleets from Norway and the UK, and later by fleets from Japan and other nations. As a result the Antarctic marine ecosystem became unbalanced, and populations of smaller whales such as the minke, and also of crab-eater seals and penguins, increased as these species occupied the niche left vacant by the removal of the

large whale species. Introducing a sanctuary for all whale species would only perpetuate this imbalance in the ecosystem.[30]

The pamphlet then suggests that this imbalance could pose a threat to any chance of recovery for the blue: 'Strong suspicions have been expressed that the recovery of the blue and other large baleen whales might be hampered by the rapid increase of fast-breeding minke whales and crab-eater seals.' This argument is supported by an incompetently contrived graph that suggests the mean age of sexual maturity for minkes has been declining over the years while the baleen whale biomass has also been declining. Riddled with Japanese-to-English translation problems and with scientific jargon clearly intended to impress the uninitiated, another Institute of Cetacean Research pamphlet makes the outrageous claim: 'Establishment of sanctuary will obstruct access to knowledge on changes of the earth environment.' Finally, because of the relatively pristine condition of the various antarctic ecosystems, 'we believe that positive use of living resources in the Antarctic should be promoted as the least polluted resources from the global point of view.' There's little doubt that statements such as these did more to win hesitant voters over to the sanctuary position. At any rate, Japan has objected to the sanctuary and continues to conduct its scientific hunt within the area.

The Southern Ocean sanctuary has important implications for the future of whaling, international environmental organization, and human-cetacean relations. First, and despite continued resistance by Japan and Norway, large-scale commercial whaling remains unpalatable to world opinion. The sanctuary is designed to protect whales, but it is principally intended to stop whaling in the area should a commercial whaling industry regain its economic potential in the future. The more sanctuaries in existence, the less likely this outcome becomes, because the sanctuary idea establishes a vivid symbol of international protection. One IWC commissioner (who requested anonymity) told me he sees the Southern Ocean sanctuary as part of 'the idea of a World Antarctic Nature reserve (comparable to the Environmental Protection Protocol, Madrid, 1991).' If the oceans of the world remain polluted (and as a result of increased trade, this will probably be the case), then a non-hunting sanctuary will not help species whose very habitat is threatened. Thus, symbolic victories can often be deceiving, since they might deflect attention from the harder tasks that lie ahead. Agenda 21 made clear what type of commitment is required to reduce the chances that habitat destruction will make all sealife precarious.

Second, the sanctuary further divides the clashing ideologists within the IWC. At a follow-up conference in mid-October 1994, this point was obvious, when the two nations that expressed reservations regarding the sanctuary – Japan and Russia – failed to attend. At the First International Conference on the Southern Ocean Whale Sanctuary in Auckland, New Zealand, Foreign Minister Don McKinnon declared the establishment of the sanctuary as a 'triumph.'[31] New Zealand had lobbied hard for its realization and the Australian government played a fundamental role at the conference; in fact, the New Zealand Department of Conservation was the official host. Several New Zealand business firms provided the necessary sponsorship, with environmental groups such as Greenpeace, World Wildlife Fund (New Zealand), Project Jonah, and the Royal Forest and Bird Protection Society contributing as well. Private businesses involved included Air New Zealand, Sheraton-ITT, United Dairy Foods, Hewlett-Packard Ltd., and Montoana Wines Ltd. These corporate sponsors were attracted to the whaling issue, since, at least in New Zealand, the issue still has great symbolic value. Then again, New Zealand is not known as a particularly magnetic site for international conferences, and this fact may account for some of the surrounding enthusiasm.[32] The conference was modest, with about 150 attendees from Australia, the United States, the United Kingdom, New Zealand, and the South Pacific Regional Environmental Programme. (In Australia today, a debate is ongoing about whether the South Australian government should proclaim the Great Australian Bight, southwest of Tasmania, a whale sanctuary.)

This conference was not expected to produce any significant outcomes following the adoption of the sanctuary earlier in May. It did recommend additional research, such as enhanced DNA analysis and the development of photo-identification catalogues for species that are individually identifiable, such as humpbacks and southern rights. It supported the increasingly popular idea of using remote-sensing developed by military institutions to learn more about the migratory and acoustic patterns of cetaceans. It called for cooperation among nations whose waters are adjacent to the sanctuary, including Argentina, Australia, Chile, New Zealand, and South Africa. And the conference explicitly condemned so-called scientific whaling. This position is in line with the New Zealand stance on the issue. A press release of 15 February 1995 stresses: 'Although we acknowledge scientific whaling is within the rules of the IWC, we have continued to register our concerns with the Japanese ... We have expressed particular concern that this year's programme is being conducted not only in the agreed Southern Ocean Sanctuary but, more specifically, in the Ross Sea.'[33] These protests have not changed the Japanese policy position. Greenpeace boats confronting scientific whaling expeditions in the area have been similarly unsuccessful.

State Actors: The Short List

Whaling has been a widespread practice in many parts of the globe and in fact was a chief contributor to the early economic and industrial development of many modern nation-states. Even if we limited our scope to whaling activities and purposes, we would need an entire series of volumes to begin detailing the history of each nation-state. It is necessary, in other words, to create for our immediate purposes a short list of states, those that have become heavily involved in whaling or in the political struggle to conserve whales.

Thus, we choose the following: Japan, Norway, and Iceland, representing the pro-whaling lobby; Russia, now a question but once one of the biggest whalers; and the United States and the European Union, representing the anti-whaling lobby. We also mention other states that have taken both pro- and anti-whaling positions.

Japan

The state most closely associated with whaling remains Japan, which is the home of the only substantial market for whalemeat. This demand keeps the Japanese whaling industry, which has been decimated by the moratorium, alive in principle, if not in fact. There is, of course, a broader context here for global ecopolitics; as Fred Pearce notes, 'when it comes to easily identifiable enemies, the Japanese have served the environment movement well, beginning with the scandal at Minamata in the 1960s,' when mercury in factory waste into Minamata Bay contaminated fish and poisoned unborn children. Before and, many suspect, even after the ban on elephant product trade through CITES, Japan was the world's largest ivory trader. Gall bladders of North American and Asian black bears are known to find their way there. Japan has been condemned for trading in kangaroo skins and labelled 'a prime market for trade in the endangered hawksbill turtle from a British dependency, the Cayman Islands, and the trade has continued in spite of an international ban in force since 1979.' Even more infamous is the Japanese consumption of tropical timber (more than a third of the total world trade) from rainforests in places like Borneo, Malaysia, and the Philippines.[34] Yet Japanese domestic environmental policies have been impressive, protecting forests and producing relatively clear air above mega-cities such as Tokyo.

Japan has always been heavily dependent on the sea for protein. Its population of 123 million still derives approximately half of its protein from fish, despite increases in beef imports; and Japan remains the world's largest importer of seafood. This dependency permeates even foreign development assistance policies. Peter Weber writes that the Japanese government is initiating links with developing countries that can supply seafood: 'The Japanese semipublic Overseas Fishery Cooperation Foundation (OFCF) coordinates attempts by fishing and trading companies to set up commercial links with developing countries. OFCF offers cheap loans, and the trading companies offer technical assistance.'[35] This initiative is significant for the connections between Japan and developing nations within the IWC, as many feel that recent mood swings can be attributed to Japanese aid policies. Indeed, the use of funds for political persuasion opens an entirely new can of worms. According to one researcher, Brazil may be offered as a case in point. In the early 1980s, only one whaling operation existed in Brazil, COPESBRA, which was in fact a subsidiary of Nippon Reizo Kabashiki Kaisha of Japan, located in the underdeveloped northeastern state of Paraiba. A politician from the area, Humberto Lucena, fought against any anti-whaling bills presented in the Brazilian Congress from 1976 to 1985. (A presidential decree in 1985 halted whaling in Brazil in compliance with the IWC moratorium.) Brazil thus voted against the moratorium but eventually accepted it.[36]

Postwar Japan was, of course, an occupied state. The Americans had more to do with the development and realization of the ICRW than any other governmental representatives. American influence would in effect permit the resumption of Japanese whaling. Nigel Bonner writes of a Lieutenant-Colonel Winston Waldron of the US Army, MacArthur's personal representative in charge of the First Fleet of the 1947-8 Japanese Antarctic Whaling Expedition, which was 'being run by MacArthur as a sort of private empire.'[37] This autonomy may be less surprising to students of the megalomaniacal MacArthur than to those of Japanese whaling, an industry that often assumes the cloak of national pride today. In short, the tremendous postwar increase in pelagic whaling was facilitated by American involvement in a global whaling regime that reinstated the Japanese whaling community to its former place within the broader Japanese fishing sector.

Because Japan has consistently opposed the moratorium and today wishes to resume whaling, it is inevitably considered the prime cause of anxiety in the cetacean issue-area network. There is no doubt that the moratorium has put traditional whalers in Japanese coastal communities out of work. According to a consultant to the Japan Whaling Association, a pro-whaling lobby group with representatives in New York, accepting IWC demands for reduced minke whale quotas in the early 1970s 'was not easy ... The cost to the Japanese whaling industry ran to well over $100 million in scrapped vessels and facilities' and involved massive layoffs in the thousands.[38] IWC annual meetings have been replete with Japanese lobbying on behalf of the coastal whaling communities, typically listed as Taiji, Wadaura, Ayukawa, and Abashiri.

Every year since 1988, the Japanese delegation has asked the IWC Annual Meeting for an 'interim relief allocation' of fifty minke whales for its coastal whaling communities. The request is presented as an attempt to limit the economic displacement caused by the commercial whaling moratorium. This allocation would require an amendment supported by a three-quarters majority, which the Japanese delegation has consistently failed to achieve. Japan has also presented studies to the IWC, including a plan for ensuring non-profit whaling should the moratorium be lifted. A 1995 IWC Resolution (not supported by the United States) recognized this work as a positive step. There are in fact deep roots of fisheries management in Japanese coastal history. During what is known as the Edo Period, from 1603 to 1867, local sea tenure was institutionalized:

> For example, seaweed harvesting was banned during spawning season to protect the fish eggs attached to seaweed, gill nets for bottom species were outlawed, and night fishing with torches was limited during the mid-nineteenth century. As the government of Japan became increasingly centralized, local communities nevertheless continued to control coastal fisheries.[39]

The present system was formalized with the creation of the Fishing Cooperative Associations (FCAs), a somewhat unusual decentralization within Japanese government. Japanese domestic authorities therefore regulate the catch of Baird's beaked whales and pilot whales, but the great whales (including the minkes) remain clearly within the IWC's mandate. The main speaker of the Japanese delegation to the 1995 IWC Meeting believes the institution 'is not keeping its legal integrity' since the original convention calls for the 'orderly development of the whaling industry.' Perhaps more to the point, he feels this issue concerns the rational utilization of sea resources, obviously a vital issue-area to Japan: 'If we give up [sustainable use of whales] in the field of whaling this creates a bad precedent for Japan which has major fleets for fisheries other than whaling.'[40]

To the Japanese, the transition of the IWC has been orchestrated by the Americans from the beginning, and the power of the American market in particular. Former whaling nations, such as Chile, Argentina, Peru, South Korea, and the Philippines, were forced to join the IWC by the United States and the 1979 Packwood-Magnuson Amendment (discussed later), lest they face severe American sanctions applicable to nations not dedicated to conservation regimes. (Taiwan, another whaling state, could not join because of China's membership, in yet another absurd reflection of China's unwillingness to recognize that state.) At the same time, explicitly anti-whaling positions were favoured by most of the new members, such as Monaco, Switzerland, Oman, India, Germany, Sweden, and Jamaica. Whether this majority reflected growing worldwide public opinion against whaling or quiet American pressure is an open question, but, for the Japanese, the United States appeared instrumental in this development.

Japan seems firm in its insistence that Japanese coastal whalers should be allowed to resume a limited minke hunt. It is also intent on continuing its small scientific-whaling minke hunt, which attracts widespread scorn. And, within the IWC, the Japanese-American clash has become a political fixture. Arguably, the Japanese government may be asserting independence on the issue, since a return to large-scale whaling is almost unthinkable. For the most part, the whales aren't there; the whalemeat market, while extant, is unstable; and another form of cetacean-human interaction, whalewatching, has grown in popularity in recent years. These changes are part of a broader process, part of the internationalization of the population through the spread of cosmopolitan values, information, person-to-person contact, and the development of skills for interaction.[41] However, all this discussion sounds rather patronizing to the Japanese delegations to the IWC. The coastal whaling communities may be what Canadians might call a Newfoundland issue; that is, while the Japanese government is quick to defend the communities at the IWC, it should instead focus on retraining and creating alternative employment for those displaced, which is a more expensive and long-term prospect.

We should avoid exaggerating the global significance of the Japanese-American split on the issue. Though the two nations share an American security arrangement, Japanese-American relations since the Second World War have been subject to a great deal of tension, with trade issues in general being the subject of heated concern. The Japanese market remains elusive to many American products. It is doubtful that the Americans would be willing at this time to risk further damage to the relationship by insisting on a hard-line anti-whaling stance. In 1985, Ronald Reagan declared, 'There is no relationship more important to peace and prosperity in the world than that between the United States and Japan.'[42] True declaration or not, the foreign policy of Japan within the cetacean issue-area network remains a thorn in the side of that relationship.

Norway
Another state with a firmly established whaling tradition and a pro-whaling foreign policy is Norway. Indeed, though the two states have little in common, Norway and Japan have become allies on the whaling issue, usually presenting a united front within the cetacean issue-area network. If there is any single name in the history of whaling that evokes pride amongst Norwegian whalers, it must be that of Svend Foyn, who invented the harpoon grenade-tipped gun. He also pioneered the idea of using cable to secure the rorquals he was fond of shooting, which otherwise sunk when killed. Foyn's first ship, equipped with such technological advances, was named *Spes et Fides*, or Hope and Faith. He hunted the waters north of Norway, and, by 1880, eight companies with twelve steam catchers operated there.[43]

Another famous Norwegian whaler was Carl Anton Larsen, who noticed the large blue, fin, and humpback populations in the Antarctic during an exploratory trip with the Swede Otto Nordenskjold. In 1904, he began whaling from the harbour of Grytviken in South Georgia. This operation was prodigious, and soon other whaling companies joined Larsen, working from floating ships. Yet another Norwegian, Petter Sorlle, began the practice of flensing and cooking whale flesh on factory ships. Thus was introduced the so-called stern-slip factory ship, which included a slipway set in its stern, used for hauling the carcass aboard for processing. The first modern factory ship, named *The Lancing*, left Norway in June 1925. No longer would whaling crews have to climb down from the ship and flense while the whales were pulled and floated alongside. No longer would the land-based whaling station, relatively easily regulated, be necessary.

Norwegian whaling today is coastal, not a factory-ship operation but a limited minke hunt. Though the hunt is legal, since Norway registered a reservation to the moratorium, it is roundly condemned by anti-whalers. Norwegian officials resent this condemnation and indeed the IWC's preservationist stance itself. At the 1992 IWC Meeting, Norway's representative stated: '[Norway] no longer accepts what she perceives as cultural imperialism imposed by the majority of the members of the IWC on the local communities of the nations and peoples who want to exercise their sovereign cultural right to be different.'[44] International condemnation of this refusal to accept the IWC's dictates can be seen especially in western media, although those participating in relevant Internet discussion groups seem much more divided on the issue.[45] The *Times* of London has commented on the interesting spectacle of renowned environmentalist Gro Harlem Brundtland leading a nation committed to whaling:

> Norway's coastal population, which has suffered declining fish catches because of the international protection of whales (because whales compete with the fishermen for fish),[46] has prevailed on Prime Minister Gro Harlem Brundtland to defend Norwegian whaling despite her role as Chairman of the World Commission on Environment and Development and European Community criticism of its stand.[47]

Nonetheless, a small hunt continues. On 22 June 1995, Norway extended its commercial catch to compensate for bad weather. On 5 July, it announced that 213 minke whales had been taken in the 1995 season and that one ship continued to whale in order to catch two more.[48] This total fell short of the 232 harvest quota that had been set by the Norwegian government under the terms of the reservation to the IWC moratorium. Earlier estimates of the minke whale population in the Northeast Atlantic, which Norway was using to justify a proposed take of over 300 whales, were rejected by the IWC Scientific

Committee as flawed due to problematic computer programs.[49] Norway again reduced the 1995 quota to 232, but the anti-whaling community accused the Norwegians of duplicity in a numbers game. Norway has threatened to leave the IWC altogether if the RMP is not finally put in place so that regulated commercial whaling can resume.

In fact, Norway will probably leave the IWC, and this withdrawal would be highly problematic for the legitimacy of the institution. It is conventional wisdom that Norway has stayed for one reason: to maintain the policy option of joining the European Union, formerly known as the European Community. Since the European Community has a ban on whale products and insists on the legitimacy of the IWC as the main multilateral authority in the issue-area network, this strategy makes some sense. However, a recent referendum on joining the European Union was not accepted by the Norwegian populace.[50] This rejection was related to fears that Spanish and Portuguese fishing fleets (and their reputations for overfishing) would gain considerable access to Norwegian waters. Meanwhile, Norway is a member of the new marine mammal management organization discussed below, which Norwegians and others argue could manage whaling as effectively as the IWC. Only American sanctions, which have not been applied despite Norway's continuation of its small minke whale hunt, can possibly coerce Norway into IWC adherence now. A regime based on coercion may not offer a promising prospect for marine management.

Iceland

Icelanders set up their first whaling station as early as 1883. The nation is surrounded by sea, and this point is reflected in popular consciousness of the whaling issue, which has become a matter of national pride. Iceland, like Norway and Japan, voted against the moratorium in 1982 and continued scientific whaling thereafter. Iceland was in fact the first state to initiate the scientific hunt, in 1986, of 117 sei and fin whales. As the meat derived from the hunt was clearly going to Japan, anti-whalers were outraged by this development. Jeremy Cherfas argued, 'There are not enough Icelanders to eat all the whales they plan to kill for science.'[51] Iceland has had whaleboats attacked and sunk in Reykjavik (rumoured widely to have been the work of Paul Watson's Sea Shepherd Society). It has been condemned in the IWC. And it has recently quit the organization, placing faith instead in a new regional body, the North Atlantic

Marine Mammal Commission (NAMMCO), and continued to assert its right to whale.

NAMMCO was established through a 1992 agreement signed by representatives of the Faroe Islands, Greenland, Iceland, and Norway, and titled Agreement on Cooperation in Research, Conservation and Management of Marine Mammals in the North Atlantic. Iceland's Gugmundur Eiriksson stated at NAMMCO's inaugural meeting that the organization was 'born out of dissatisfaction with the IWC's zero-catch quota, lack of IWC competence to deal with small cetaceans, and the need for an organization to deal with other marine mammals such as seals.'[52] It has its own scientific committee (which relies on the RMP for whaling), though management committees for various species can only 'propose' conservation measures to members. Notes Caron: 'In developing its own data base of marine mammal populations in the North Atlantic, NAMMCO will challenge the legitimacy of the IWC's decision making by contradicting the science and expertise that is the foundation of such legitimacy.'[53] Its regional character and multi-species approach makes it the front runner for conceptions of alternative international organizations to the IWC. No non-whaling members belong, thus directly challenging the notion that the commons should be managed by as many states as possible. Should Iceland resume commercial whaling, that state, and perhaps Norway, would use NAMMCO either to pressure the IWC into finally accepting the RMP or to provide a management mechanism for the area. This development is perhaps the most visible challenge to IWC legitimacy. Despite a consumer boycott that could grow if Iceland does resume whaling, the Icelandic government is determined to pursue an autonomous foreign policy in this area.[54]

Many within the cetacean issue-area network hope that Iceland will rejoin the IWC, since the institution has less credibility when states that are determined to whale do not participate. The main reason Iceland will not rejoin the IWC seems to be the inability of the IWC to adopt the RMP as a formal amendment to the ICRW schedule. However, rejoining the IWC has its own political implication: for example, what type of sentiment is expressed when a nation that doesn't like an organization's approach drops out, only to return when conditions are more favourable. (Many people were upset with the United States when it retired from UNESCO, and from paying UNESCO dues, in the 1980s, demanding a change in that UN agency's agenda.) As a coastal state, Iceland has a decided stake in preserving the oceanic commons and, in fact, is willing to cooperate in this endeavour. For example, in March 1995, Iceland put forth a proposal with the United States regarding national-level actions to combat coastal pollution. This proposal was presented at a meeting in Reykjavik in preparation for the formal adoption of the Global Programme of Action to Protect the Marine Environment from Land-Based Activities. The programme was adopted in Washington in early November 1995.

One thing is certain: Iceland will not let the matter rest. The whaling issue has in fact become an integral aspect of Iceland's identity. One author concludes that whaling is part of the three key symbols in Icelandic nationalist discourse, which celebrates 'a pure and ancient language, a pure and beautiful land, and the sagas, a body of medieval historical and heroic literature.'[55]

Russia

Though Russia's whaling tradition predates this century, it became a serious threat to several species of Cetacea during the age of the factory ship. Indeed, alongside Japan, the Soviets were the biggest whalers when the market remained even somewhat lucrative. Currently, Russia does not whale (save for the aboriginal whaling mentioned earlier), but it remains a central figure in the IWC, not only because of the Russian Federation's international status as a great power, as well as the threat that a resumed Russian whaling operation could very well erase many decades of stock recovery, but also because of ongoing rumours that the Soviets did not accurately report whale catches during the Cold War.

There is now no doubt about those rumours: the Soviet Union, and in particular the KGB, the infamous secret police established in March 1954 following Stalin's death, provided deliberately false kill-figures to the IWC. The KGB (Komitet Gosudarstvennoi Bezopasnosti, or Committee of State Security), which was preceded by a less sophisticated and even more violence-prone creation of Vladimir Lenin (1870-1924), the Cheka, was indeed a pervasive force in Soviet society. Its main purpose was to investigate state crimes, such as treason, espionage, smuggling, organized crime, and political dissent. The KGB was therefore a counterintelligence and an intelligence organization, much like the CIA and FBI combined. It was controlled by the Communist Party (CPSU) until Mikhail Gorbachev began the perestroika program, which gave the USSR Supreme Soviet control of the

KGB.[56] The service was disbanded altogether after the attempted coup of August 1991, replaced with a dual apparatus, the Russian Ministry of Security and the Foreign Intelligence Agency. That the KGB was involved in whaling record duplicity was made clear by Russia's current whaling commissioner, Konstantin Shevliagin, at the 1994 Norfolk Island Conference held to discuss the Antarctic moratorium. In fact, Shevliagin suggested, in an astonishing, and for many heart-breaking, revelation, that Soviet reports from the 1960s to the 1980s may have to be doubled to gain any accuracy. The following quotation from a related Associated Press article recounts some of these discrepancies:

> Alexei Yablikov, a whale biologist and environmental adviser to president Boris Yeltsin, used declassified Soviet Ministry of Fisheries records to find that one Soviet factory ship told the IWC during the 1960s that it [*sic*] had killed 152 humpback and 156 blue whales.
>
> In fact, the ship had taken 7,207 humpbacks and 1,433 blue whales and illegally killed 717 right whales, a species protected by the whaling commission since the 1930s.[57]
>
> Ernst Cherny, a former Soviet whaler who now heads Russia's Union of Independent Fishery Workers, offered similar examples.
>
> Scientists aboard the whaler Sovietskaya Rossiya told the fisheries ministry that ship alone killed 1,568 humpback whales in the 1961-62 season. The Soviet Union told the IWC that all four Soviet whaling fleets killed only 270 humpbacks that year, Mr. Cherny said.
>
> During that period, the Sovietskaya Rossiya also took 1,200 right whales and reported none, Mr. Cherny said: 'It is worth mentioning in this connection that the Soviet fleets were specially designed and built so the deck could be covered by steam, hiding from the view of any outside observers the carcasses of protected species.'[58]

Notwithstanding the problematic statement by Cherny, this revelation raises at least three questions. Most immediately, what does it mean for present stock projections? Though this new knowledge makes the survival of certain species (most notably the humpback, blue, and right) all the more remarkable, it suggests their initial numbers may have been underestimated. That so many more whales, and especially in such vulnerable populations, were taken may suggest that there are presently fewer whales than projected, since current projections are often based on assumptions about the recovery of former population levels. Also in question is the accuracy of all whaling reports, which lends support to arguments that whaling cannot resume unless a highly visible – and some would argue obtrusive – verification/observation system is in place.

Second, why would the Soviet Union go to all this bother? The USSR has, of course, been a state with paranoid leaders and the KGB had tentacles in most forms of economic activity. But if the IWC was as inconsequential as some have decided, surely the USSR would not bother to reduce the figures so drastically. The role of the KGB in this issue suggests an intriguing Cold War aspect that should be the subject of future historical analyses.

Third, is this situation a case of a new Russian regime unearthing previously classified information, then earnestly attempting to set a precedent of openness by releasing the information to the world? Or has the information been circulating for some time – as the apparent extent of Ernst Cherny's knowledge might suggest – and its release was timed to coincide with the Norfolk Island Conference or with an intention to resume whaling? Rumours that Russia might resume whaling, principally to supply the Japanese market, would be supported by openness, only if the release of this information was pre-emptive. In other words, if Russia intended to resume whaling, it could not risk exposure by anti-whaling states or groups of the falsified statistics, and therefore it provided the information to pre-empt charges that such deceptions could happen again.

However, any resumption of large-scale Russian whaling is unlikely. The largest single reason is the gravity of world opinion. Russia today is in no condition to seriously upset any trading partners, especially western sources of aid. The dilapidated Russian whaling fleet, including massive ships such as the *Sovietskaya Rossiya,* is rotting in dry dock or employed in other capacities. To resume commercial whaling, the Russians would have to revamp an antiquated whaling fleet or even begin all over again. This initiative would require a large capital investment, and, given the dire needs of the rest of the country, whaling fleets are unlikely to receive that type of governmental assistance. The start-up costs of large-scale operations alone would no doubt prove prohibitive. However, small-scale coastal whaling remains a distinct Russian possibility.

In the end, the Russian position is difficult to assess without more detailed information and a clearer picture of where Russia itself is going. American officials noted a marked change in Russian behaviour at the IWC during 1995. Russia blocked NGO participation in some important areas, and it claimed that some of the more accurate data presented by Russian scientists to the IWC Scientific Committee should be deleted from the record. The Russian federation 'refused to accept a ruling by the Chairman that the Commission had no choice but to accept the SC Report, since it was a record of what had occurred during the two-week Scientific Committee meeting. Russia's objection was to three sections of the report dealing with data submitted on past Soviet catches. The Russian delegate ... said his government would consider a vote for the adoption of the report as a "hostile act" against the Russian Federation.'[59] The only member to vote against adopting the report was, in fact, Russia.

The United States
Though American whaling interests are a thing of the past, this fact does not dilute the importance of whaling in American industrial history. Not only did whaling provide oil, fertilizer, and other products, it provided folklore.

Since the early 1970s, the United States has presented a consistent anti-whaling policy to the world, at the IWC, and in other contexts. The US has clearly played the major anti-whaling role in the cetacean issue-area network; and, in general, no other nation-state has as much influence on marine issues. By contrast, the United States has proven relatively intransigent in response, for example, to reducing carbon emissions to stem global warming. In a short study of the past twenty years of US environmental foreign policy, Robert Paarlberg contrasts 'convenient environmentalism' and 'committed policies.' He concludes that American policy has largely focused on the former, a style of convenient environmentalism that involves the 'use of international action to *extend to others* the relatively high standards of environmental protection that the US has embraced at home.'[60] This focus would especially include those policies whose real applications were abroad; in the case of whaling, this was obviously the case. In the United States, the last commercial whaling operations, gray hunting off the southern coast of California, stopped nearly three decades ago, and the Americans banned the sale of whale products in 1971. The United States Marine Mammal Protection Act, passed in 1972, reflected concern over the millions of spinner, spotted, common, and striped dolphins that had been killed in tuna-fishing operations. The US was instrumental in the establishment of CITES in February 1973 in Washington. It also played a leading role in allowing NGO access to the process involved in the creation of the Global Environment Facility.

Proactive wildlife policy is largely the result of the concentrated energy of NGOs, for whom the whaling issue became so important in the early 1970s, though the strength of environmental lobbyists in the United States is much more evident in some issue-areas than others.[61] Despite a small whaling operation off Richmond, California, closed in 1972, a significant national pro-whaling lobby did not exist in the United States, and suitable replacements for whale products had been discovered. US administrations, prodded by growing public pressure articulated by conservationist groups, scientists, and even labour unions, would lead the fight against whaling both by participating in the IWC arena and by resorting to less diplomatic, or more economic, means of statecraft.

The latter involved the essential ban in 1970 on imports of products derived from endangered great whales, and the enactment of relevant legislation that threatened the commercial interests of whaling nations.[62] Two amendments to older American legislation are of particular significance. The first relied on threatening access to what has always arguably been America's greatest asset, its internal market. The Pelly Amendment to the Fisherman's Protective Act (1971) gives the president the option of banning any or all fisheries imports from a country certified by the US secretary of commerce (who is ultimately responsible for whaling policy) as conducting fishing operations in a manner or under circumstances that diminish the effectiveness of an international fishery conservation program. The amendment was originally enacted 'in response to Danish [as well as Norwegian and West German] depletion of North Atlantic salmon in violation of the total ban put on that stock by the International Convention for the Northwest Atlantic Fisheries.'[63] All three states agreed to phase out their salmon fishing after Pelly was adopted, giving the amendment immediate political currency. In 1978, the act was amended to include bans on imports from states engaging in trade that diminishes the effectiveness of any international program for endangered or threatened species. Such bans would apply regardless of whether the conduct is legal under the laws of the offending country. In 1988, Congress added the possibility of imposing penalties on states regardless of whose nationals caught the fish.

The second amendment is commonly known as the Packwood/Magnuson Amendment to the Fishery Conservation Management Act

(1976), which blocks access to US coastal waters for nations that are violating bans on killing endangered marine mammals. This restriction is of great significance since Japan takes some 75 per cent of the bottom fish caught in Alaskan waters, worth around $750 million annually; the US in 1983 withheld 171,000 tonnes from Japan's fish allocations within the American 200-mile coastal zone in retaliation for Japan's initial objection to the 1982 moratorium.[64] While certification under the Pelly Amendment is supposed to be mandatory, presidential discretion is needed to impose sanctions. Under the Pelly-Packwood/Magnuson system, the United States reserves the right to mandate certification for trade in whales, even though the whales may not be endangered.

In 1974, the US certified both Japan and the USSR for exceeding the IWC's quota for minke whales the previous whaling season. However, because both states had earlier objected to the quota and were therefore not bound by it, then president Gerald Ford decided against imposing sanctions. The Japanese and Soviets both adhered to the quota the next season. Other achievements partly resulting from the threat or implementation of sanctions include the changed policies of the Republic of Korea, which in 1980 banned the use of cold harpoons (i.e., harpoons without explosives, which damage less meat but result in considerably more suffering for the whale); Taiwan, which (officially) ended 'pirate' (not IWC-regulated) whaling in 1980; China, which in 1982 banned whaling; Chile, Korea, and Peru, which in 1979 joined the IWC (though they may have joined the IWC only for the right to legally sell whalemeat to Japan, which in 1979 agreed to stop importing meat from non-IWC nations); Spain, which in 1979 was forced to observe a fin whale quota; and Norway, which in 1987 temporarily ceased commercial whaling after US Commerce Secretary Baldridge certified Norway for continued catches of minke whales.[65]

The Pelly-Packwood/Magnuson system has led to conflicts among anti-whaling groups that argue the American government does not go far enough in implementing the sanctions it calls for. Since the sanctions can be applied regardless of the international legality of whalers' actions, they could in theory be quite widespread. A side agreement with the Japanese, who did not officially adhere to the moratorium until after 1986, raised a great deal of controversy in the American domestic arena. This agreement went to court, as environmentalist groups charged that the conservation statutes prohibited the US commerce secretary from not invoking sanctions. In turn, the secretary's office argued that his duties, in this case, were in fact discretionary: he was not obliged to apply sanctions if the office felt more was to be gained by accepting promises of eventual adherence to IWC dictates. The court found in favour of the secretary. The finding was greeted with predictable dismay by conservation groups such as Greenpeace, but many analysts might conclude, as did Scott Larson, that since 'international schemes function better on cooperation than on coercion, the executive's interpretation of certification may be best for whale conservation.'[66] In other words, flexibility in such cases is better for regime building, but it may also reflect a slowly turning perspective on the whaling issue. The Clinton administration has also been very reluctant to impose sanctions on Norway, despite calls for them from NGOs.

Aside from a certain reluctance to implement the full possible weight of sanctions,[67] the record of American leadership has some notable exceptions. The ongoing debate over subsistence whaling periodically 'neutralized' American determination, especially in 1977-8, until it was agreed that aboriginal whaling (in Alaska, Greenland, and Siberia) could take place provided the hunters involved maintained IWC quotas. The political problem that the US faced was an acute one: could they actually stop the Alaskan Inupiat Eskimos from subsistence hunting if they accepted the IWC Scientific Committee's call for a total ban on bowhead kills? Apparently, the decision was made that, though the Eskimos were expected to reduce their takes, they would not be stopped altogether. The controversy over aboriginal subsistence whaling is heated, but it alone does not explain a temporary change of American heart in the late 1970s. David Day reports that soon after his replacement in 1980, Richard Frank, who was the US commissioner during this time, was hired as a pro-whaling lobbyist for Japanese commissioner Kunio Yonezawa.[68] Nonetheless, willingness on the part of successive American administrations to take a high-profile approach with the whaling issue was obviously instrumental in the evolution of the moratorium and its continued observation by most states, including Japan.

What remains impressive, as usual, is American resource. The American delegation to the IWC annual meetings, in contrast to most nation-states that may send three or four representatives, consists of twenty advisers, including representatives from the Departments of Commerce and State, congressional staff, and eight invited representatives from NGOs. The only nation with a larger delegation is

Japan. The American delegation to the IWC Scientific Committee consists of thirteen scientists. American delegates play varying roles in all IWC committees and subgroups, including Finance and Administration, Infractions, Aboriginal Whaling, Southern Hemisphere Baleen Whales, and North Pacific Minke Whale Management Trials.[69] This large commitment is not free, of course, yet the US doesn't pay much more in IWC fees than other states. The IWC payment structure is based essentially on differing shares according to the number of delegates sent to the previous year's annual meeting. The Japanese, who usually have the largest contingent, are one of the biggest, if unhappiest, contributors to the IWC. Should commercial whaling resume under the Revised Management Procedure, there would have to be agreement on who pays for the tighter observation and more involved research component of the organization. Whaling nations believe these costs should be shared by those who seek conservation; the American position, of course, is that the whalers should pay the entire cost.[70] At present, a 30 per cent charge is levied on all nations that continue aboriginal whaling, and arguably the same condition should apply to those that resume limited, but IWC-approved, commercial whaling.

The success of American positions at the IWC stands in contrast to its disenchantment in a body dealing with broader North-South issues, such as the United Nations Educational, Scientific and Cultural Organization (UNESCO), from which the US withdrew in the mid-1980s, citing what it perceived as an anti-free market political agenda. In the case of UNESCO, paying annual dues proportionate to the huge American GNP caused great concern among decisionmakers in Washington. The IWC avoids both this approach and the preferred American system of weighted voting, where the highest absolute contributors are awarded the greatest number of votes, the model followed by the World Bank and International Monetary Fund. Although we should be very cautious concerning generalization here, the IWC fees/voting structure resolves some of the more obvious problems inherent in the divided UN system.

As well, the split between the Americans and the Japanese reflects different styles of government. The Americans, who have to deal with public opinion in a visible fashion, became quite dominated by public pressure groups with the rising tide of second-wave environmentalism in the early 1980s. For the Japanese, government plays a much different role: that of the firm guide of the economy. In fact, the idea of an IWC delegation from Japan divorced from or even impartial to industrial interests is unthinkable. Many would characterize the current conflict as between NGOs and the Japanese fishery industry. Obviously, governments play roles that allow these groups to be so influential and, as in the case of Norwegian sanctions, the American government is also concerned with establishing the liberal trading regime of tomorrow.

The European Union
The European Union, formerly the European Community, is also an active anti-whaling coalition. However, states represent themselves individually at the IWC – they do not appear under the aegis of the EU as they do, for example, in the Northwest Atlantic Fisheries Organization or in negotiations for the Climate Change Convention – and there are important divisions among them.

Interestingly, the first official attempt to regulate deep-sea whaling was likely made by a British administrator. When the Norwegian whaler Carl Anton Larsen set up camp in South Georgia, his initial success at taking humpbacks encouraged a stream of ambitious whaling operations, which operated out of South Georgia and the South Shetland Islands. Shore stations for the new whaleboats were constructed in areas administered by the United Kingdom (through the controversial British dominion over the Falkland Islands). Sir William Allardyce served as governor to the islands at that time, and, foreseeing the 'possible, indeed, likely, destruction of the whale stocks, as had happened in the North, Allardyce limited the number of licenses granted to operate whale catchers and the number of leases for factory sites. He made requirements to utilise the carcases as well as the blubber, and provided protection for young whales and whales accompanied by calves.'[71] This effort is remarkable, since it represents an attempt to regulate whaling conducted by a number of states and competitive firms.

Presently, with the exceptions of Spain and Portugal, who have wavered over the years and have indigenous whaling populations of their own (Portugal is not at present an IWC member), European states are as a whole opposed to whaling, though in varying degrees. Most routinely vote with the Americans at IWC annual meetings. France has been vocal, pushing for the Antarctic whaling sanctuary in the early 1990s. Again, some might find this position ironic, given the French nuclear tests conducted in 1995. In fact, the IWC commissioner for France claims that his main concern at the IWC was 'to make sure that the preoccupations of the French population, massively in favour of the protection of cetaceans, are taken into consideration.'[72] In most European states, public opinion is very influential; a strong animal rights lobby and limited Green party success exists in Germany, Belgium, Italy, Luxembourg, Switzerland, and Sweden. Tony Brenton argues further that, in 1989, 'environmental dissatisfactions played a major role in bringing down the [government] in the Netherlands.'[73] The EU has come away from recent confrontations with Canadians divided over straddling stocks of turbot off the latter's east coast. Although the EU was forced to defend the actions of Spanish fishermen in the area, a large intra-EU split was revealed. Many, in particular the British, were very divided on the issue. A united front at the IWC, since no precedent has been set for such an approach, seems unlikely in this context. Another crucial division is Denmark's support for the Faroe Islands pilot whale drivery, widely condemned as a savage annual hunt in which pilot whales are herded into shallow lagoons and then slaughtered.[74] Because of these differences, a common EU front at the IWC seems far off. More likely, European states will continue to represent themselves and vote accordingly, perhaps differently, on the issues.

Nonetheless, the effects of European integration in the cetacean issue-area remain difficult to predict. The concept of subsidiarity, which implies that the diplomats in Brussels should not make decisions that could be made at lower levels of governance, is the cause of some concern. While subsidiarity was vital as an institutional inducement, and while the overcentralization of political affairs is always stifling and inefficient, the problem is that this concept moves the European Union further from, instead of closer to, one of its chief goals: universal standards in areas like environmental protection. The 1972 decision of the then-European Community to ban whale products was viewed as an instrumental development towards restricting the whale market. As the United States had already taken this step, the European Community's decision in effect limited the marketplace to Japan, though some whale consumption occurred in older whaling communities elsewhere (notably Norway and Iceland), and the Soviet Union continued to use whalemeat in its notorious fur industry. The important point is that the European Community's decision was assumed, without any doubt, to apply to all active and future EC members, some of whom were not even members of the IWC. As

Michael Bond reports in the *European*, such blanket acceptance of legislation or policy may be nearing its end. Since December 1992,

> European Union environmental directives have been high on the list of the Brussels legislation that London would like to see 're-nationalised.' Environmentalists fear ... the [European] Commission ... is giving in to considerable political pressure from Britain and France to scale down Brussels' interference in their affairs. Of particular concern is a Commission plan to recast the regulation governing trade in endangered species. Under this proposal the bans on whale and seal products would be scrapped and amalgamated into a new regulation. This could then be amended by the Commission without going through the European parliament. The International Fund for Animal Welfare claims this is an attempt by the Commission to 'repeal laws by stealth.'[75]

Given the weight of public opinion on the seal and whale issues, the International Fund for Animal Welfare may be a bit anxious on this issue.

A final point should be made concerning the willingness of the United Kingdom to host the IWC, at some expense, on its soil. By and large, there does not seem to be any widespread concern that this location prejudices the commission.[76] Since the IWC's activities centre on the annual meetings, which are held in places as diverse as Ireland, Japan, and Mexico, its home location is probably not a major factor in public opinion. Nonetheless, the anti-whaling lobby in the United Kingdom itself is strong, and we should not dismiss this fact.

Non-State Actors in the Cetacean Issue-Area Network

In addition to the state membership of the IWC, some states maintain observer status but do not officially belong to the commission. At the 1994 IWC Meeting in Mexico, these states included Canada, Iceland, Italy, Morocco, and Zimbabwe. Other intergovernmental organizations represented included the European Union, the UNEP, the Commission for the Conservation of Antarctic Marine Living Resources, the Inter-American Tropical Tuna Commission, the NAMMCO, and the World Conservation Union. And close to 100 NGOs (of quite divergent stripes) were also in attendance, actors now ubiquitous in the cetacean issue-area network.

Before describing their continuing involvement in detail, we might briefly discuss the more general question of the role of non-state actors in world politics today. While there is considerable consensus that governments are no longer the only important players in international diplomacy and relations, how we can systematically examine these new players is much less clear. The conceptual haziness here is worth clarifying before proceeding. There are two main groups of non-state actors that have international implications. The first includes private sector representatives: multinational firms, international private lawyers, advertising firms, and lobbyists for industrial concerns. Their principal goal is the creation and maintenance of profit. The multinational firm, in particular, acquired an extraordinary degree of policy relevance for government decisionmakers. Some have called our times the age of global capital in which firms are often seen as the extensions of American or Northern dominance of the world economy.[77] Large multinationals, such as General Motors, the Royal Dutch/Shell Group, Ford, International Business Machines, Toyota, IRI (Italy), British Petroleum, Mobil, General Electric, Daimler-Benz (Germany), and Hitachi, all have greater sales than the GNP of many nation-states.[78]

The second group, which has much more relevance here, includes non-governmental organizations, often organized along international (or, as some would prefer, transnational) lines but not operated for profit. These organizations are oriented towards issue-area involvement and often have an overriding ideological vision. The environmental issue-area has been a primary source of NGO action and organization. As several authors have argued, the environmental NGOs have been able to fill a niche after the Cold War, one that they 'have simultaneously helped create and fill to influence both state and society.'[79] They play the twin roles of advocate and observer, and some suggest they even have the potential to become the 'conscience of the world,' providing information and advocacy where governments fear to tread.[80]

Among the most visible environmental crusades has been the international campaign to stop whaling, and its visibility is due not to the low-key affairs of IWC meetings or periodic foreign policy statements on the issue, but rather to the publicity captured by the more vocal anti-whalers who work for non-governmental organizations. We consider these groups to be non-state actors because they operate outside the formal context of diplomacy, unless they are let inside for official meetings, and because their members are not responsible to governments. Nonetheless, the American delegation to IWC annual meetings has evolved to include NGO representatives. This development is a selective precedent for the United States. The whaling issue has generated much interest in and support for these groups, suggesting that an almost symbiotic relationship has evolved between them and cetaceans. However, pro-whaling governments and lobby groups are not so impressed: they feel that NGOs, staffed typically with middle-class North American and European white males, reflect a privileged western environmental ethic and seek to impose this perspective on the rest of the world. To some they may be saviours, but to others they are cultural imperialists. As well, they are viewed with mixed appreciation by the scientific community; some regret the 'Tarot-card-reading faction' of groups like Greenpeace, which supported New Zealander Paul Spong in his post-Stockholm anti-whaling campaign. The reference here is to so-called new-age environmentalists who seek greater connections with the earth through communicating/interacting with mammals.[81] Others, however, not only accept the NGO activity as urgently necessary, but have even dedicated their professional lives to serving the cause. Even the relatively conservative World Wildlife Fund has been reported as a financial supporter. According to Fred Pearce, 'In 1978, the Dutch branch of the World Wildlife Fund paid for the new London office of Greenpeace to send a mission against Icelandic whalers. This was the first of many little-publicized contributions by the WWF, with its staid image and royal patronage, to their more wild-eyed brothers.' The WWF also paid some of the expenses for Sidney Holt, a well-respected cetologist and avid anti-whaler, to represent Seychelles at the IWC.[82]

We have already discussed the large role played by NGOs in moving the American foreign policy position towards preservationism. During the 1970s, NGOs were able to create a direct economic threat to whalers by supporting consumer boycotts of products, especially Japanese products, within the United States. This action coincided with growing resentment of Japan's protectionist trade policies, and a perception that Japan was flooding the United States with foreign products. At some point, the whaling issue became subsumed by a larger, anti-Japanese movement and fears about America's industrial future. Indeed, in addition to lobbyists working in Washington, the Japan Whaling Association at one point contracted with an American public relations firm to deal with this controversial issue.[83]

By now, the participation of non-governmental organizations in whaling is famous. The groups include Friends of the Earth, Greenpeace, the International Society for the Protection of Animals, Project Jonah, the World Wildlife Fund, and many others, mainly of North American origin. The whaling issue became a rallying point for these groups, figuring prominently in many of their itineraries. They were able to capture public imagination through peaceful protest and the distribution of information. Specific events also made headlines, such as a wild ten-hour chase scene when Soviet authorities tried to capture film of the 1983 landing and arrest of activists at the Lorino whaling station on the Bering Sea in Siberia. The British-based Whale and Dolphin Conservation Society also makes important headlines, for example, their recent assertions that whalemeat trade is widespread, based on a series of genetic tests conducted on whalemeat taken from major cities in Asia, including Tokyo and Seoul. The group claims a virtual smuggling triangle exists between South Korea, Japan, and Taiwan. Whalemeat fetches up to $100 (US) per pound. (Of course, this high price-incentive factor can also support an argument for cancelling the moratorium.)

Much media attention has focused on incidents that involved violence, such as the ramming of the notorious pirate ship *Sierra* by the renegade self-described 'lead *Kamikaze*'[84] Paul Watson and the destruction of Icelandic whaling property in October 1986. Other bombings in Portugal and Spain followed. While the topic of 'monkey wrenching' (or deliberately sabotaging equipment used to utilize natural resources) is beyond the scope of this chapter, cetacean survival has provided a strong stimulant for its advocates.[85] We may also note the instrumental role played by Greenpeace and other non-governmental actors in exposing both illegal and pirate whaling. The conventional distinction between pirate and illegal whaling is interesting: the former is usually construed as all whaling that takes place outside the regulatory scope of the IWC; the latter refers only to member-state violations of those regulations. This distinction raises interesting jurisprudential problems for international law specialists, as well as the question – tantalizing to regime theorists – of what, exactly, is a prohibitionary regime (discussed in Chapter 2).[86] The extensive Japanese whaling empire worked in and out of the IWC's jurisdiction: Japanese companies have been accused of establishing, through the export of capital and expertise, pirate 'whaling colonies,' primarily in South America (Peru, Brazil, Chile), but also in Taiwan,

South Korea, and the Philippines. In the absence of any international state-sanctioned system of surveillance that could efficiently cover such widespread operations, non-governmental organizations, and their motivated members, were essential participants – despite continuous confrontation with state authorities – in the emerging cetacean issue-area network. Edith Brown Weiss even writes of NGOs as 'informal ombudsmen for the environment' and, by extension, for future generations. Brown Weiss mentions in particular the Sierra Club, the Natural Resources Defense Council, the Environmental Defense Fund, the World Wildlife Fund, and the International Union for the Conservation of Nature and Natural Resources.[87]

Some groups, such as Greenpeace, clearly played a direct role in inducing some of the many states that joined the IWC from 1978 to 1982 to vote for the moratorium. According to Francisco Palacio, he and David McTaggart gave immense help to states prepared to join the IWC. Palacio, currently a Colombian living in Miami, was the commissioner for St. Lucia. His lawyer, Richard Baron, was a representative for Antigua. McTaggart's friend, Paul Gouin (a Moroccan-born French expatriate living in Nassau), represented Panama. The Japanese, roundly condemned for their efforts to support anti-moratorium states, point quickly to these instances of Greenpeace /United States support and influence. Members of Greenpeace, of course, would argue that almost any technique is valid when the future of a species is at stake.[88] For the most part, the NGO role has surfaced around active campaigning, inside but also outside of the IWC. Friends of the Earth (FOE), for example, held a series of outdoor demonstrations in Europe immediately preceding the adoption of the moratorium. One demonstration, held in Trafalgar Square in July 1979, attracted 12,000 people. During the IWC Meeting in London that year, FOE exceeded 300 press article mentions in a single month.[89]

It is difficult to decide how much of an impact the NGOs had on state policy: they demonstrated considerable lobbying skills in persuading non-whaling nations to join the IWC, they generated unprecedented media coverage for environmental politics with their publicity stunts, and they attracted large numbers of highly educated individuals who legitimated their cause for many previously sceptical observers. Perhaps the best testament to the importance of NGOs in conservationist politics, both local and global, is their impressive growth and resilience. NGOs continue to play a large role at IWC annual meetings. Though they are not given voting status, they can sit in as observers and, in this capacity, engage in considerable 'arm-twisting.'[90] The whale and interested NGOs have, as mentioned, established a unique symbiotic relationship, since the issue helped galvanize and popularize the once-peripheral promotional efforts of the latter. For example, as two activists explain, 'Greenpeace cut its teeth on whaling.'[91]

Greenpeace, in particular, has become a large transnational organization, with offices in thirty countries and an annual income of well over $100 million (US). Its income reached a peak of $179 million (US) in 1991 but has been declining since. Nonetheless, the sheer scope of Greenpeace activities remains impressive. For example, in the summer of 1995 alone, 'the group's campaigners humiliated Royal Dutch/Shell, Europe's biggest company, over its plans to dump the redundant Brent Spar oil platform at sea ... It has turned its fire on France's plans for nuclear tests in the Pacific. And on 15 August, five senior Greenpeace campaigners were arrested in Beijing after protesting against Chinese nuclear testing. Greenpeace was also heavily involved in the formation of the Basle Convention, an agreement to restrict exports of hazardous waste from rich to poor countries.'[92] Meanwhile, as Table 3 indicates, the number of NGOs at the IWC has increased drastically over the years. Indeed, some of the NGOs are private firms that pursue consultancy work for others, and, even, pro-whaling groups from Japan, such as the Citizen's League for Preservation of Whaling, represented by K. Takeuchi.[93] (In such cases, the line between NGOs and government representatives is especially unclear.)

Told from their perspective, the NGOs can claim credit for the struggle to achieve the moratorium. At the same time, the IWC meetings gave the NGOs a focus, for themselves and for the public. As well, governments have been essential in financing the IWC and in imposing its preservationist ideology on the few remaining whaling states through, in the American case, the threat of sanctions. Lowe and Goyder conclude that, in certain issue-areas at least, 'it was not until the emergence of political internationalism and the creation of international governmental organizations that international non-governmental organizations achieved any relevance and permanence.'[94] Put bluntly, they needed some form of political organization to lobby. And, as Norway, Iceland, and Japan have made clear, attitudes towards whaling have not undergone a universal shift.

Table 3

List of Non-Governmental Organizations attending the 1994 IWC Annual Meeting in Puerto Vallarta, Mexico

African Wildlife Foundation
Alliance of Marine Mammal Parks and Aquariums
American Friends Service Committee
American Zoo and Aquarium Association
Animal Kingdom Foundation
Animal Protection Institute of America
Animal Welfare Institute
Antarctic and Southern Ocean Coalition
Appel pour les Baleines
Arnold A. Finn P.E. Inc.
Association for the Protection of Wildlife and Amazonia-Caribbean
Beauty Without Cruelty
Campaign Whale
Center for Action on Endangered Species
Center for Marine Conservation
Centro de Investigaciones Marinas y Acuaticos de Colombia
Cetacean Society International
Citizen's League for Preservation of Whaling
Coalition Clean Baltic
Comite Nacional pro Defensa de la Fauna y Flora
Cousteau Society
David Shepherd Conservation Foundation
Dolphin Connection
Dolphin Research Center
Earth Island Institute
Earthtrust
Environmental Investigation Agency
European Bureau for Conservation and Development
European Environmental Bureau
Fauna and Flora Preservation Society
Friends of the Earth
Friends of Whalers
Fundacao Brasileira para a Conservacao da Naturezza
Greenpeace International
Group to Preserve Whale Dietary Culture
High North Alliance
Human/Dolphin Foundation
Humane Society International
Indigenous World Association
Institute for European Environmental Policy
Institute for the Study of Animal Problems

List of Non-Governmental Organizations attending the 1994 IWC Annual Meeting in Puerto Vallarta, Mexico

International Association for Aquatic Animal Medicine
International Association for Religious Freedom
International Coalition of Fisheries Associations
International Commission of Jurists
International Dolphin Watch
International Environmental Advisors
International Fund for Animal Welfare
International Institute for Environment and Development
International League for the Protection of Cetaceans
International Marine Animal Trainers' Association
International Marine Mammal Association, Inc.
International Ocean Institute
International Transport Workers' Federation
International Wildlife Coalition
International Wildlife Management Consortium
International Work Group for Indigenous Affairs
Inuit Circumpolar Conference
Inuit Circumpolar Conference Environmental Commission
Island Resources Foundation
Japan Anthropology Workshop
Japan Fisheries Association
Japan Whaling Association
Minority Rights Group
Monitor
Monitor International
Nordic Council for Animal Welfare
Nordic Ecoforum
Ocean Advocates
Patagonia 2000
Project Jonah
Riches of the Sea
Robin des Bois
Rondor Music International Inc.
Royal Society for the Prevention of the Cruelty to Animals
SAVE International
Save the Children
Seafinding Associates
Sink or Swim Stitching
Special Expeditions
Survival International

continued on next page

Table 3 (continued)

List of Non-Governmental Organizations attending the 1994 IWC Annual Meeting in Puerto Vallarta, Mexico

TRAFFIC International
Tusk Force
Waterlife Association
Werkgroep Zeehond
Whale and Dolphin Conservation Society
Whale Issue Network
Whaling Problem Discussion Committee
Women's International League for Peace and Freedom
World Council of Indigenous Peoples
World Wide Fund for Nature
Zoo Check

Source: IWC Annual Report, Document IWC/46/3, Cambridge, UK

Looking Ahead

Fears that Iceland's withdrawal from the IWC, Norway's limited resumption of minke hunts, and the establishment of NAMMCO signal the beginning of the end of the current whaling regime are understandable. The RMP, as mentioned in Chapter 2, would offer the IWC a very conservative regulatory structure which, however, would need to secure funding for its implementation. Its establishment would also involve lifting the moratorium, and this step seems unlikely to gain the support of the western nations.

One of the most serious challenges facing the IWC, then, is the question of cost. Demands have been made that, if the RMP is accepted, it should include a very tight monitoring regimen, including observers, preferably international, on every vessel; DNA testing of all whalemeat landed; the use of enforcement vessels; and ongoing research by the IWC Scientific Committee. The government of New Zealand released a report in November 1994 outlining what was needed to add a workable enforcement regime to the IWC Revised Management Scheme. The report suggests the following principles take priority: transparency of operations, full reporting, and 'confidence' in reporting. 'To confirm that illegal whaling is not occurring, this should include regular use of vessel monitoring systems, independent observers and inspectors, and DNA analysis of whalemeat and products.' This tricky verification issue brings to the fore questions of trust and intrusion. The DNA question relates to recent advances in determining which species are being sold, largely in local markets in Japan.[95] New Zealand called for 'the capacity for autho-rised independent personnel to halt their particular activities and for the IWC to impose penalties for any significant infractions of the RMS'; and only those states whose nationals or flag vessels partici-pate in whaling operations should be made to pay the related costs.

Ultimately, the Japanese and others argue, such measures are intended primarily to make whaling as economically unprofitable as in the days when rapid and massive stock reductions made whaling journeys a financial drain and not a bounty. Assuming fairly wide-spread support for a strict observation regime, however, the especially difficult question of payment arises. Who should pay for this scheme: whalers, as the American camp insists; or all members, who presum-ably benefit from a system that preserves whales for the enjoyment, or intellectual comfort, of future generations? If whales are an inte-gral aspect of ocean ecosystems, and we all need oceans, should we all pay for the conservation of cetaceans? And should all members pay the same, regardless of large differences in their internal econo-mies? According to the present payment structure, nations that con-tinue to whale, even in the case of aboriginal whaling, pay more than others. St. Vincent, a tiny Caribbean island that has taken two hump-back whales in the last three years, pays more than $21,000 per year in dues, while France, Germany, and the United Kingdom, three of the most powerful economies on earth, pay only $12,000.[96]

The IWC still entirely relies on the contributions of its members and, like any other modern institution, is affected by the financial currents in which it swims. For example, in 1993, the IWC agreed to an approximate 15 per cent increase in contributions; this agreement was necessary partly because of the lower interest rates in the United Kingdom (where the commission does its banking); interest generated by the IWC General Fund was down. (The goal of this fund is to keep operating expenses for six months held in reserve in case of emer-gency.) As well, salaries of IWC officials are pegged to International Maritime Organization standards and had to be increased by 8 per cent that year. Finally, the expanding agenda of the IWC Scientific Committee would require more funding in the future.

The IWC is becoming increasingly involved in a much broader research agenda. A working group on whalewatching now exists, something rather unimaginable just ten years ago, when the IWC was popularly labelled a 'whalers club.' Whalewatching is a growing industry and represents a new outlook on human-cetacean interaction, an emphasis on what some have labelled 'non-consumptive utilization.'[97] However, it is not without potentially harmful effects. In fact, the Mexicans are actually limiting the activity with respect to the famous gray whale winter migration into the Baja California lagoons. Noise, pollution, propellers, harassment of whales – all these dangers may be quite secondary to the harpoon, but they are a cause for concern. Are universal regulations necessary? Should the IWC play a role here? A meeting on whalewatching, organized by NGOs but also attended by IWC officials, was held in Venice in March 1995. For now, however, the IWC maintains that the regulation of whale-watching activities is the responsibility of relevant coastal states.

There is another call for the IWC to play a large role in the management of smaller cetaceans, such as dolphins and porpoises. Given the organization's financial constraints, the IWC is unlikely to expand in functional terms. This development would also involve further intrusions into sovereign regulatory jurisdiction.[98] However, the IWC is increasingly involved in habitat protection efforts, especially those related to ecosystem health studies. We return to this new, and vital, responsibility in the next chapter.

In terms of international antagonism, then, the lines are clearly drawn. One of the American delegates to the 1992 IWC Meeting was Michael Sutton, a senior program officer at the World Wildlife Foundation; one of the Japanese delegates was Kazuo Shima, the deputy director general of the Japanese Fisheries Agency.[99] On 21 May 1995, two weeks before the IWC Meeting in Dublin, the Global Guardian Trust, which supports Japanese whaling interests, took out an ad in the *Sunday New York Times,* arguing that the crisis of whale endangerment is over and that beliefs about whale intelligence are mythological. ('Cetacean scientist David Gaskin ... concluded that there is little evidence of behavioural complexity beyond that of a herd of cows or deer.') The ad also complains that the US and some other IWC member-nations 'under pressure from animal rights groups, oppose the sustainable utilization of non-endangered whales by nations traditionally dependent on it. The US, however, makes an exception for its own Alaskan Eskimos.' Since they have treaty whaling rights, the Makah will be another exception should they persist in reviving the gray whale hunt.

4
Whale Ethics: A Normative Discussion

> The history of the intermingling of human cultures is a history of trade – in objects like the narwhal's tusk, in ideas, and in great narratives. We appropriate when possible the best we can find in all of this.
>
> – Barry Lopez, 1986[1]

One of the most impressive stories in cetacean survival has been the comeback of the Pacific gray whale (*Eschrichtius robustus*). Threatened with extinction at the turn of the century, these magnificent, forty-foot, unassuming bottom feeders have recovered to their pre-exploitation levels of more than 20,000. The Atlantic gray whale was not so lucky; the species was extinct by as early as AD 500 along the coast of Europe, and followed suit in the early 1870s in North America. The western North Pacific variant, which travels between the Sea of Okhotsk, the Kamchatka Peninsula, and the Aleutian Islands southward to Korea and Japan, remains very scarce.

As noted in Chapter 2, a great deal of uncertainty surrounds much of our knowledge of whale populations; the current debate over minke whale populations in the northeast Atlantic reflects this uncertainty. However, due to active groups of whale enthusiasts along the West Coast and the proclivity of giant baleen whales to stay within sight of shore, the celebrated gradual increase in the gray whale population is reasonably certain.[2] Although they have a very understandable fear of the killer whale, Pacific grays are no longer the object of the harpoon. One cetologist was able to assert as early as 1978 that 'the gray whale has shown a surprisingly quick restoration to reasonable abundance in the comparatively short period of complete protection, and may be an example of what can be expected if the populations of other over-fished species are left in peace to recover their numbers.'[3]

Like many enchanted authors and even more tourists, I've had the privilege of seeing these mammals up close, both feeding calmly in a shallow lagoon and pushing northwards in stormy seas during their annual migration off the coast of Vancouver Island. The bulky mammals are dedicated bottom feeders and can often be observed for hours on end in areas such as Clayquot Sound. They are well suited for this feeding exercise: the gray whale's tongue can weigh up to 3,000 pounds. The annual 20,000-kilometre (13,000-mile) journey from the Chukchi and Bering seas to Mexico's Baja peninsula is conducted at an average speed of 185 kilometres (115 miles) per day; it is the longest known migration of any mammal in the world.[4] The passing whales provide tourist dollars to many coastal towns along the American and Canadian coasts, and the Mexican government has – so far – protected the Baja California lagoons that serve as birthing grounds. The most famous of these, Scammon's Lagoon, named for an overproductive whaler, was once the scene of an unmitigated slaughter of gray whale mothers and calves. Now, it is a highly regarded tourist area and whale sanctuary, though industry threatens its ecological integrity. The whales are familiar symbols in travel guides up and down the coast; their annual appearance marks a festive occasion in many areas. They symbolize conservationist progress and resiliency. What if someone wanted to resume killing them?

Two Central Positions: Ideologies in Cetapolitics

The gray whale is cited here because it is so recognizable to western Americans and Canadians, and because a coastal aboriginal group, the Makah of Washington State, has expressed an interest in resuming a subsistence hunt.[5] But cetacean management is not by any means only a local issue. Because of the IWC global moratorium on commercial whaling, all great whales are formally protected from commercial whaling. As we have seen, the smaller minke whale (*Balaenoptera acutorostrata*) is taken by the Norwegians and the Japanese (the latter take them for 'scientific' purposes), but their catch is limited. The question, however, remains: when whale species have recovered from the slaughters of the past, as the minke and gray certainly have, should whalers resume their occupation, albeit at reduced rates that reflect a new awareness of maximum sustainable yields?

There are many aspects to this question, including the perplexing ethical dilemma associated with aboriginal whaling. However, two immediate dimensions to commercial whaling stand out: one is practical, the other ethical, and though the two are closely related, we separate them for the purpose of this discussion and focus on the latter. The practical question is whether the market for whale products economically justifies a resumption of whaling. Arguably, though whale products had a central role in the industrial development of the

United States, Great Britain, Australia, and many other nation-states, the only contemporary major market is Japan, and the only product in great demand is whalemeat, now considered a delicacy. It is conceivable that this situation could change, yet rather unlikely, not just because the European Union and United States have banned the commercialization of whale products, but also because of the ethical question discussed here. In the meantime, demand from Japan is sufficient to keep the diminished whaling industry active in lobbying the IWC (and Washington) to drop the moratorium and at least allow small-scale coastal whaling of the minke. Assuming some demand is maintained for whale products into the next century, we are left with what is essentially an ethical, and not a practical, dilemma.

Three central positions have emerged with regard to whaling, though this generalization simplifies the debate rather drastically. The main question is whether the consumptive utilization of whales is acceptable. The conservationist perspective seeks to save whales from extinction and keep them at current levels; however, killing whales is considered acceptable, although this acceptance varies depending on the purpose of the killing. The preservationist camp holds that, given the whales' high level of intelligence and place in the ocean ecosystem, killing them is always improper, regardless of its purpose. The term preservationist may have been adopted for lack of a better one; anti-consumptionist would perhaps be more fitting. A third position, however, dominates American governmental policy on the issue: those opposed steadfastly to commercial whaling but supportive of subsistence whaling. This stance raises acute controversy, since the Japanese whale lobbyists claim that their coastal communities are attempting to maintain an important cultural heritage through resuming whaling; the American policymakers have been inclined to disbelieve them.[6] To some, it is highly hypocritical to permit aboriginal whaling in Alaska (and, perhaps in the future, along the West Coast) while denying it to Japanese and Norwegian whalers, through a set of possible sanctions and the ideological domination of the IWC. Worse, some even suggest that 'whaling has become a convenient symbol for those who try to create anti-Japanese feelings in western countries where many people already blame the Japanese for many of the economic problems found in the west.'[7]

As literary deconstructionists are constantly reminding us, there is much in a word. How we choose to describe certain activities, carried out by humans and non-humans alike, will influence our perception of those events. M. Brock Fenton, referring to the success of conservation groups in obtaining the desired reaction in Europe to the Canadian Atlantic seal hunt in the 1970s, writes that 'situations are often coloured by the choice of words: "killing" versus "harvesting"; "seal pups" versus "baby seals."'[8] Pro-whaling groups are sure to call themselves conservationists, while speaking of the sustainable utilization of natural resources. Their opponents, especially in the non-diplomatic context of environmental activism, prefer to refer to 'whale slaughter' or 'killing,' not 'utilization.' In perhaps the most extreme version of semantic flexibility, Michael Tobias refers to the lamentable fact that in 1992 the Japanese *'cannibalized* 2000 tons of whale meat.'[9]

We search in vain for neutrality here; the two sides are diametrically opposed. One group sees the use of whales by humans as perfectly legitimate, providing that use doesn't cause the same type of ecological disaster as early whaling did. The other group within this network sees the whaling issue as an almost closed one: all whaling is as unnecessary as it is gruesome. Within these groups, further splits are detectable: those few who would have commercial whaling resume its former scale, if physically possible (and it is not); those who would limit whaling to medium-sized operations, such as Japanese coastal communities; and those who believe the answer lies in technology, the discovery of better and quicker ways to kill the mammals. Among preservationists, the ideological differences reflect the environmentalist community itself. The whale is sacred, according to some: its intelligence and rarity should make it immune from human destruction. For example, a recently published collection of such sentiments begins: 'If we can destroy such remarkable marine mammals – beasts who do not compete with us for living space, who are not predators on our domestic livestock, who are not physical threats to us in any way, and whose beauty is impressive and enriching – then nothing is safe from our destructive impulse.'[10] At the same time, many support aboriginal whaling, which is often viewed as reflecting a pre-European environmental paradigm, similar to the Plains Native Americans' reliance on the buffalo. There is also the further question of dealing with the implications of the preservationist perspective while being fully aware of the intersocietal problems raised by cultural relativity. To kill or not to kill is only part of the question; we must also ask what is the ethical basis for enforcing such a decision on a global scale.

The long and convoluted story of the international politics of whale conservation has been told elsewhere. Certainly, attitudes towards whales have changed remarkably in this century. In economic terms, whales have shifted from being 'stocks giving rise to private goods' to public goods with an 'existence value.'[11] Once the source of oil for reading lamps and for industry, the whale outlived this usefulness and became hunted largely for meat; it also provided food for mink ranches in the former Soviet Union. Tens of thousands were taken on the high seas despite the existence of the regulatory IWC, which many referred to as a 'whalers club' before the organization underwent its own normative transition, obtaining a three-quarters majority needed for the 1986 complete moratorium on commercial whaling.[12] And the IWC has also created commercial whaling sanctuaries in the Indian and, more recently, Antarctic oceans. At least in the western public mind, whales have become symbolic of the larger need to preserve the natural environment. As mentioned, the US Air Force formerly shot at killer whales for target practice. Such actions would be unacceptable today. Indeed, accounts such as the following, told by Nigel Bonner, sound bizarre:

A 30m (98 foot) 'Blue Whale,' probably a female, swam into the Panama Canal from the Caribbean on 23 January 1922. For some unexplained reason ... it was killed by machine-gun fire. The carcass was towed out to sea and abandoned, but drifted ashore again at Nombre de Dios Bay. It was towed out again and the US Army Air Force used it for bombing practise. Parts of this whale (the 2nd and 3rd cervical vertebrae) were rescued from the shore by an English explorer and big-game fisherman, Mitchell Hedges, who presented them to the British Museum (Natural History).[13]

At least in the western public mind, then, whales have become symbolic of the larger need to preserve the natural environment. Their condition is interpreted as an indicator of the modern state of the biosphere as well as human-nature relations. Norman Myers points to the October 1988 incident of three gray whales trapped in Arctic ice that led to great public support for their salvation, including $800,000 (US) spent by government bodies and conservation agencies. 'It is this role of whales,' he writes, 'to stand as a measure of our global conscience, that should give us hope ... Whales ... are universal standards by which we can assess our stewardship of the planet.'[14] This is a tall order indeed, and such statements need to be tempered by an explicit analysis of relevant ethical and political considerations.

Not much has been published that deals directly with the ethics of whale conservation, though an essay by James E. Scarff, who once served as an official American observer to the IWC, provides an excellent starting point.[15] Significantly, this essay was published before the acceptance of the present moratorium on commercial whaling. We are in a new era now, rather different from that of 1980 when whale populations were still declining. We examine this contentious issue from five perspectives: interspecies ethics, resource utilization, aboriginal whaling, small-scale coastal whaling, and habitat protection. We refer to literature on international ethics and to differing conceptions that have emerged over the last few decades. If the whale is to be a symbolic player in the quest for achieving consciousness of Barbara Ward's Spaceship Earth, surely we must have some sort of idea of the resulting ethical implications? On the other hand, if the whale is a resource we should harvest, what does this proposition say about human-nature relations and how far the conventional stewardship model can travel?

Interspecies Ethics

Here we might launch into a protracted discussion of the origins of ethical thought in our own species. Any such discussion would be inevitably inconclusive. While many have considered commonly held assumptions about morality to be the product of divine inspiration, others, such as those who study in the realm of biopolitics, suggest 'conative beings emerge because mobile parasites on plants [i.e., us] not only need orientation but guidance as well ... Ultimately, the vector of their will is pointed toward the survival of their genes ... "Good" and "bad" are entirely related to individual survival.'[16] While we are well advised to steer clear of discussing the 'vector of will,' even this conception of human ethical development, which is based more on self-interest than on collective environmental concerns, blends the two motivations. In other words, a cold calculus of survival chances (perhaps slowly transmitted through gene structures) nonetheless lends itself to a concern for environmental decay, including species impoverishment.

Environmental issues have ethics at their heart: questions of what constitutes proper human behaviour and proper relations between people and nature. In discussing human behaviour, David Sarokin and Jay Schulkin write of 'environmental justice,' a hybrid between environmental concerns and civil rights issues. In the United States, blacks, Hispanics, American Indians, and the poor generally are at greater risk than others from environmental contamination and/or nuisance (for example, by living adjacent to waste management facilities and noisy airports). They are often excluded from policy-making and decision-making processes, and this exclusion applies both within and beyond the relatively prosperous United States.[17]

But ethics need not stop at human-human relations. What about the voice of non-humans, either of select mammals or, in yet more complicated fashion, of entire ecosystems? Generally, the very idea of such a voice has been rejected. Thomas Hobbes, who is often quoted by classical realists in the international relations discipline, believed that mammals' lack of speech rendered political/ethical relations with them impossible. (This viewpoint makes the debate over cetacean and primate communicative abilities even more interesting.) 'To make Covenant with bruit Beasts, is impossible; because not understanding our speech, they understand not, nor accept of any translation of Right; nor can translate any Right to another; and without mutual acceptation, there is no Covenant.'[18]

Others argue that all species must be treated as perfectly equal.[19] This argument has interesting consequences for the whaling issue. If whaling is viewed as inherently wrong, why not the annual killing of hundreds of millions of cows, or billions of chickens? A vegetarian might not quibble over different species, though even they often make qualitative distinctions, for example, between fish and other animals. At any rate, we hardly live in a vegetarian world. Why not eat whales?

Are whales that special? Many clearly feel they are, though this belief is closely tied no doubt to the level of endangerment experienced, by whales and by us. Robert Payne writes that he 'used to wonder what had become of the two *Sovetskayas*. A recent article in an Australian newspaper reports that they are to be spruced up for use as floating slaughterhouses for sheep in transit between Australia and the port of Vladivostok (the *Sovetskaya's* home port). According to the article [which Payne does not cite], ten million sheep per year will get a final cruise aboard these ships, interrupted only by their own deaths. It's a bit tough on the sheep but at least keeps these vessels off the whales' backs for the nonce.'[20] Indeed, it is tough on the sheep.

If blue, humpback, right, and bowhead whales are threatened with extinction, then we may have a moral obligation to save these species. At the very least, we may be obligated to future generations to avoid

driving today's species into extinction; the imperative of intergenerational ethics was even accepted in the Rio Declaration emerging
from UNCED.[21] This logic certainly applies to the question of today's
habitat protection for all living things; but it is challenged by the
recovery of once-endangered species, such as gray whales and African
elephants. In favouring popular mammals, such as whales, for protection beyond the mere fact of their rarity, we make certain assumptions
operational: that whales are intelligent, magnificent, capable of teach-
ing us much in terms of marine biology and perhaps even sociobiology,
and – not least important – capable of attracting curious tourists.

Such logic does lead to some problems, however, as Scarff pointed
out in his 1980 article. If intelligence is the defining characteristic –
if killing whales is wrong because they are closer to us in intelligence
than most mammals, save perhaps primates – then questions arise concerning the intelligence of various cetaceans. (Generally, Mysticeti or
toothed whales, which include dolphins and porpoises, are considered
brighter than Odontoceti or baleen whales, though this conclusion is
open to dispute.) Further, we have yet to arrive at an acceptable universal standard for measuring human intelligence, much less nonhuman intelligence. The Japan Whaling Association insists that whales
exhibit no more intelligence than that of cows or, in social terms,
herds of deer. Regardless, their place in the marine ecosystem food
chain certainly warrants extra concern for their future.

In a recent article in the journal *Environmental Ethics*, William
French, a theologian at Loyola University in Chicago, carefully ana-
lyzes the biological egalitarianist perspective, which insists that all
species should be considered equal in all ways. He concludes:

> I think it is best not to think of rankings as an assessment of some
> 'inherent' superiority, but rather as a considered moral recognition
> of the fact that greater ranges of vulnerability are generated by
> broader ranges of complexity and capabilities.[22]

Neither conservationist nor preservationist would argue with this
point. Whales are special. However, this fact does not mean that they
are necessarily unhuntable. Aboriginal societies have often been
praised by western environmentalists for their intrinsic connection to
their habitat, reflected in cultural artifacts and tradition. This praise
can be exaggerated. Nonetheless, many coastal aboriginal societies
have historically taken whales or, in the case of the Makah, wish to

resume limited whaling, while simultaneously believing whales are very important in a profound spiritual sense.

If avoiding cetacean extinctions is now an ethically acceptable priority on a universal scale, a priority both conservationists and preservationists would support, this goal is inextricable from habitat protection itself. There is little use in long-term thinking about saving the great whales in captivity. The promise (or, as some might think of it, the necessary evil) of *ex situ* conservation – striving to replicate natural conditions, maintaining genetic diversity, inducing procreation – is barely mentionable in this context.[23] Though scientists might experiment with genetic material, whales are here appreciated for their social as well as biological distinctiveness; and the captivity of even smaller cetaceans raises great concerns about this ethical dimension. If whales are truly intelligent, should we use them (and other mammals) to attract visitors to theme parks? And their size alone makes the question of the captive breeding of the large whales an entirely academic one.[24] Therefore, the species must be preserved at sea; and therefore, the sea must be preserved as the irreplaceable habitat of these mammals. This imperative would be axiomatic to anyone determined to continue or resume whaling and to anyone determined to stop or preclude it. After this temporary convergence, however, a rather large divide opens, chiefly around the question of resource utilization.

Resource Utilization
In a letter to the United States Congress dated 4 October 1993, Bill Clinton reacted to charges from the late secretary of commerce Ronald Brown that Norway was threatening the effectiveness of an international marine mammals agreement. By means of the Pelly Amendment, American sanctions could be applied to Norway. The response was characteristic: Clinton insisted that the US would wait until world opinion has a chance to influence Norway's behaviour. A list of potential sanctions, including Norwegian seafood products, has been drawn up, and the letter stands ready for implementation. Perhaps most noteworthy, however, are these two lines: 'The United States recognizes that not every country agrees with our position against commercial whaling. The issue at hand is the absence of a credible, agreed management and monitoring regime that would ensure that commercial whaling is kept within a science-based limit.'[25]

Many doubt that this point is really the issue at hand. The Japanese, the Norwegians, and, prior to their withdrawal from the IWC, the

Icelanders, have consistently claimed that the American position has little to do with science and everything to do with the imposition of the current American value position – the preservationist or anti-consumptionist ideology – on other IWC members. To be fair, the majority of IWC members agree with the American anti-whaling position. But it is certainly true that commercial whaling is viewed by the American IWC delegation as inappropriate behaviour, even if limited aboriginal whaling by the Alaskan Inuit is not. (See Appendix C for the current IWC-endorsed aboriginal whaling quotas.)

Commercial whaling in part receives this assessment because of its awful track record, especially in this century. The eastern coast of the United States heavily depended on commercial whaling in the 1700s and 1800s. But whaling had diminished as an economic activity by the 1900s as other nations began to dominate the industry in the deep seas. This development led to the race towards extinction that characterized the years before and after the Second World War. Radical groups like the Sea Shepherd publicly proclaimed their right to resort to violence to save whales from this onslaught. Should commercial whaling be widely allowed again, should the Japanese develop their extant whale market and again employ even part of their whaling fleet, the floodgates could open.[26] In addition, despite the years of American whaling and despite their romantic representation in classics such as Melville's *Moby Dick*, we knew very little about whales, which were considered rather large fish. As we now know much more, we are inclined to believe that selling whale products is unacceptable. The Japanese and the Norwegians have not yet come to the same conclusion, but given time they might.

Conservationists do not accept these points. They do not believe that commercial whaling is inherently bad, that it will necessarily lead to an unmanageable tragedy of the commons, or that the whaling nations have somehow steered themselves down a delinquent ethical path. Indeed, whales may be special, and we should take extra care not to endanger them. The long-sought RMP, which the IWC could eventually put in place, does so. It will also eventually include tough observation formulas: better to have legitimately regulated activity than to rely on groups with limited resources and preservationist agendas (such as Greenpeace) to monitor illegal commercial whaling. The revised scheme fulfils the original mandate of the IWC, which is to regulate, not stop, whaling. Members of the IWC Scientific Committee have expressed dismay over their inability to have the RMP implemented. As mentioned, the committee chairman recently resigned over this contentious matter.[27] Anti-whalers retort that the IWC should represent whatever is the majority opinion within its membership, and if this opinion is against commercial whaling, then so be it.

More broadly, an explicit anti-preservationist tone characterizes the conservationist perspective. The environmental activist movement, which prides itself on protecting seal pups with the help of celebrities like Brigitte Bardot, may ignore the real cultural importance of people dependent on subsistence hunting.[28] Whales, in particular, have been used as a convenient symbol for the environmental movement as a whole, without due regard for the complexity of marine ecology. The power of the symbol has distorted not only the necessary rigours of science but has indiscriminately cast whalers as the bad people of the sea. The domination of the IWC by the American position has even led a rather scathing essayist to coin the phrase 'Management by Totemization.'[29] Perhaps the IWC should get out of the business altogether, and regional organizations, such as the recently created North Atlantic Marine Mammals Commission (Faroe Islands, Norway, Iceland, and Greenland), should take over. Nations without an interest in whaling have an easy time pontificating about whales, while their citizens consume hamburgers and drive polluting vehicles to work in their resource-consuming modern cities, no doubt with 'Save the Whale' bumper stickers above the exhaust pipe.

Obviously, a wide gulf separates these two positions on the utilization of whales. Whales have been seen as our brothers and sisters in the sea; they have been seen as resources that should be carefully harvested. Is it possible that one of these positions will dominate the other? Many western nations demonstrate a preservationist stance, but others, protective of their sovereignty, argue that to impose such a value system is tantamount to cultural imperialism. This argument will provide a constant criticism of future global environmental policies that affect trade and economic activities that cut across regions. As Daniel Esty notes in his recently published book on the General Agreement on Tariffs and Trade:

> North-south disputes arise when the developed world tries to advance through trade restrictions environmental policy judgements or moral values not shared in the developing world ... drawing on recent US-Mexico experience, the tuna-dolphin dispute presents a classic

example of a North-South values clash. From the point of view of the developing world, why should Mexico forgo fishing tuna with efficient purse seine nets, which produce a valuable source of low-cost protein for poor Mexicans and modest export earnings on US sales, just because America has a dolphin fetish? As the Mexicans are quick to point out, the dolphin population in the Eastern Tropical Pacific Ocean is not endangered [though the eastern spinner and the northeastern offshore spotted dolphins are listed as 'depleted' in the US Marine Mammal Protection Act], and fewer than 30,000 dolphins a year have been killed out of a population that numbers in the millions.[30]

As long as people are interested in resuming whaling, the issue will not go away. Perhaps that interest will be diminished by taking seriously the Precautionary Principle – which translates into refusing to engage in projects with unknown ecological effects – but there is no guarantee of good results.

A related question concerns the nature of whaling itself, which is often seen as an especially cruel form of hunting. This perception is based on another: whales are extraordinarily intelligent mammals, capable of great suffering, and harpoons rarely kill instantly. One of the many questions Scarff raises concerns the humaneness of killing techniques. He quotes Alistair Hardy of Australia: 'What an outcry there would be if we hunted elephants with explosive harpoons fired from a tank and then played the wounded beasts upon a line.'[31] Great whales in this century were killed with explosive harpoons which, ideally, ruptured near enough to the whale's brain to kill it instantly or at least render it unconscious. Of course, this outcome was not always the result: as anti-whalers point out, whales can survive the initial blast and struggle for life before finally succumbing. This prolonged death was more the case, of course, before modern technology rendered the battle between the sea's leviathan and its human hunters a decidedly one-sided affair.

At the Workshop on Humane Killing Techniques for Whales held at the 1980 IWC Meeting, participants noted that the 'development of a means of achieving a rapid, painless death would also and incidentally increase the efficiency of the whaling operation and improve the quality of the meat obtained (by reducing the stress caused to the whale).' Twelve years later, the Humane Killing Working Group at the IWC Meeting in Glasgow recommended that appropriate governments and national agencies 'develop procedures for ... representative samples of blood, brain and other tissues from selected animals, to allow assay of stress indicators and other physiological parameters in animals killed in whaling operations.'[32]

In a victory of sorts for whale enthusiasts, the last few decades have seen the near-elimination of the particularly cruel non-explosive cold harpoon, which was used primarily for smaller whales such as the minke, to minimize damage to the meat. (The harpoon was shot out of a fifty- to seventy-millimetre canon.) However, aboriginal whaling methods, which often involve the tracking of harpooned whales for hours on end, may be even more cruel. Alaskan Eskimos have begun using penthrite projectiles, small grenades designed to ensure a quick death when a whale is harpooned. At the 1994 IWC Meeting, both the Norwegians and the Japanese claimed that 'survival time' (i.e., how long a whale lives after being harpooned) has diminished over the years. The average is apparently around four minutes. This claim raises some problems: the statistics refer to minke whales, which are small and would appear easier to kill. However, as any statistician will tell you, radical exceptions to the average always exist, and that means prolonged agony in the case of some harpooned whales. Questions also arise concerning the possible accuracy of the timing itself. How do we know a whale is dead when it is in the water? Some debate ensued over New Zealand's presentation of preliminary evidence suggesting that the electric lance, often used to finish off struck whales, could cause 'unnecessary pain and suffering.' Japan insisted that the lance was humane. An IWC resolution discouraging the use of the electric lance (to which Japan objected) was adopted. Naturally, for those opposed to whaling in principle, the debate over humane killing may appear absurd. For those who accept the possibility of a resumption of commercial whaling, developing quick killing techniques should occur now.

As mentioned, another form of utilization has been so-called scientific whaling, a device employed by the Norwegians and the Japanese when the moratorium finally came into place. The newly established Southern Ocean sanctuary (for which Japan has entered a formal reservation) bans all commercial whaling except scientific whaling. Every year the Japanese demand and receive a small quota of minke whales for this purpose. Leaving aside the scientific issue of possibly learning more by studying the social behaviour of living whales, and by unobtrusively collecting living tissue samples, an ethical dispute arises over killing animals in order to study them. Many IWC delegates and environmental activists find the entire concept of scientific whaling to be a sham. Nonetheless, banning it entirely might push the Japanese beyond their patience on this issue. After all, the Japanese can voluntarily leave the IWC, and even the United States is unlikely to risk a major trade war over a few minke whales.

Finally, human utilization of cetaceans includes non-consumptive activities. Whalewatching has become big business in many places, especially along North America's West Coast. Should the IWC be involved in regulating this activity? At present, it is clearly unable to do so because of its limited mandate according to the International Convention for the Regulation of Whaling and because of practical limits to the scope of the IWC's work. However, it has established the Working Group on Whalewatching.[33] Since whalewatchers can be irresponsible and harass whales, the activity is not always considered benign, though it hardly represents an ethical dilemma of similar stature to the killing question. Importantly, the whalewatching industry itself forms yet another interest group in the cetacean issue-area network. Its impact will become evident in the case of the Makah gray whale hunt.

Any regulation of this further utilization would have additional costs. After the 1993 IWC Meeting in Kyoto, US commissioner Michael Tillman said: 'World opinion has influenced the IWC to broaden its focus. I am pleased that the IWC has agreed to expand its agenda to address non-lethal uses of marine mammals such as whale-watching, the study of environmental threats to living marine resources, and increased international cooperation on conservation of small cetaceans.'[34] This support does not necessarily imply, of course, that the United States is willing to pay for this increase in activities.

The question of financing has North-South implications for rich-poor member contributions. As mentioned in Chapter 3, nations that allow aboriginal whaling pay around 30 per cent more in dues. This assessment upsets states like St. Vincent and the Grenadines, which have difficulty making even regular payments and have an extremely small aboriginal whaling effort, with as few as one or two whales taken per year. Shouldn't the Americans pay more? Again, if commercial whaling does resume, should those states engaging in the activity pay the monitoring costs? Or should all IWC members pay to help conserve what is, after all, often touted as a global resource

– a part of the commons? And would this financing question affect IWC membership levels?

All controversies aside, one conclusion is inescapable: few, if any, observers or whalers would advocate a return to full-scale commercial whaling, as in the notorious days of Soviet and Japanese dominance from the 1950s to 1970s. There is no short-term economic rationale, and there is no long-term benefit involved in driving species to extinction. Whatever success a resumed whaling industry might achieve depends on its careful maintenance of conservationist principles, specifically as dictated by the RMP of the IWC, which, if implemented, could involve obtrusive observation/verification designs. Commercial whaling, as it once was, is dead. But this fact hardly settles the question, since smaller operations, such as aboriginal and small-scale coastal whaling, remain either in effect or in demand. Some environmentalists fear that these operations, which would or do involve limited hunts and shore-based processing techniques, can open the door to legitimizing mass commercial hunting. Others insist that we have learned our lesson, and that small-scale whaling projects can be essential to local cultural values and to subsistence. It is to these forms of whaling that we now turn.

Aboriginal Whaling

Aboriginal whaling is one of the more contentious issue-areas on the IWC agenda. It certainly remains so for its ethical implications alone. What has become the accepted cetapolitical ideology for American policymakers is that whaling for commerce is bad, but whaling for subsistence and cultural purposes is justified. This position leads to many questions. Who determines this distinction between commercial and subsistence whaling? At this stage, governmental authorities do. Though the distinction is discussed at length at IWC meetings, no appointed judiciary decides the question. The Japanese can thus claim that their coastal communities have ancient cultural links to whaling activities. And this attachment is similar to those of North American aboriginal whaling communities, which, at last count, numbered ten. Further, the American delegation accepts aboriginal hunting of gray whales in the Russian federation, fin whales off Greenland, and humpbacks off St. Vincent and the Grenadines. However, it considers the resumption of Japanese coastal whaling or Norwegian small-scale whaling as unacceptable. The difference, the Americans insist, is that aboriginal whaling does not involve killing whales for 'commoditization,' but for personal consumption. Many argue this point amounts to a mythical distinction and is a convenient one for the American delegation to make.[35]

Although the aboriginal quota determined by the IWC is always very low, even it may not be fulfilled on any given year. It is nonetheless a cause of great political competitiveness and bargaining, a fixture of the American position at the IWC. The absolute insistence on Alaskan whaling rights continues today as a matter of sovereign prerogative. The delegation to the 1993 IWC Meeting in Kyoto, Japan, made this point in its subsequent report:

> The possibility of a Canadian hunt for bowhead whales outside the IWC regime is a matter of great concern to the United States because of possible attempts to subtract Canadian takes from the aboriginal subsistence quota granted to Alaska Eskimos. The U.S. made it clear that Canada's takes should not be counted against the aboriginal subsistence quota granted Alaskan Eskimos because that quota was based on a documented need approved by the IWC.[36]

Aboriginal whaling in the United States is regulated at numerous levels. Though the American government ultimately relies on IWC approval before allowing catches, its authority is obviously limited. And, though the IWC, like other international regimes, does set important norms and standards, it has little regulatory muscle.[37] Therefore, the question of sovereign jurisdiction, inevitable in international affairs, arises. The US has insisted that, if limited commercial whaling resumed, part of the RMP would involve an active observer scheme wherein whaling vessels would be accompanied by observers from other nations. However, Norway's and Denmark's delegations (the latter speaking for Greenland, though perhaps with the Faroe Islands' pilot whale hunt in mind as well) 'made clear that a universal observer scheme would not be feasible for aboriginal whaling.'[38] In the mid-1970s, when it became apparent that the IWC Scientific Committee would begin opposing any take of the extremely rare bowheads, Alaskan whalers formed their own group, the extant Alaskan Eskimo Whaling Commission (AEWC), which did not initially recognize the authority of, but now cooperates with, the IWC.[39]

Canadian aboriginal whalers, meanwhile, operate outside the jurisdiction of the IWC; and the Inuit Tapirisat of Canada is an important group that denounces the preservationist stance of the IWC. And, as a recent case demonstrated, the Tapirisat does not necessarily conform with Canadian domestic regulations either. Consider this recent newspaper report:

> Some Inuit hunters in the Eastern Arctic have decided that the wishes of a beloved elder carry more weight that some laws written on paper. Four hunters from Igloolik [Northwest Territories, Canada] went to sea in two boats last week and, using traditional means, killed a bowhead whale. The bowhead, one of the largest creatures in the Arctic Ocean, is regarded as an endangered species. It is against [Canadian] law to hunt them in Eastern Arctic waters. [An Inuit spokesman] said Noah Piugatuq, 94, of Igloolik had said on the radio recently that he wanted to taste bowhead muktuk (whale skin) again before he died. Mr. Piugatuq had killed a bowhead in the 1960s ... Some government officials and some Inuit organizations have expressed disapproval. Ben Kovic, chairman of the Nunavut Wildlife Management Board, said the board cannot support any harvesting activities that do not follow the rules set out in the Nunavut land-claim agreement. The agreement says the board must conduct a study on the bowhead ... The Inuit Tapirisat of Canada and the Baffin Region Inuit Association have also said they cannot support the hunt.[40]

The related debate in the late 1970s concerned whether the United States should agree with conservationists who called for the outright prevention of killing any Alaskan bowhead and Greenland humpback whales because of their relative scarcity and because of the new status the environmentalist movement had bestowed upon the whale. The American IWC delegation argued, to the contrary, that the hunt should be increased, since the cultures dependent on whaling were themselves threatened with extinction. Indigenous peoples argue, entirely correctly, that whale hunting has been an intrinsic part of their spiritual life for over 2,000 years, and that only after contact with commercial whalers in the late 1800s did the bowhead (or, on the Pacific coast, the gray whale) become endangered. The same circumstances are evident in other aboriginal whaling histories, including those in the Caribbean and Siberia.

At the time, the Americans even conceded to increased quotas of sperm whales to achieve agreement over the aboriginal hunt. In 1977, the Americans, then unable to obtain the three-quarters majority needed for the complete moratorium on whaling, agreed to an enormous increase in the sperm whale quota for Japan and the USSR – from 763 to 6,444 kills. This increase was derided by environmentalists at the time, but reflects the sincerity of American delegations towards Alaskan aboriginal whaling rights. Thus, we have the added ethical dilemma of whether biological extinction is worth risking if and when cultural extinction becomes a possibility. (The bowhead has survived, but it is still endangered.) In the case of gray whales, however, it is difficult to stretch the biological argument to claim that a limited resumption of whaling by the Makah would even remotely threaten the species with extinction. It is also unlikely that such a development would lead to an uncontrollable increase in demand for whale products, even among aboriginal coastal peoples. American officials would have a difficult time arguing that the Alaskan Inuit have a greater need for hunting the endangered bowhead than the Makah do the gray. As Makah tourist guides will proudly tell visitors, whaling was once an integral aspect of their culture, though they have not hunted since the 1920s. Tourist guides seem to like to tell this story as a part of a glorious wild history. But it is also told as a thing of the past; the bigger story of Europeanization, apparently, rendered such activities unnecessary. The Makah are now suggesting that this assessment is not necessarily the case, opening up a rather messy ethical frontier.

The embryonic Makah situation will probably prove highly illustrative of the sort of ethical policy problem outlined here. The Makah's request is too late to be put effectively to the IWC in 1995, but it will certainly be an issue in 1996, and indications are that the American government will support the initiative.[41] Ultimately, this situation will pit those who accept the conservationist position and those who argue strongly for the cultural sovereign rights of aboriginal groups, against those who advocate non-consumption. The former group will include the Makah leadership, who now believe the community can survive only with a return to ancient traditions. There is also a growing 'wise-use' movement in the United States, popular among Republican members of Congress, which opposes typical preservationist perspectives. These perspectives will clash with radical environmentalists who accept the egalitarian interspecies argument discussed earlier, as well as tour-boat operators who see the whales as beneficial resources. This already complex ethical dilemma also has an international dimension, since the Makah claim an ancestral right to hunt in British Columbian waters, off Canada's West Coast. Ironically, the United States – the most ardent supporter of the preservationist stance at the IWC – could end up negotiating a deal with Canada, which pulled out of the IWC because of that stance, in order to allow aboriginal whaling.

Small-Scale Coastal Whaling

Meanwhile, the Japanese delegation has been upset at IWC annual meetings because its 'community-based' whalers have not been allowed to take an interim quota of fifty minke whales. The Norwegians are publicly scolded and sanctioned for refusing to observe the moratorium and for taking some 300 minke whales per year. (This take, as we have indicated, is perfectly legal under the IWC's weak framework, since Norway registered a reservation to the moratorium.) The population of the minke whale is, of course, the subject of much debate. However, the total population is now probably well over 700,000.[42] The American aboriginal whaling total, approved by the IWC, will come to 204 whales in the next four years, with a major difference. These whales will be the much larger and more endangered bowhead (*Balaena mysticetus*) in the Bering-Chukchi-Beaufort seas, a species decimated by American and Russian nineteenth-century Northeast Pacific whaling fleets. Estimates vary, but there are probably fewer than 8,000 remaining, and almost certainly fewer than 10,000.

To many, these population estimates point to a problem of equal access to the ocean's resources. As mentioned, Japan has argued that its coastal whaling villages have a long and noble history, and that if aboriginals are permitted small takes each year, then Japanese villagers should be as well. The argument is supported by assertions that the intended prey species, minke whales, is not endangered. At the 1994 IWC Meeting, delegates to the Working Group on Socio-Economic Implications and Small-Type Whaling listened to statements by the mayor of one such village, Oshiko Town, and the chairman of the Japan Small-Type Whaling Association.[43]

To avoid commercial whaling, if the moratorium is lifted, the proposed Japanese Action Plan intends to limit coastal whaling by using a 'non-market distribution system to remove profit motivation from production and distribution of whale products.' However, according to the IWC 1994 Annual Report, this innovative foray into what could almost be termed socialistic whaling is viewed with some scepticism by many IWC members, who doubt that a 'non-commercial harvest could ... coexist with a well developed high value market for the same product.' Since the moratorium, prices for whalemeat have risen dramatically, and there is concern that Japanese coastal whalers would be strongly tempted to sell the meat, rapidly increasing their total take before prices evened out again. Urban Japan remains the only substantial market for whalemeat in the world, and DNA sampling has indicated that meat from even the endangered great whales, such as humpbacks and fins, is making its way to market.[44]

That the Japanese will eventually lose their fondness for whalemeat is an idea with some merit, since this change may be gradually occurring and whalewatching itself is becoming more fashionable. Given the restrictions imposed by the global moratorium and the fact that only southern minke meat can be legally sold in Japan, the Japanese might change their outlook towards whales entirely. But the argument that the Japanese need to become civilized on this matter is obviously based on a rather condescending cultural orientation, one resented by the Japanese and used publicly by the Japan Whaling Association, a lobby group with consultants in New York, backed by Japan's strong fisheries sector.

Cultural relativism surfaces here. The anti-whaling lobby has often pushed the idea that stopping whaling reflected a new global consciousness. This is powerful imagery. Yet the Japanese remain as the vociferous leaders of what is very clearly a small minority of nations that still advocates commercial whaling. But does this position, in itself, make them wrong? In the environmental policy world, there are no angels. Surely the most consistent and powerful proponent of the anti-consumptionist stance, the United States, the world's biggest industrial and military polluter, the mecca of wasteful consumption-oriented culture, is subject to rather harsh criticism regarding its own environmental policies. Even more problematically for American delegates, the idea that Japan can be 'internationalized'[45] on a host of issues related to and reflecting its increasingly important position on the world stage may be sensible. But to suggest this transformation will occur in the cetacean issue-area through integration into some international consensus begs a question: shouldn't modern Alaskan or coastal aboriginals be similarly integrated, so that they, too, overcome their insensitive urge to kill advanced mammals such as whales and seals?

The Japanese delegation considers the moratorium an insult to Japanese sovereignty, and fears remain that the Japanese might follow the Icelanders, who left the IWC in 1992 over this issue. Several states, including Grenada and St. Vincent and the Grenadines, have formed a small supportive cast for Japan. As mentioned, anti-whaling activists insist this support is related to promises of increased Japanese development aid. The Japanese certainly have a point when they refer to the economic hardship caused by the dislocation of small-scale whalers, with the ban inevitably helping drive an underground trade. But, as the Swiss delegation and others have insisted, any quotas allowed outside the conventional definition of aboriginal whaling would require lifting the moratorium, and the majority of members are simply unprepared to do so. Creating a new category of legitimate whaling for the coastal small-scale whalers might satisfy those who see the American insistence on aboriginal whaling rights but denial of Japanese rights as self-serving. It would also mean abandoning a preservationist policy.[46]

We can, with some certainty, accept the proposition (troubling to some, perhaps comforting to others) that whaling in some form will continue into the twenty-first century. It will certainly not look anything like past efforts made by the major whalers, the Japanese and the Soviets. Indeed, the whale populations and product markets don't exist for this scale of operation. But, regardless of the outcome of the Japanese coastal whaling debate, small-scale whaling will occur in the aboriginal context. Although the preservationist or anti-whaling stance attracts many adherents from environmentalist movements around the world, its appeal doesn't make for a universal shift. If the governments of some nations insist that some whaling, some of the time, is legitimate – and both American and Japanese policy-makers agree – then it may be best to arrive at the implementation of the RMP. We can then dedicate ourselves to effective multilateral management for a very limited and strictly controlled, if often lamented, kill.

Habitat Preservation: The Ultimate Ethical Responsibility

Cetapolitics is an expanding issue-area. It is, as Lyster writes, unclear whether the 1946 convention covers small cetaceans.[47] At present, there are obvious lapses in the observational powers of an organization like the IWC. Estimating whale stocks remains a haphazard endeavour. Monitoring catches is similarly arduous, since the IWC cannot even appoint its own inspectors but must rely on those supplied by various members, who then board declared whaling vessels.[48] In other words, the nations are to watch each other, and this practice leaves a lot to faith (and makes the vigilance of groups like Greenpeace significant). As mentioned, some members are calling for an extension of the IWC mandate to include monitoring and regulating populations of small whales, even if that task must be done on a regional (and more expensive) basis. The Americans may be pushing for this extension of IWC jurisdiction in the near future.[49] Martin Harvey, the current IWC executive officer, is quick to point out the considerable organizational and financial difficulties decentralization would entail, especially if current membership levels do not rise.[50] Decentralization also raises questions about sovereign jurisdiction.

There is an example of a regional whaling commission, to which Peru, Chile, and Ecuador belonged, that was very similar to the original IWC (in other words, it facilitated whaling) and that disintegrated when these nations joined the IWC in the late 1970s. This organization was the not-so Permanent Commission of the Exploitation and Conservation of the Marine Resources of the South Pacific. Meanwhile, renegade Iceland, with Norway and others, established NAMMCO, discussed in Chapter 3. Aside from the logistical challenges, an expansion in the IWC mandate to include small cetaceans raises interesting ethical questions: if it is wrong, for reasons other than ensuring their future consumption, to kill great whales, what does this position imply about small whales, marine mammals, and other forms of wildlife? Where is the line drawn? A flurry of further debate is expected on this issue, but other immediate threats exist.

One is the continuation of driftnet fishing, which is among the least sustainable methods of fishery harvesting ever devised, inadvertently killing dolphins, porpoises, and other small whales, along with anything else unfortunate enough to enter the path of the miles-long nets. Driftnet fishing has always been a special problem for smaller cetaceans. In 1924, historian Charles Boardman Hawes wrote of the bottlenose porpoise, found in Cape Hatteras, 'where whole schools of them are taken at once in nets of extra heavy twine.'[51] But driftnets represent a quantifiable difference, for they have measured up to sixty-five kilometres and run to a depth of ten metres. In 1989, a United Nations General Assembly resolution called for a global moratorium on driftnet fishing by mid-1992, and Chapter 17 of Agenda 21 reiterates this demand.[52] Japan has agreed to halt this practice, and the Convention to the Prohibition of Fishing with Long Driftnets in the South Pacific has been created; Taiwan, South Korea, and Mexico continue to be problem states in this respect.[53]

More generally, overfishing has become an epidemic in this century. There are as many as fifteen major marine fishing regions on earth, most of them coastal areas in the Pacific and Atlantic, with others in the Mediterranean and Black seas and the Indian Ocean. In all but two regions, the catch has fallen from past peak years. In four regions, the catch has fallen by more than 30 per cent.[54] This decrease is not from lack of trying, as more fishing vessels operate today than at any other time in history: between 1970 and 1990, the UN's Food and Agriculture Organization recorded a doubling in the world's fishing fleet, from 585,000 to 1.2 million large boats, and from 13.5 million to 25.5 gross registered tons.[55] This capacity far exceeds the available catch. Peter Weber, a fisheries expert with the Worldwatch Institute in Washington, believes this mismatch is because fishers are too good: modern technology makes mass fishing too easy, and, what's worse, 'counterproductive government policies ... have led more people and boats into the business even after the point of no return.'[56]

It is well known that fishers also waste vast quantities of their catch, with strict quotas in fact encouraging this loss since all non-targeted species are often thrown back, dead, into the water. For example, for every tonne of wild shrimp trawled, an estimated four tonnes of fish are discarded. This kind of mariculture has resulted in the loss of 25 per cent of the world's mangrove forests, which grow in shore-mud. Trawlers routinely disturb seabeds by dragging nylon nets weighed down with chains, and driftnet fishing drowns dolphins and whales as well as takes everything else in its path. There is also a disturbing trend towards fishing the deep seas, which has already decimated fish stocks such as orange roughy, and is now harming more exotic fish such as smooth oreos. In the Pacific, the sablefish (or blackcod), which reproduce very slowly and can live up to seventy years, are fished at depths of up to a mile.[57] The long-term effects of this trend remain to be seen, but disturbing the deep-sea ecosystem will have an impact on the squid and many species of whale (most notably, the deepest diver of all, the sperm). The effect of countless 'ghostnets' – which have escaped their moorings and continue to 'fish' nonetheless – is unknown.

Yet another threat related to human extractive activity is the diminished food supply resulting from the increased harvesting of krill from the Southern Ocean of Antarctica. The krill issue demonstrates just how interdependent ocean ecology really is: whaling reduced the larger krill consumers, which in turn led to increased populations of 'seals, seabirds, squid, and those baleen whale populations that had not been exploited.'[58] Conversely, 'any success in efforts to ... [encourage] the growth of stocks of great whales will have important implications for arrangements governing the harvest of renewable resources, such as krill, in the Southern Ocean.'[59] The world's oceans and connected seas cover 71 per cent of the planet's surface, with deep-sea areas accounting for a full 55 per cent; less than 1 per cent of the continental slope and deep-sea areas are fully conserved as protected areas, despite the fact that the Biodiversity Treaty signed at UNCED 'is legally situated to set aside protected areas in the oceans beyond national boundaries and in contested waters.'[60]

No doubt, the world's oceanic ecosystems are fundamentally changing as a result of human activity. As M. Brock Fenton writes: 'Habitat destruction is the main cause of species impoverishment, indiscriminately causing the demise of endangered, common, little-known, and unknown organisms.'[61] Global warming could be biggest threat of all. Polar temperatures increasing disproportionately to equatorial ones are reducing the temperature differential that now drives ocean currents. Who knows what effect this change will have on various organisms? Rising sea temperatures could be contributing to the premature bleaching of highly sensitive coral reefs, and increased storm activity could damage coral reef and kelp-bed ecosystems. The depletion of the ozone layer presents similar uncertainties:

> The thinning layer allows increased amounts of ultraviolet radiation (UV-B) to reach Earth's surface; and few groups of organisms are more susceptible to UV-B injury than phytoplankton in the seas' surface layers (other marine species vulnerable to UV-B injury are copepods among other primary consumers, plus the larvae of several fin and shellfish species).[62]

As Myers points out, first, the extreme loss of phytoplankton would be devastating throughout the food chain but particularly at its top, the cetaceans. Second, and even more importantly in the long run, if the oceans do in fact absorb about half of all carbon emitted into the global atmosphere, as many scientists believe, then the loss or mutation of the main source of this photosynthetic absorption would probably enhance the greenhouse effect.

Toxic pollutants constitute another grave threat to cetacean survival. Bonner reports that 1,796-2,695 parts per million of DDT has been discovered in bottlenose dolphins off California. 'Sublethal effects may cause a failure to breed (this has been shown in some seals) and this, of course, spells ultimate extinction for a stock as surely as acute poisoning.'[63] The sea is awash in chemicals made for land-based activity, including DDT pesticides; dieldrin; PCBs (poly-chlorinated biphenyls), used in plastics and a cause of liver damage; and heavy metals, such as mercury, lead, cadmium, zinc, and copper. High levels of toxic chemicals have been found in dolphins, seals, and polar bears. As mentioned earlier, the carcass of the St. Lawrence beluga is even classified as toxic waste.

Oil pollution is perhaps the most visible problem of all. Televised footage of gray whales swimming through oil slicks has brought this point home to western Americans in recent years. However, an article on the physiological and toxic effects of oil spills on cetaceans suggests that this problem is not as urgent as might be expected.[64] In January 1969, Union Oil's undersea well near Santa Barbara sprung a leak; by 31 March that year, recorded discoveries of dead whales in the area included six grays, one sperm, one pilot, five common dolphins, and one Pacific white-sided dolphin. However, toxicological evidence did not provide a direct link to the spill. The infamous *Exxon Valdez* spill, which released eleven million gallons of Prudhoe Bay crude oil in March 1989, had a similar impact: many dead cetaceans were found, including twenty-five grays, two minke, one fin, and six harbor porpoises, but such findings are not extraordinary. As well, a study in captivity indicates bottlenose dolphins can easily distinguish between oily and uncontaminated water surfaces.[65] The biggest threat to whales is most likely the vapours from spills, intentional and unintentional, absorbed through inhalation. The effect of tanker traffic on cetacean behaviour remains largely unknown, though several studies have been conducted. Boat traffic in general threatens the sound system employed by whales of all types, and tankers with regular routes might offer a special threat because they could permanently discourage travel in certain migratory routes. A related controversy emerged in the Canadian North. Offshore oil and gas exploration began in the Canadian area of the Beaufort Sea and, in 1981, commenced in the Alaskan waters. Since bowheads are hunted by aboriginals there, and these rare whales summer and migrate through the Beaufort, immediate concerns arose over the effects of developing offshore oil and gas industries in the area. A recent agreement promises to limit the amount of related industrial activity.[66]

The physical evidence of habitat degradation seems rather over-whelming, and indeed it is. But the spectre of uncertainty still hangs over pronouncements about global warming, coastal flooding, icecap melting, and other long-term threats to environmental security. There can be little doubt that the oceans, vast and full of life, are under great threat from habitat encroachment by the human species. Thus, the cetacean survival story is far from complete, irrespective of the future of whaling. In the case of the oceans, it is extremely difficult to provide solutions comparable to those developed for land, such as land management, the United States Endangered Species Act, eco-tourism, game management integrated with subsistence farming, and the establishment of conservation parks. And even those solutions are not without considerable controversy, though whaling sanctuaries are interesting to note here. We must also rely on multilateral institutions, which must in turn be guided by a minimal ethical consensus; for example, habitat degradation is not only dangerous to all of us, but insults nature as a concept that all societies, in their own way, hold precious. Thus, we have a widely accepted, if necessarily imperfect, consensus on which to base future multilateral and domestic policy action.

Whales play a special role in this ethical imperative. Perhaps more than any other creature, they have come to symbolize the commons, though we have defined this role in an anthropocentric manner to mean our commons, susceptible to the vicissitudes of our exploitation. The negotiations at UNCLOS III made this point clear: the conservation of marine biota was 'considered an economic measure – to assure continued availability of the resource – rather than an ecological measure – to maintain the health of the marine environment.'[67] The Rio Declaration restates this perspective.

The two ideological positions that presently shape the cetapolitical debate, as described here, have few meeting points. At the level of international discourse, it is difficult to argue one position while supporting the other. Some might argue that the United States does: preservationist for whales, exploiter of most other global resources, protector of its right to do so. But an obvious point of convergence exists between preservationist and conservationist, which, arguably, we should capitalize upon.

This is the concern for the cetacean habitat, a concern which all participants in the complex web that is the cetacean issue-area network share. Of course, the appeal to ecosystem conservation could be as non-universal as any other environment-related approach to social and public issues. Alastair Gunn notes in a searching essay entitled 'Why Should We Care About Rare Species?' that a concern with restoring natural habitat 'is really no answer to the person who cannot see why it is better to have a natural ecosystem than an airport, and who prefers Los Angeles to the Vermont mountains.'[68] This critique may be telling, but over the years, many people have developed a stake in the survival of cetaceans, small and large alike, and they will have to confront the larger threat facing whales in this age. The divisions within the IWC do not help us work towards addressing this current imperative.

Where, then, does the human responsibility rest for this aspect of cetacean survival? The obvious answer is that it lies within all of us. This answer sounds sufficiently global but avoids the much more difficult political questions about degrees of responsibility for the state of the oceans, the depleted fisheries, the pollution threats from oil tankers, and the even broader threat to phytoplankton (and thus the entire marine food chain) associated with ozone-layer depletion. American anti-whaling policy is less impressive if we realize that American industry has led the world in contributing to these types of threats. As Norman Myers laments: 'Given the way we run our planetary affairs and exploit our biosphere, we are effectively saying there is no room on Earth for both ourselves and whales. And "we" means all of us, not just the Japanese.'[69]

For intergenerational equity, for the sustainable use of ocean resources, and for the sake of preserving all marine life – from plankton to sea star to whale – we have a primary imperative to preserve the oceans. For years, the whaling industry advanced self-justifying arguments about impending world hunger. The argument, despite its problematic nature (because all the whales in the world could hardly feed those affected by malnutrition), is still alive. As world population increases and fisheries are depleted,

> many people may [begin to] recognize whales as food, or a competitor for the [world] fishery. Whales consume a large amount of prey species which are also a target of fisheries. One calculation is that minke whales alone consume 70 million tons of prey species annually (and the world fisheries product is 80 million tons annually).[70]

This estimate seems high on the minke side and low on the human side.[71] But the point is that, in terms of public opinion and policy, environmental ethics are situation-specific. Unless the biological diversity and resource level of the seas is maintained and managed, and we are clearly failing to do so, whales may well become endangered again.

All the platitudes in the world about sharing the earth with our brothers and sisters in the sea won't change this fact. Wildlife conservation will always have to struggle with hard choices over resource utilization. To some, labelling a mammal or even any other life form a 'resource' is itself an act of epistemological violence. Though I don't concur entirely with this perspective, I must confess to wincing when whale populations are constantly labelled as 'stocks' in the IWC and other literature, and resent the fact that I often find myself doing so as well. Speaking of 'fish stocks,' on the other hand, seems perfectly acceptable to me in my species-hierarchical world. The use of such language may help justify dangerously expansive human intervention in ecosystems, and, in the long run, the destruction of human habitat itself. This is, of course, the minority viewpoint, interesting but far from convincing. What is needed is human responsibility, even stewardship.

In this context, whales are special. They are widely admired for their biological and social characteristics. However, it is difficult – ethically, politically, legally – to deny all human beings everywhere the right to eat them. If, for what must be viewed respectfully as cultural reasons, aboriginal whaling proceeds, it should be well managed and, within the limits of custom, utilize advanced killing-technology. Then we must consider if Japanese and Norwegian coastal communities have the right to similar operations. As the preservationist perspective continues to clash with Japanese and Norwegian opinion, American policy will be particularly strained. In the end, an anti-consumptionist argument based on threatened species carries its own seeds of destruction: if the argument is widely accepted, and it has been in the cetacean case, whale populations will rise. Therefore, the central thrust or rationale of the perspective is no longer relevant. Ironically, there would be less controversy over the minke hunt if minkes were endangered. This realization is uncomfortable for whale enthusiasts but deserves much reflection before dogmatism begins to determine thought.

5
Conclusion: Whales and World Politics

> International institutional mechanisms are not necessarily a reflection of globally shared norms. They can also reflect self-interest on the part of actors who find they must engage in cooperation if they wish to come to terms with the challenges of the postindustrial order. If the underpinnings of a genuine global culture are to evolve, there must be a sharing of basic values pertaining to how the world is perceived and how conflicting loyalties are managed.
>
> – James Rosenau, 1990[1]

This final chapter revisits themes introduced in the first chapter in light of our previous discussion. We have seen that the IWC evolved over time, and that the broader cetacean issue-area network increased in both scope and influence after the Second World War. Perilously close to extinction at one stage, several endangered species have made a comeback, especially the gray and minke whales, which are the object of two separate debates about the resumption of their hunt. Others, however, remain very far from recovery, especially the bowhead, right, blue, and humpback whales. These whales were even closer to extinction than we realized, thanks to misreporting by the Soviet Union. Both the whale and the IWC are in trouble, however. The legitimacy of the commission continues to be challenged on several fronts, most notably by Norway's refusal to observe the moratorium and the establishment of an alternative multilateral regional body, NAMMCO, which may in time regulate an Icelandic and Norwegian hunt.

For this writer, it has been a difficult journey towards the following conclusions. As an avid whale fan, I have been fascinated by these creatures since an early age and have been thrilled to witness gray whales feeding in bays on Vancouver Island. As a political scientist, I found that the symbolic power of the whale was worth exploring in an analysis such as this book. As an environmentalist, I found this project had a progressive research agenda, for the death of large-scale whaling ushered in a new era of human-nature understanding. The IWC had demonstrated the results of what we might, with some measure of optimism, consider nothing less than a normative transition. A post-industrial age was dawning, with the story of whaling more than anything else conveying this message. The moratorium, in particular, heralded the establishment of a new global prohibition regime,

which should naturally be a permanent fixture. Those that felt otherwise were wrong, obstinate, and even regressive.

I am still entranced by whales and wish no one would whale again,
but I find it impossible to continue to support a permanent moratorium for three related reasons. First, I have come to respect that, in
some cases, there is great cultural resonance behind whaling. The
American delegation argues this position for its aboriginal subsistence
whalers, but surely Norwegian, Icelandic, and Japanese whaling communities can make the same point. Second, I believe that the IWC
has achieved an RMP that, if implemented, would result in a very
conservative regime. Though this stance may sound overly prudent,
whalers are better served by an international organization with a
strong scientific component and non-whaling members than by an
alternative such as NAMMCO. At the same time, the IWC should
strive to incorporate a multi-species perspective, if not a mandate
broader than cetacean management. In becoming increasingly concerned with ecosystem questions, the commission is already doing so.
Finally, I am less convinced of the symbolic power of whales. Though
whales can easily capture our hearts, using them this way might dis-
tract from concern for their habitat, which is the critical survival issue
for the cetacean issue-area network in the late 1990s.

We can draw a plethora of conclusions from the study of the intersection of whales and human international relations. At this point,
we revisit the central components of the framework for analysis introduced in Chapter 1.

Whales: Biology and Folly

It is difficult to underestimate the increased importance of science in
environmental management. Governments will learn from scientists
and, yes, they will manipulate findings to their liking. This fact makes
it all the more important to have international organizations that
have a scientific component and members representing various
nation-states. However, the legitimacy of this component may in the
long run depend on how its findings are implemented. In the case
of the IWC, as the recent resignation of the Scientific Committee
chairman indicated, western states are very reluctant to grant the
committee the credibility it obviously needs if we accept the fact that
some form of whaling will occur in the future.

As Haas, Williams, and Babai write with regard to the UNEP,
learning 'must imply that governments come to redefine their initial

objectives in response to demonstrations that the character of the physical world does not permit them to attain all their objectives simultaneously, at least not without eventually paying an exorbitant price in the deterioration of the quality of life. This demonstration must be the work of scientists.'[2] The ability of the IWC Scientific Committee to finally rid the regime of the disastrous Blue Whale Unit may be seen as evidence of this redefinition process; its current inability to get the IWC to implement the RMP, however, may be seen as indicative of the entrenchment of a new ethical position among a majority of IWC states. In a later work, Ernst Haas contrasts *organizational adaptation*, which implies either incremental growth by taking on new tasks and using old methods, or turbulent non-growth with major changes and disintegrating internal consensus on means and ends, with *organizational learning*, which suggests managed interdependence where 'the reexamination of purposes is brought about by knowledge-mediated decision-making dynamics.' The IWC might well be in a stage of turbulent non-growth at present. Certainly, the organization lacks the cohesion for the type of learning Haas describes. Regardless, as Haas concludes,

> change in human aspirations and human institutions over long periods is caused mostly by the way knowledge about nature and about society is married to political interests and objectives.[3]

As Patricia Birnie writes, scientific advice can be incorporated in international environmental regimes in several ways, including the use of scientists who are in effect national delegations, such as with the North Atlantic Fisheries Organization (NAFO) and the IWC; scientists who stay in residence or 'in-house' to advise, such as the International Pacific Halibut Convention; and scientific organizations that play a non-formal role in advising nations, such as the International Council for Exploration of the Sea and the Scientific Committee on Antarctic Research.[4]

Within the cetacean issue-area network, cetologists have been instrumental in helping develop our knowledge of both cetacean biology and human folly. Only with patient and careful study can we do so. I cannot, personally, see any valid reason for ongoing scientific whaling or lethal research. This issue presents many questions, but widespread belief is that scientific whaling is little more than a 'camouflaged commercial operation.' This criticism is offered by the

IWC commissioner for Spain, which in fact favours limited scientific whaling 'on a case-by-case evaluation.'[5] Much better to allow Japan a small minke quota, provided they drop this pretext altogether, though such an arrangement would no doubt be rejected by both the preservationists and the Japanese. Meanwhile some IWC members continue to argue not only that the Scientific Committee is constrained from performing its true duty, but that the original convention is abrogated by the insistence on a post-scarcity moratorium. Typical is Joseph Edmunds, who was St. Lucia's ambassador to the United Nations from 1984 to 1989, and is currently both ambassador to the United States (Washington, DC) and IWC commissioner for St. Lucia:

> The policy of my government is to defend the science of whaling and the Convention governing the IWC. We believe in the sustainable utilization of whales and feel very strongly that the IWC must be guided by these three basic principles: a) the Convention governing its very existence; b) the facts of science and the guidance of the Scientific Committee; and c) the sustainable utilization of marine resources including whales. As a scientist and a scholar, I leave it to you to judge whether the IWC lives up to the three principles above.[6]

The role of science in global ecopolitics is certainly expanding, but are we moving towards some sort of technocratic organizational mode, perhaps similar to what the neofunctionalists and epistemic community analysts either propose to or seem to imply would solve our problems? Michael Ignatieff argues, 'Science has always driven the economy. It will now begin to drive politics.' Other authors have focused on the role of science, especially as it relates to the diminishment of uncertainty, and also from the critical perspective of discursive analysis.[7] However, we do not appear to be approaching an age where scientists will become the chief decisionmakers in global ecopolitics. This is not necessarily terrible, however, since science itself is hardly value-free. It can be used for various ends, not all of them environmentally friendly by any means. At the level of world politics, sovereignty will remain a crucial factor that limits the development of supranational technocratism.

Issue-Area Networks in World Politics

When whalers had the IWC to themselves, how relatively tranquil it must have been. There would be some debate about which stocks needed extra protection, perhaps. Though whalers probably had a better idea of this requirement than anyone, they may have been blinded by the economic imperatives of their operations. There was no doubt some confrontation based on the allocation of quotas, which took place outside the IWC but would certainly affect deliberations within it. However, the acrimony that accompanies the annual general meetings today would make the old days seem good indeed for the whalers, too good to last.

Most of the whalers have moved on. They have spread into other sectors of the fishing industry or found work and investment opportunities elsewhere. But we shouldn't forget the remarkable transition the IWC has undergone as non-whaling states have joined and become participants in the issue-area network. Again, the organization was originally a whalers club, set up to perhaps mitigate the worst excesses of the industry but not to manage its members' activities. This origin should not be surprising, since it is common for industry to initiate such ventures. The Tropical Forestry Action Plan, for example, has been labelled a loggers charter, since, according to some estimates, 'one-third of the aid it distributes goes into commercial logging projects and virtually none of it to tackle the basic causes of deforestation.'[8] The transition of the IWC might provide a rough model for other issue-area networks.

Then again, it may not: the politics of whaling are fairly peculiar, due to the unique market involved, the emotional nature of the issue, and the extent of the tragedy before the moratorium. As John Gerard Ruggie wrote in 1970:

> The devolution of existing structures appears to be an issue-specific and actor-specific process. It is asymmetrical, reflecting differences in national capacities to perform different tasks, as well as discontinuous, reflecting the differential impact of interdependence costs in different issue areas and for different states. Moreover, it appears to generate issue-specific and actor-specific collective arrangements, existing at different levels in the interstate system, and compensating for different imperfections ... The resulting international order promises to be both highly differentiated and exceedingly complex.[9]

Looking at the world politics of cetacean survival suggests, among other things, that no single paradigm or, to use a less demanding and perhaps preferable term, no theoretical package is sufficient to provide a convincing route to understanding the events and structures that have developed in this issue area. Rather, the framework for the study of global environmental problems, introduced in Chapter 1, demands that we obtain both theoretical direction and, equally important in a case study, empirical direction from various schools of thought, even if the problem of the commons would appear at first glance to be a neoliberal institutionalist dilemma. We search in vain for permanent concepts, since the human mind is a reflective one. Even a rational-choice theorist such as Robert Keohane has come to this conclusion. He writes in his 'Personal Intellectual History':

> As I understand it, historicity refers to the social process of reflection on historical experience that human societies undergo. This social process alters societies' understandings of themselves and, hence, the actions in which they engage. 'Meaning matters.' As a result, ahistorical accounts of human action, which attribute unchanging utility functions to their members, fail to capture the essentially historical and reflective nature of human collective life.[10]

It would seem impossible to escape the analytic primacy of the nation-state on the international stage, and the power relations this entails. However, many transnational actors with quite different agendas (saving whales, saving the planet, saving whaling jobs) are involved, and we must go beyond a purely state-state analysis to capture the inherent complexity of international organizations today. Moreover, and related to the regimes for the commons literature introduced in our first chapter, we should revisit a few specific issues, in particular those of leadership and compliance.

The Leadership Question
Much of the literature on international institutions is concerned with the role played by leading states in regime formation. There is no question that American leadership has been pivotal at the IWC. Not only did the United States initiate the entire regime back in 1946, it was by far the most powerful influence in creating the environment in which the moratorium vote could be taken.

Yet, in a world where states still exercise what is at least formal sovereignty, the United States does not always get its way. For example, there is currently a debate within the IWC regarding its competence to make recommendations or even amendments concerning small cetaceans (dolphins and porpoises). The IWC Scientific Subcommittee on Small Cetaceans has been looking into this matter. At the 1995 meeting, a resolution noted that many members will not accept any resolutions related to small cetaceans, although they made an obvious exception to make this statement. Only three nations voted against the resolution, which passed easily, and one of them was the United States. The issue of sovereignty is central here, since small cetaceans will be found within the 200-mile exclusive economic zones of many Caribbean members (St. Vincent and the Grenadines, St. Lucia, Dominica, and Grenada). According to Ray Gambell, 'Small cetacean management continues to be a problem for the IWC – the Eastern Caribbean states may now refuse to accept advice or Resolutions from the IWC because of their concerns over sovereignty.'[11] Of course, rumours persist that Japanese assistance to the fishing industries in these areas was a causal factor.

More to the point, Norwegian whaling and Icelandic non-cooperation with the IWC are direct challenges to the institution and also to American leadership. We may see a change in American philosophy regarding conservation issues, though the whaling issue seems to demand the strongest adherence to a preservationist position. Abram and Antonia Chayes suggest, 'It seems plausible that treaty regimes are subject to a kind of critical-mass phenomenon, so that once defection reaches a certain level, or in the face of particularly egregious violation by a major player, the regime might collapse.'[12] American leadership may be becoming more problem than solution, which would certainly be the case if the IWC breaks down entirely as an effective institution. It has even been suggested that the United States has acted like an 'international bully' on the issue, in effect behaving like its own 'whale protection industry.'[13]

None of this suggests we should dismiss the importance of structural power in global ecopolitics. Plenty of room remains for state-centric power analysis within the scope of global environmental security, but power has taken on a new form. India, China, and Brazil all present a threat to future generations, if they follow the development paths of the West, and, as such, the populous southern states wield considerable leverage. This North-South dimension will dominate related diplomacy in the future. This trend was evident in the negotiations following the Montreal Protocol, which established a complicated ozone-protection regime contingent upon including a technology-transfer clause. The very threat to biospheric integrity posed by the future use of chlorofluorocarbons by heavily populated southern states lent the South what may be epiphenomenal, but by no means ephemeral, bargaining power.[14] Yet the ecological crisis does confront the logic of the model of a zero-sum world of states (where one state's gain is necessarily another's loss) that previously dominated the discipline of international relations. Further, the North-South divide is assuming greater importance than the overall division of the world into territorial states.[15] In fact, any case study of global environmental security invariably deals to some degree with the North-South dynamic. It has become as contextual as the anarchical nature of the international system itself, although taking the North-South divide as primary has its problems, which transnational class analysis reveals.

The regime that has evolved on the whaling issue suggests that market forces are initially predominant in questions of the commons. However, they may eventually bow to interest-group pressure and, more specifically, to the diplomatic weight of a powerful nation such as the United States. Nonetheless, returning to the idea of counterfactual analysis, it does not necessarily follow that, without American leadership, whaling would have continued unabated. The simple economics of whaling finances would have resulted in the industry's end, because at various times in its history, whaling reached a saturation point and became no longer remotely profitable. That point is reached when the available whales no longer justify the investment in ships, equipment, and labour, which modern pelagic whaling operations entail. And there were other national contingents to the IWC that made firm decisions to pursue an explicit anti-whaling policy. Chief among these groups was Australia as well as numerous European nations, such as France and Great Britain. The European Community ban on whale products in the early 1970s – a highly problematic political development – was also a vital conservation measure taken when adequate whale stocks could encourage further kills. The Stockholm Conference itself was almost hijacked by an environmental movement that used the whale as its most potent symbol and involved groups of unorthodox youth who probably had not even thought of the potential leadership role of the American policy establishment. (It is still somewhat awkward to think of Washington's elite as whale lovers!)

Regardless, and despite the immense amount of non-American effort that went into establishing a non-whaling regime, little doubt remains over the importance of the United States in this issue-area.

It is the American fish market that gives the threat of sanctions any realistic bite. We might see this area as state activity where the unilateral and multilateral converge, much like many foreign policy questions in a closely networked but still-divided world. Daniel Esty writes of

> cases where the imposition of environmental trade measures appears somewhat more unilateral but still has elements of multilateralism ... When the US imposed trade restrictions on Norway for violation of the IWC's whaling moratorium, the standard (no whale killing) had been set multilaterally, but the trade measures were unilateral ... The trade actions were taken in the context of a multilateral environmental program and were therefore condoned in some senses by the other parties to the accord ... These parties could have disagreed with the US trade penalties, rejecting either the judgement about Norway's noncompliance or the severity of the measures imposed by the US.[16]

Yet American intransigence, much to the dismay of pro-whalers like Norway and Japan, ensures the continued application of the moratorium (barring unforeseen events).[17] While the American position on aboriginal whaling has often been portrayed as a hypocritical technique to maintain harmony between Washington and parts of Alaska, the American delegation has managed to institutionalize aboriginal whaling while outlawing commercial whaling. Small coastal whaling, such as the Japanese practise and advocate, falls between the cracks, and the American delegation still seems unwilling to deal with the issue. At the very least, more dialogue is needed. It is certainly not unprecedented. For example, New Zealand, which has pursued a relatively strong anti-whaling policy for some time, has taken initiative in this matter: while in Norway in 1994 for an intercessional meeting on supervision and control, IWC commissioner J.K. McLay 'took the opportunity to meet with local whaling groups. While we did not agree, the local people appreciated the chance to exchange views, and publicly acknowledged our initiative in arranging the meeting.' The Hon. McLay, a former deputy prime minister, notes also that public opinion polls indicate that over 90 per cent of New Zealanders are opposed to commercial whaling.[18]

Finally, we should add that states alone do not provide leadership. We have seen this fact clearly in the case of the anti-whaling movement, spurred on by combative NGOs that learned early on how to use the media for their purposes. Though the unequivocal insistence on the moratorium causes many problems, the role played by these dedicated, and often necessarily brave, participants in the cetacean issue-area network deserves acknowledgment.

The Compliance Question

An equally important question concerns compliance to a regulatory regime. By and large, with several obvious gaps, the IWC still commands compliance from most states, including Japan, which is the most outspoken opponent to the moratorium and yet has observed it since 1988. As Patricia Birnie suggests, the two approaches to international environmental law with regard to the compliance question are hard versus soft regulation. Hard regulation demands the imposition of mandatory obligations on states, which must implement and enforce such laws in their own national legal systems. Soft law depends on resolutions, declarations, and other foreign policy statements, which 'are not really law at all, *strictu sensu*; the term is paradoxical.'[19] Customary law, similarly, becomes legally binding 'only if accompanied by a subjective belief on the part of the state concerned that it is under a legal obligation to conform to custom.'[20]

In his article outlining a framework for multilateralism study, Robert Keohane suggests that the impact of 'institutions on interests' can be examined best by the identification of 'situations in which institutional rules are "inconvenient"; that is, in which they conflict with governments' perceptions of what their self-interests would be if there were no such institutions.'[21] The whaling issue suggests that the IWC, which is now the centre of regulatory efforts, indeed has an impact, since the moratorium was adopted in that body and, after great reluctance, accepted by the Japanese. However, as noted, the external pressures applied by the American government were in fact instrumental in gaining worldwide acceptance of (if not formal acquiescence to) the moratorium. The legitimacy of the IWC, if measured entirely by an ability to enforce the collective decision-making it facilitates, is limited.

After all, trade in whale products continues. The smuggling of whalemeat is not, technically speaking, an infraction of IWC rules. However, the IWC Infractions Subcommittee has taken to discussing smuggling operations in the hope that embarrassment can still promote their mitigation. For example, at the 1994 IWC Meeting, participants noted the discovery of 232 tons of Bryde's whalemeat, which had been brought to Vladivostok in a Honduran-flagged vessel. The meat was originally from Taiwan and was apparently headed for illegal shipment to Japan. The Russian Ministry of Environmental Protection did not allow the meat to be re-exported.[22] This incident, one of the few that are actually detected, illustrates the inherent complexity of modern smuggling operations and the difficulties – without direct and enthusiastic national governmental cooperation – involved in tracking them down.

However, compliance at this level is not a job for the IWC. On the international level, an institutional network is already dedicated to such activity, CITES. In 1979, CITES had agreed not to issue a certificate of introduction from the sea for primarily commercial purposes, or any import and/or export permit for any species or stock protected by the IWC moratorium.[23] (Of course, this restriction currently includes all species.) As well, the committed NGOs are actively pursuing smuggling operations. However, as a forum that can be used to exert moral pressure on those involved in smuggling, the IWC will remain useful. During the IWC annual meetings, the world media pays very close attention to the issue.

Finally, the question of financial commitment must be raised, because the RMP will not be cheap to implement (though probably well worth the price if it ensures future compliance by whalers to a strict regime). Financing international organizations is a difficult prospect regardless of the institution involved, as observers of the United Nations know all too well.[24] The IWC can hardly afford to be harsh on those members that do not pay dues on time. As stated in Appendix 19 of the 1994 Chairman's Report:

> If a Contracting Government's annual payments have not been received by the Commission by the due date ... compound interest shall be added to the outstanding annual payment at a rate of 10% per annum with effect from the day following the due date and thereafter on the anniversary of that day. The interest, calculated to the nearest pound, shall be payable in respect of complete years and continue to be payable in respect of any outstanding balance until such time as the amount in arrears, including interest, is settled in full.

In fact, this policy is weak. Any increases in fees are dealt with rather gently as well. The regular due date for fees is 28 February, but the IWC Financial Regulations also contain a clause which leaves it 'open to any Contracting Government to postpone the payment of any increased portion which shall be payable in full by the following 31 August, which then becomes the due date.'[25] We can only hope that all states with a perceived interest and stake in cetacean survival – and that can afford the dues – will pay them accordingly.

Ethical Questions and Environmental Consciousness

Beyond these analytical questions, we have explicated the ethical dilemmas within the cetacean issue-area network.

While we must be careful about universalizing this point, we have nonetheless seen a substantial shift in perspective regarding the whale. As mentioned in Chapter 4, the US Air Force apparently had a habit of firing upon killer whales, ostensibly to help Icelanders get rid of the orcan menace in the 1950s and for simple target-shooting in the 1960s.[26] This practice occurred when whaling was still a legitimate economic activity in most areas of the world. As a normative transition took place, reflected by initiatives at the Stockholm Conference and eventually by an expanded and pro-moratorium IWC, such behaviour would now be unthinkable. Recently, a military exercise illustrates the caution exercised during operations that threaten ocean wildlife, though many marine biologists are not satisfied with the ultimate result. In November 1994, the Canadian military conducted a test on the test frigate *HMCS Halifax* near Sable Island (about 300 kilometres off the coast of Nova Scotia). In the largest test, 5,000 kilograms of explosives were detonated underwater to see how the frigate would respond. Of immediate concern were the acoustic implications, for cetaceans in particular. As our discussion of whale biology points out, whales depend heavily on sound for communication, direction, and feeding. The Canadians went to extensive lengths to ensure that no whales were within five kilometres of the blast. One 545-kilogram test was actually delayed two hours 'until pilot and sperm whales spotted seven kilometres away moved out of range.'[27] The military could be criticized for conducting the tests at all, or at least for doing so during what is traditionally a rich feeding season. But a public relations effort was certainly made, and additional safety measures taken, because of the public's concern for marine life and, in particular, whales.

At the same time, the ethical polarization of the debate within the cetacean issue-area network may in time be disastrous. The fall of the whaling industry was related to the rapid and perhaps irreversible

decline in whale populations and the rise of environmental consciousness in the Western world. But much of this consciousness has
been predicated upon a simplified understanding of issues that have
generated much compassion and citizen participation. Over time, the
whale could become an old, almost stale, symbol of a movement that
has lost its ability to gauge and counter the threats to the earth. As
one social scientist, writing in another context, states: 'Ideology is
ideology precisely because it presents the existing world as a litany
of eternal verities.'[28] Whalers are bad. Whales are good. But what
about the health of the sea?

I agree that whales are good, in fact marvellous, creatures. It is very
unfortunate that they have been slaughtered in the past, and that
some want to continue hunting them for profit. At the same time,
provided that a return to large-scale pelagic whaling is avoided – and
the best way to do so is to keep the IWC legitimate in the eyes of
potential whalers – I am much less comfortable with the crusade to
eliminate all whaling than I once was. My changed attitude reflects
not only the unfortunate consequences the moratorium is having for
the IWC, but also a rejection of the double standard that the American
delegation insists on projecting – if small-scale coastal whaling is
bad for the Japanese, Norwegians, and Icelanders, then it is bad for
the Alaskans. We need a middle ground to pursue conservation and
habitat protection among industrialized states, and a more holistic
perspective on all marine affairs.

Again, the net has been cast. The qualitative shift in attitudes
towards whales – or towards killing them – is admittedly a comparatively romantic and non-universal instance of a normative transition
in human-nature relations. Environmentalists might consider this shift
as resulting from a happy coincidence where power and ethics fused
to create an anti-whaling American foreign policy. A whalewatching
industry is gaining momentum in Japan, and it will be interesting to
see if a pro-whaling foreign policy will survive into the next century.
Judging by current Japanese policy, it will. But an undeniable shift in
values has taken place, which could tend towards a new holism.

Many observers and commentators cringe at the very mention of
the word 'holistic.' They argue, not without justice, that the word
conveys images of an impossible politics. It is not that ecologists have
done anything wrong, but to transplant the idea of a holistic perspective to the real world would require a degree of political control
not achieved by humanity. Some sort of totalitarian state might, and

only might, be able to enforce such a vision. Thus, we have fears of 'ecofascism' expressed by opponents of the often-misunderstood writings of scholars such as William Ophuls. These fears are reinforced by Garret Hardin's wretched thesis about lifeboats. Whereas some of the ecology-based political literature appears to encourage authoritarianism, if only to rid ourselves of the burden of bad choice, others present a starkly elitist conception of who should be allowed to repopulate, and who should have control over decisions with collective impact. Thus, the Malthusian perspective continues, and, as Karl Marx suggested in his critique of Malthus, the rationalization of the oppression of the poor continues as well.

Another criticism of the holism concept is rooted less in concerns about future political systems and more in conceptions about what is achievable in political life. The international system remains, at best, what Hedley Bull and others have called an anarchical society. Many analysts continue to find even the word 'society' problematic in this respect, since a state-bound society is usually based on a greater degree of commonality than can be claimed about the world system, even in this age of supposed globalization and approaching homogeneity. It is fanciful, therefore, to expect a vision of the commons, much less of the entire biosphere, which includes sovereign territory, to be an effective political symbol. The divisions of humanity – race, state, ethnicity, religion, class, even gender – will ultimately preclude the realization of a unified approach to environmental issues. The oceans are no different in this regard, as the painful and often contradictory processes surrounding the establishment of a virtually meaningless Law of the Sea regime for nodule extraction demonstrates. And even if the deep seabed mining regime were effective, surely it merely encourages the type of economic activity that challenges any valuable conception of marine-life conservation.

A further largely ontological factor must be mentioned. Western science has dealt with the world by cutting it up; by reductionism, atomism, and processes of experimentation that encourage achieving predictive capability on limited scales. In presenting what has become a standard dichotomy, David Suzuki and others claim that traditional knowledge about nature (for example, that of the American indigenous peoples) involved not taking nature apart but maintaining a holistic perspective related to daily survival.[29] Put yet another way, knowledge may be about reducing nature to understandable components, but the wisdom necessary for long-term survival is about putting the pieces back together. While the weight of modern scientific tradition promotes reductionism, this orientation is to a certain degree now changing. In fact, much of the scientific literature on global environmental problems is in some ways at odds with traditional scientific inquiry, since it draws inferences on such a massive scale. For example, the greenhouse effect is most certainly in operation, but arguments about global warming, though enticing because they represent a modern variant of apocalypse theory, remain inconclusive. As discussed earlier, we are also predicting its impact on marine life, but we are taking a leap of faith in doing so. While our knowledge is extremely limited, growing acceptance of the Precautionary Principle might be changing this. This principle is endorsed in the consensus-based Rio Declaration (Principle 15), Agenda 21 (Chapter 17, paragraph 17.2), the United Nations Framework on Climate Change (1992), the Convention on Biological Diversity (1992), and the Montreal Protocol on Substances that Deplete the Ozone Layer (1990). The principle insists that governments have an obligation to prevent environmental degradation, and that, in the absence of scientific certainty regarding the future impact of human activity, we should err on the side of caution and resist taking risky actions.[30]

None of these agreements alters the fundamental political difficulty of achieving a meaningful holistic viewpoint, one that produces changes in short- and long-term policies and may or may not develop towards the political integration anticipated by functionalists. But we do have, as a minimum, Chapter 17 of Agenda 21, and its inclusive outline and research agenda, as a basis for future national and multilateral decisions.[31]

Chapter 17 is labelled 'Safeguarding the Ocean's Resources.' Several environmental problems applicable in a variety of contexts are mentioned, such as sedimentation, pollution, harmful fishing practices, and climate change. It calls for an estimated $6 billion (US) per year for implementing a coastal management program, allocating at least $200 million per year to protect the marine environment from degradation resulting from sewage, agricultural chemicals, synthetic organic compounds, various forms of litter, radioactive substances and hydrocarbons. (If the damage caused by the ex-Soviet Union's radioactive contribution to the seas is any sort of accurate measure, this figure is far too low.)[32] Another $200 million is suggested for new programs aimed at reducing overexploitation of migratory fish; for example, requiring nations to monitor more effectively and ensure compliance by any ships flying their flags, no matter how inconvenient such supervision may be. And, as mentioned, the IWC is given explicit responsibility for large cetacean management, in a document signed by over 150 states, most of which do not belong to that organization.

We also have the troubled but hopeful Global Environment Facility, which is administered by the World Bank, United Nations Development Programme, and UN Environmental Programme, with funding commitments of $1.2 billion in 1990-3 and $2 billion in 1994-8. The facility focuses on four areas: climate change, biological diversity, stratospheric ozone depletion, and, most relevant to this book, the pollution of international waters. France and Germany have been the largest donors. (All are voluntary.) The US has contributed $150 million through the US Agency for International Development to 'parallel finance' projects, and the Clinton administration has committed to larger contributions. These commitments were made at a March 1995 meeting in Reykjavik, in preparation for the formal adoption Global Programme of Action to Protect the Marine Environment from Land-Based Activities. As previously mentioned, this program was adopted in Washington in early November 1995. We must keep in mind, however, that the 'most striking analogy to Hardin's medieval tragedy of the commons in contemporary international affairs is the problem of managing the oceans.'[33]

Finally, another dilemma encountered by wildlife preservationists as a whole deserves discussion. This ethical as well as practical problem was raised earlier in this book, but it is worth returning to here. From a holistic perspective, is the symbolic strength of the whale or any other endangered species not counterproductive in the long term? In other words, does the focus on individual species, regardless of their position on the food chain, not threaten to belittle habitat concerns? The stardom of the 'charismatic megavertebrates'[34] might cause two basic problems. First, the mammals are often conceived as noncontextualized abstractions, shown in zoos, and reduced to movie-promotion posters and stuffed animal toys. This tendency can lead to ignoring the vital link between truly wild mammals and habitat. Whale researcher Jim Darling knows public awareness has its limits. If you wish to save whales, he says, 'I think 90 percent [of people] you talk to would agree with that. But probably 5 percent of the people realize that means you have to save their food supply too. Probably only 1 percent understand that saving the food supply means maintaining the integrity of the system which supports the food.'[35]

The second problem relates to success. If the public focus on a particular species rather than habitat concerns, then success at conserving the species may in fact result in a loss of overall concern. Therefore, if whale stocks are slowly recovering, haven't we achieved something, and can we now turn attention to other mammals, such as elephants?[36] Then after implementing a (highly controversial) ivory ban through CITES, instead of looking at the cramped living conditions of today's African elephants, perhaps we can next move on to the next star, such as the panda bear? In other words, success can become a problem, minimizing the larger concerns that in time will determine the fate of all species. Ultimately, the whale's symbolic importance shouldn't be lost on us, but cetaceans must be recognized for what they are: intelligent creatures who live in a threatened environment, irrevocably linked to all the other organisms in that ecosystem. This perspective may not be a bad way to conceptualize ourselves.

The IWC and the Future

In this final section, we reflect on three critical issues for the future of the IWC. One is the divisive moratorium, another the question of the IWC mandate, and the third the need for increased funding.

First, although it is unlikely to happen, the absolute moratorium should be lifted. Again, this conclusion is extremely difficult for a self-confessed whale lover. However, the moratorium is undermining the scientific legitimacy of the IWC. If the RMP is not put into effect, the commission could very well lose the compliance it already elicits. The American position is also an increasingly untenable one, partly because of the insistence that only some forms of small-scale coastal whaling are morally acceptable, and partly because of the discernible shift within the United States from preservation-oriented environmental policies towards a so-called wise-use philosophy.

In my opinion, this ecological philosophy is misguided, a defence of property rights much more than a valid outlook on human-nature interaction. But it is there and could well affect the future direction of an increasingly isolationist American foreign policy. A probable exception to this influence, however, is the National Oceanic and Atmospheric Administration of the US Department of Commerce, whose position has been constant for the past twenty years but which may not survive restructuring in the new political climate of Washington. The Clinton administration has not imposed costly sanctions on Norway, and Japan's membership in the IWC remains tenuous. If regional organizations such as NAMMCO become the centre of decision-making related to the North Atlantic minke hunt, this development would be regrettable. Such organizations are welcome innovations, though they are probably limited in their ability to deal with issues of the commons. As for preservationist forces, nothing stops them from continuing campaigns for consumer boycotts against whaling nations. For other conservationist measures, the RMP sets a tough standard, and the problem of paying for it remains a sticking point. As the Korean IMC commissioner argues, the RMP 'would be absolutely perfect, but implementing it will be practically difficult without a great [increase in] budget, manpower, and equipment.'[37]

Second, at least one observer has suggested that the true mandate of the IWC should be environmental monitoring; catches could then be regulated by regional organizations such as NAMMCO.[38] His reasons are fairly sound: those nations rejecting the preservationist perspective still need a regulatory body, and they are rather tired of waiting for the IWC to lift the moratorium; NAMMCO can engage in multi-species management, unlike the single-species IWC; the IWC has no jurisdiction over small cetaceans, whose management is increasingly necessary; coastal states reject the 'creeping jurisdiction of the part of an international organization'; and a regional body can help disseminate information on conservation.[39] The counter-arguments are many. The IWC need not take a single-species approach to conservation issues, and it is in fact embedded in much broader multilateral efforts for marine preservation. As well, whales remain part of the global commons, and, as such, the IWC should strive to manage and protect them in as global a fashion as possible. Smaller cetaceans are usually found within coastal jurisdictions and should remain beyond the IWC's regulatory reach until coastal states are willing to cooperate with the IWC and/or sufficient funding is available for this massive expansion in mandate. However, the IWC can certainly conduct some research and give related advice, as indeed it does now.

Beyond the symbolism of sanctuary zones is the more striking development of whalewatching as a substantial economic activity. Even the government of Oman is promoting whalewatching 'to attract tourism.'[40] This phenomenon fills the hearts of many whale enthusiasts with hope, but it can also be quite hazardous to whales. Economists may argue that whalewatching increases the value of preserving whales. In their parlance:

It is generally recognized that direct viewing of wildlife provides an economic value to the participant. However, preservation of the species for viewing is a joint product for the 'users' and also may provide value to non-viewers, from the continued existence of the species for both themselves and (in many cases) for others in the future ... Existence of a species is a public good and, like any other public good, its total economic value should be included when calculating benefits and costs of proposed policies.[41]

Specialists argue that whalewatching in the wild is important because it bonds the whales and the public, encourages respect for whale habitat (though this point may be debatable), discourages captivity, and provides a counter-argument to those who insist that old whalers need to whale to survive. This latter point may sound patronizing to whalers and aboriginal communities alike, but whalewatching certainly has economic potential. It will be interesting to see if the IWC does in fact play a large role in this relatively new sector. Without doubt, guidelines are needed. For example, a group of North American specialists have developed commandments concerning 'How to Behave around Killer Whales.' The guidelines include: always view from a distance, first determining the travel direction and diving sequence of the whales; approach whales from the side, not from the front or rear, and approach and depart slowly; maintain low speeds and a constant direction when travelling parallel to whales, taking care to avoid crowding them near shorelines; keep noise levels down ('no horns, whistles, or racing motors'); limit the time spent watching any group of whales to less than thirty minutes; and be conscious of sudden changes in whale behaviour that might indicate the whales want to be left alone.[42] (Ramming boats would be an obvious, but thankfully rare, sign.) Mexico declared Laguna Ojo de Biebre a gray whale refuge, banning tour boats, as early as 1972. The IWC is looking at the whalewatching issue in an upcoming meeting involving NGOs and whalewatching operations. For now, however, coastal states are responsible for implementing measures related to tourist access and cetacean safety.

Assuming large-scale whaling is a thing of the past (and this book certainly does), community-based approaches are necessary for small-scale whaling. When subsistence whaling does occur, it must be linked to a broader vision of community planning and sustainability. This point is as true for whaling as for salmon fishing, waste disposal, and environmental education; the latter can benefit from cross-cultural experience as well.[43] The international sexiness of the whaling issue should not detract from attempting to gain a broader understanding of other issue-areas. Here the IWC has a key role to play in disseminating information, acting as the key gathering place for cetological studies. To do this work, we need a truly international institution and the IWC needs more voluntary funding.

This requirement leads to the next and final point. The forecasted 1995-6 expenditures of the IWC stand at £1,090,800.[44] Clearly, this amount is not enough. We must encourage all governments to either become full members of the IWC or at least make voluntary contributions. Unfortunately, an opposing trend appears to be under way, as fewer states feel the whaling question is urgent, and as many states consider withdrawal from the IWC, given their frustration over the divisions discussed in this book.

For the sake of the magnificent whale, and the even grander sea where it lives and travels, we must reverse this trend.

Appendixes

APPENDIX A
An Essential Chronology of Whaling

50 to 25 million years ago
According to some accounts, primitive whales evolve into carnivores who live on the African shorelines and then return gradually to the seas via rivers and estuaries. Three suborder of Cetacea emerge: Mysticeti, Odontoceti, and Archaeoceti.

25 million years ago
The Archaeoceti becomes extinct in the Lower Miocene period.

2200 BC
Very early drawings of whales date back to this time.

1500 BC
Some experts believe the Alaskan Inuit began whaling.

AD 800-1000
Norsemen begin whaling, followed by the Basques in the Bay of Biscay. Right and gray whales are hunted.

1400
Basques begin whaling in the North Atlantic.

1550
Basques begin spending summers at shore stations along the north shore of the Strait of Belle Isle in Labrador.

1578
Basque ships hunt bowheads near Greenland.

ca. 1600
In Japan, coastal whaling using a net fishery develops.

ca. 1611
Dutch and British whalers travel northeast to Spitzbergen, where they compete to control the grounds.

1613
Dutch merchants form the Noordsche Compagnie, gaining a monopoly over the northern whaling grounds that lasts until 1642.

1617
Dutch whalers on Amsterdam Island build a shore station at Spitzbergen. This station develops into a whaling town named Smeerenburg that thrives and is then deserted by the 1640s.

1650
Shore whaling begins on Long Island, New York.

1712
After a Nantucket whaling captain kills a sperm whale, American whalers begin hunting them in the open ocean.

1720
Dutch whalers take increased numbers of bowheads from Davis Strait.

1749
The British government uses a subsidy to encourage British whaling.

1750
Development of the spermaceti candle.
Introduction of tryworks on American vessels, allowing the crew to boil blubber at sea, which facilitates longer voyages in the South Atlantic.

1775
The American Revolution stops American whaling for a decade.

1788
A British whaleship rounds Cape Horn, returning in 1790 to England with a full cargo of sperm oil from the South Pacific.

1789
North American and European whalers reach Cape Horn in pursuit of sperm whales, then begin whaling in the Pacific. Hawaii would become a major whaling base in the early 1800s.

1800-50
A fishery for right whales develops off New Zealand, Australia, and the Kerguelen Islands.

1805

The first Australian-built deep-sea whaler is launched.

1813

An American naval vessel attacks and destroys almost half of the British Pacific whaling fleet.

1830

In Davis Strait, nineteen British whaleships are destroyed by ice and storm.

1835

Right whales are discovered in the Northwest Grounds (presently, the coast near British Columbia, Canada).

1840

Right whales are hunted in the North Pacific and eventually in the Bering, Chukchi, and Beaufort seas.
Gray whales are hunted in the lagoons of Baja California.

1851

First publication of Melville's *Moby Dick*.
First shore station established by Americans on Baffin Island.

1857

Charles Melville Scammon, whaling captain and writer/artist, finds gray whales in a Baja California lagoon. This encounter results in such a rapid escalation that hunting for gray whales was uneconomical by 1861.
British whalers begin installing steam engines.

1859

Oil discovered in Pennsylvania.

1860

Sperm whaling drops off and attention turns to right whales in the Southern Hemisphere.

1863-8

Norwegian Svend Foyn invents the harpoon gun and explosive harpoon, using them on a steam-driven vessel. Modern methods are also employed at his shore station in northern Norway.
The modern whaling era begins.

1865

During the American Civil War, a Confederate warship destroys thirty-four whaleships in a surprise raid in the western Arctic.

1871
Thirty-three American whaleships are destroyed in the ice off Alaska.

1872
The grenade harpoon is perfected.
Whalers focus their hunt on fast-swimming rorquals (blue, fin, sei, Bryde's).

1880
Americans start powering whaleships with steam.

1889
Norwegian-style whaling begins off the coast of Korea.

1892
The first expedition to the Antarctic fails.

1898
Norwegians are whaling off Newfoundland.

1904
The first land station opens at South Georgia in the Antarctic.

1905
Norwegians enter the Antarctic, or Southern, Ocean, and find blues and fins.

1907
The American bowhead industry dies.

1909
Hydrogenation is used to convert whale oil to soap and margarine.

1912
The last British whaler working in the North Atlantic returns to Dundee.

1914-18
During the First World War, most whaling operations are suspended. Stocks do not recover.

1924
The British set up the Discovery Committee to investigate whales in the Antarctic.

1924 and 1927
The League of Nations makes unsuccessful attempts to regulate whaling activity.

1925

The first factory ships with 'slipways' begin working in the Antarctic. World catches rise from 23,000 in 1924-5 to 43,130 in 1930-1.

1930

The International Council for the Exploration of the Sea asks Norway, under the Norwegian Whaling Act of 1929, to set up the Bureau of International Whaling Statistics.

1931

The first International Convention for the Regulation of Whaling is negotiated in Geneva by twenty-one countries. The convention includes protecting right whales and female whales with calves, licensing of whaling vessels, and collecting statistics. It is only partly observed. The convention also enshrines the rights of aboriginal whalers.
Almost 30,000 blue whales are taken worldwide.

1937

8 June: The International Agreement to Regulate Whaling (IARW), also known as the First International Whaling Convention, is signed in London. The agreement includes adding the gray and bowhead whales to the protection list, defining the hunting season in the Southern Hemisphere, and introducing some size limits. The signatories include Argentina, Australia, Germany, Iceland, New Zealand, South Africa, the United States, and the United Kingdom.

1938

Renewal of the First International Whaling Convention.
24 June: The Protocol to the IARW (1937) provides protection for the Southern Hemisphere humpbacks from pelagic whaling and a temporary sanctuary in the Antarctic.

1939-45

The Second World War affords a break from whaling, but stocks fail to recover.

1944-6

A series of conferences helps establish the International Whaling Commission (IWC).
The Blue Whale Unit and the idea of quotas are accepted.

1945

November: The first postwar whaling season begins in the Antarctic.

1946

20 November: A conference on the regulation of whaling begins in Washington.
2 December: The International Convention for the Regulation of Whaling (ICRW) is signed.
The IWC is created. Its original members are Argentina, Australia, Brazil,

Canada, Denmark, France, Iceland, Japan, Mexico, Netherlands, New Zealand, Norway, Panama, South Africa, the Soviet Union, United Kingdom, and the United States.
The Blue Whale Unit, with its first quota of 16,000 units, is adopted.

1956
19 November: Protocol amendment to the ICRW (1946).

1958
Hunt begins for sei whales.

1959-62
Norway and the Netherlands withdraw from the IWC, given an inability to reach agreement on dividing the IWC quota with other whaling nations. They rejoin in 1962 when an agreement is reached.

1960
IWC sets up the Committee of Three Scientists (later increased to four).

1961-2
The peak whaling activity[1] reported in this season: 66,090 whales.

1962-3
Collapse of the Australian humpback whale fisheries.

1963-4
United Kingdom ceases pelagic whaling.
The Netherlands cease small-scale pelagic whaling.
New Zealand ceases coastal whaling.

1964-9
Food and Agricultural Organization (FAO) carries out stock assessments on behalf of the International Whaling Commission.

1965
The blue whale receives IWC protection; Russia later reveals the Soviet Union continued this and other illegal hunts.

1967
US Fisherman's Protective Act is created.

1969
Norway ceases pelagic, but continues coastal, whaling.
The IWC sets catch limits on fin and sei in the North Pacific; species quota for other than the blue whale are thus set for the first time.

1970
Catch quotas are introduced for sperm whales in the North Pacific.

1971
The hunt for North Pacific Bryde's whale begins.
Catch quotas are set for sperm whales in the Southern Hemisphere.
The United States passes the Pelly Amendment to the Fisherman's Protective Act of 1967.

1971-2
A large-scale hunt for minke whales begins.

1972
The United Nations Conference on the Human Environment, with fifty-three nations, gathers in Stockholm. A ten-year whaling moratorium accepted and presented (unsuccessfully) to the IWC.
The International Observer Scheme is established within the IWC.
Mexico declares Scammon's Lagoon the world's first whale sanctuary.

1972-3
Canada ceases coastal whaling.
United States ceases coastal whaling.
BWU formally abandoned in the Southern Hemisphere with the introduction of species quotas.

1974
The IWC adopts the New Management Procedure (NMP), using Maximum Sustainable Yield (MSY) as a guideline. Put into effect for the 1975-6 season.
Japan rejects IWC quotas and an international outcry follows.
Brazil joins the IWC.

1975
Then prime minister Takeo Miki of Japan pledges to adhere to IWC quotas at a Washington press conference.
Greenpeace begins its anti-whaling campaign.

1975-6
Total reported world catch for this season down to 19,337.
New Zealand joins the IWC.

1976
South Africa ceases coastal whaling.
IWC gets a full-time office in Cambridge, England, with a full-time cetologist as its secretary, and supporting staff.
International Decade of Cetacean Research is declared.
Japan's whaling firms merge to form the Japan Joint Whaling Company.

Japan announces its intention to begin so-called scientific whaling of Bryde's whales (quota set at zero by IWC) during the 1976-7 season.

1977
Netherlands joins the IWC.

1978
Report of the Inquiry into Whales and Whaling, chaired by Sir Sydney Frost, presented to Australian prime minister Malcolm Fraser.

1979
Australia ceases coastal whaling.
Proposal to end all pelagic whaling except for minke whales is adopted at the IWC.
Sanctuary declared in the Indian Ocean by the IWC.
Seychelles, Sweden, Chile, Peru, Spain, and Korea join the IWC.
United States passes the Packwood-Magnuson Amendment to the Fishery Conservation and Management Act of 1976.

1979-80
Ramming, then sinking, of the pirate whaleship *Sierra,* with Paul Watson's *Sea Shepherd* held responsible.
Bombing and sinking of *Isba I* and *Asba II,* Spanish whaleships, in the harbour of Marin near Vigo, Spain.
Switzerland and Oman join the IWC; Panama withdraws.
The Republic of Korea agrees to stop using cold harpoons.

1981
Over Japanese objections, an IWC zero quota is set for sperm whaling in the Southern Hemisphere and North Atlantic.
Australia unsuccessfully proposes total phase-out of whaling.

1982
IWC sets zero quotas on all commercial species, to begin 1 January 1986. The moratorium passes by a 25 to 7 vote with 5 abstentions. Japan, Norway, Peru, the Soviet Union, Brazil, Iceland, and South Korea opposed. (Peru and Brazil drop their objections in 1983.)
Jamaica, St. Lucia, Dominica, Costa Rica, Uruguay, China, St.
Vincent and the Grenadines, India, and the Philippines join the IWC; Canada withdraws.
Thirty-eight members in the IWC.
China bans whaling.

1983
Egypt, Kenya, Senegal, Belize, Antigua, Monaco, and West Germany join the IWC; Jamaica and Dominica withdraw.

1984

November: Japan agrees through an executive arrangement with the US to end sperm whaling by 1988.
Finland and Mauritius join the IWC.

1985-6

Ireland and the Solomon Islands join the IWC.

1986

Global moratorium officially comes into effect. Japan, Iceland, and Norway continue limited whaling, including scientific whaling.
Whaling station in Iceland is sabotaged.

1987

26 May: The USSR announces a formal ban on commercial whaling.
Mauritius and Belize withdraw from the IWC.

1988

Japan, in eventual compliance with the moratorium, discontinues commercial whaling. Scientific whaling continues.

1989

Scientists report to the IWC that blue whale population estimates have been far too high.

1992

Iceland withdraws from the IWC.
Establishment of North Atlantic Marine Mammal Commission.
The United Nations Conference on the Environment and Development is held in Rio de Janeiro; Agenda 21 is produced, complete with Chapter 17.

1993

IWC Scientific Committee chairman Philip Hammond resigns in protest over the commission's inability to adopt the RMP.
Norway resumes a commercial minke hunt. Scientific whaling continues as well.

1994

Seychelles withdraws from the IWC.
Norfolk Island meeting on the Southern Ocean sanctuary.
Stunning revelations of past Soviet under-reporting.
Establishment of the 11.8 million square-mile Antarctic whaling sanctuary.
Japan registers a reservation, continuing scientific whaling.

1995

Demands by the Makah of Washington State for a renewed gray whale hunt.
Norway continues to take minkes; controversy surrounding stock size dominates debate; US refrains from imposing sanctions against Norway.

1996

The IWC Annual Meeting takes place in Aberdeen, Scotland; no changes to the status quo. US delegation puts off Makah request due to internal divisions; issue should resurface in 1997.

APPENDIX B
The 1946 International Convention for the Regulation of Whaling

The Governments whose duly authorized representatives have subscribed hereto,
RECOGNIZING the interest of the nations of the world in safeguarding for future generations the great natural resources represented by the whale stocks;
CONSIDERING that the history of whaling has seen over-fishing of one area after another and of one species of whale after another to such a degree that it is essential to protect all species of whales from further over-fishing;
RECOGNIZING that the whale stocks are susceptible of natural increases if whaling is properly regulated, and that increases in the size of whale stocks will permit increases in the numbers of whales which may be captured without endangering these natural resources;
RECOGNIZING that it is in the common interest to achieve the optimum level of whale stocks as rapidly as possible without causing widespread economic and nutritional distress;
RECOGNIZING that in the course of achieving these objectives, whaling operations should be confined to those species best able to sustain exploitation in order to give an interval for recovery to certain species of whales now depleted in numbers;
DESIRING to establish a system of international regulation for the whale fisheries to ensure proper and effective conservation and development of whale stocks on the basis of the principles embodied in the provisions of the International Agreement for the Regulation of Whaling signed in London on 8 June 1937, and the protocols to that Agreement signed in London on 24 June 1938, and 26 November 1945; and
HAVING decided to conclude a convention to provide for the proper conservation of whale stocks and thus make possible the orderly development of the whaling industry;
HAVE AGREED as follows:

Article I
1 This Convention includes the Schedule attached thereto which forms an integral part thereof. All references to 'Convention' shall be understood as including the said Schedule either in its present terms or as amended in accordance with the provisions of Article V.

2 This Convention applies to factory ships, land stations, and whale catchers under the jurisdiction of the Contracting Governments, and to all waters in which whaling is prosecuted by such factory ships, land stations, and whale catchers.

Article II

As used in this Convention:

1 'factory ship' means a ship in which or on which whales are treated whether wholly or in part;
2 'land station' means a factory on the land at which whales are treated whether wholly or in part;
3 'whale catcher' means a ship used for the purpose of hunting, taking, towing, holding on to, or scouting for whales;
4 'Contracting Government' means any Government which has deposited an instrument of ratification or has given notice of adherence to this Convention.

Article III

1 The Contracting Governments agree to establish an International Whaling Commission, hereinafter referred to as the Commission, to be composed of one member from each Contracting Government. Each member shall have one vote and may be accompanied by one or more experts and advisers.
2 The Commission shall elect from its own members a Chairman and Vice-Chairman and shall determine its own Rules of Procedure. Decisions of the Commission shall be taken by a simple majority of those members voting except that a three-fourths majority of those members voting shall be required for action in pursuance of Article V. The Rules of Procedure may provide for decisions otherwise than at meetings of the Commission.
3 The Commission may appoint its own Secretary and staff.
4 The Commission may set up, from among its own members and experts or advisers, such committees as it considers desirable to perform such functions as it may authorize.
5 The expenses of each member of the Commission and of his experts and advisers shall be determined and paid by his own Government.
6 Recognizing that specialized agencies related to the United Nations will be concerned with the conservation and development of whale fisheries and the products arising therefrom and desiring to avoid duplication of functions, the Contracting Governments will consult among themselves within two years after the coming into force of this Convention to decide whether the Commission shall be brought within the framework of a specialized agency related to the United Nations.
7 In the meantime the Government of the United Kingdom of Great Britain and Northern Ireland shall arrange, in consultation with the other Contracting Governments, to convene the first meeting of the Commission, and shall initiate the consultation referred to in paragraph 6 above.
8 Subsequent meetings of the Commission shall be convened as the Commission may determine.

Article IV

1 The Commission may either in collaboration with or through independent agencies of the Contracting Governments or other public or private agencies, establishments, or organizations, or independently
   (a) encourage, recommend, or if necessary, organize studies and investigations relating to whales and whaling;
   (b) collect and analyze statistical information concerning the current condition and trend of the whale stocks and the effects of whaling activities thereon;
   (c) study, appraise, and disseminate information concerning methods of maintaining and increasing the populations of whale stocks.
2 The Commission shall arrange for the publication of reports of its activities, and it may publish independently or in collaboration with the International Bureau for Whaling Statistics at Sandefjord in Norway and other organizations and agencies such reports as it deems appropriate, as well as statistical, scientific, and other pertinent information relating to whales and whaling.

Article V

1 The Commission may amend from time to time the provisions of the Schedule by adopting regulations with respect to the conservation and utilization of whale resources, fixing (a) protected and unprotected species; (b) open and closed seasons; (c) open and closed waters, including the designation of sanctuary areas; (d) size limits for each species; (e) time, methods, and intensity of whaling (including the maximum catch of whales to be taken in any one season); (f) types and specifications of gear and apparatus and appliances which may be used; (g) methods of measurement; and (h) catch returns and other statistical and biological records.
2 These amendments of the Schedule (a) shall be such as are necessary to carry out the objectives and purposes of this Convention and to provide for the conservation, development, and optimum utilization of the whale resources; (b) shall be based on scientific findings; (c) shall not involve restrictions on the number or nationality of factory ships or land stations, nor allocate specific quotas to any factory ship or land station or to any group of factory ships or land stations; and (d) shall take into consideration the interests of the consumers of whale products and the whaling industry.
3 Each of such amendments shall become effective with respect to the Contracting Governments ninety days following notification of the amendment by the Commission to each of the Contracting Governments, except that
   (a) if any Government presents to the Commission objection to any amendment prior to the expiration of this ninety-day period, the amendment shall not become effective with respect to any of the Governments for an additional ninety days;
   (b) thereupon, any other Contracting Government may present objection to the amendment at any time prior to the expiration of the additional ninety-day period, or before the expiration of thirty days from the date

of receipt of the last objection received during such additional ninety-day period, whichever date shall be the later; and

(c) thereafter, the amendment shall become effective with respect to all Contracting Governments which have not presented objection but shall not become effective with respect to any Government which has so objected until such date as the objection is withdrawn. The Commission shall notify each Contracting Government immediately upon receipt of each objection and withdrawal and each Contracting Government shall acknowledge receipt of all notifications of amendments, objections, and withdrawals.

4 No amendments shall become effective before 1 July 1949.

Article VI

The Commission may from time to time make recommendations to any or all Contracting Governments on any matters which relate to whales or whaling and to the objectives and purposes of this Convention.

Article VII

The Contracting Governments shall ensure prompt transmission to the International Bureau of Whaling Statistics at Sandefjord in Norway, or to such other body as the Commission may designate, of notifications and statistical and other information required by this Convention in such form and manner as may be prescribed by the Commission.

Article VIII

1 Notwithstanding anything contained in this Convention, any Contracting Government may grant to any of its nationals a special permit authorizing that national to kill, take, and treat whales for purposes of scientific research subject to such restrictions as to number and subject to such other conditions as the Contracting Government thinks fit, and the killing, taking, and treating of whales in accordance with the provisions of this Article shall be exempt from the operation of this Convention. Each Contracting Government shall report at once to the Commission all such authorizations which it has granted. Each Contracting Government may at any time revoke any such special permit which it has granted.

2 Any whales taken under these special permits shall so far as practicable be processed and the proceeds shall be dealt with in accordance with directions issued by the Government by which the permit was granted.

3 Each Contracting Government shall transmit to such body as may be designated by the Commission, in so far as practicable, and at intervals of not more than one year, scientific information available to that Government with respect to whales and whaling, including the results of research conducted pursuant to paragraph 1 of this Article and to Article IV.

4 Recognizing that continuous collection and analysis of biological data in connection with the operations of factory ships and land stations are indispensable to sound and constructive management of the whale fisheries, the Contracting Governments will take all practicable measures to obtain such data.

Article IX

1 Each Contracting Government shall take appropriate measures to ensure the application of the provisions of this Convention and the punishment of infractions against the said provisions in operations carried out by persons or by vessels under its jurisdiction.
2 No bonus or other remuneration calculated with relation to the results of their work shall be paid to the gunners and crews of whale catchers in respect of any whales the taking of which is forbidden by this Convention.
3 Prosecution for infractions against or contraventions of this Convention shall be instituted by the Government having jurisdiction over the offence.
4 Each Contracting Government shall transmit to the Commission full details of each infraction of the provisions of this Convention by persons or vessels under the jurisdiction of that Government as reported by its inspectors. This information shall include a statement of measures taken for dealing with the infraction and of penalties imposed.

Article X

1 This Convention shall be ratified and the instruments of ratification shall be deposited with the Government of the United States of America.
2 Any Government which has not signed this Convention may adhere thereto after it enters into force by a notification in writing to the Government of the United States of America.
3 The Government of the United States of America shall inform all other signatory Governments and all adhering Governments of all ratifications deposited and adherences received.
4 This Convention shall, when instruments of ratification have been deposited by at least six signatory Governments, which shall include the Governments of the Netherlands, Norway, the Union of Soviet Socialist Republics, the United Kingdom of Great Britain and Northern Ireland, and the United States of America, enter into force with respect to those Governments and shall enter into force with respect to each Government which subsequently ratifies or adheres on the date of the deposit of its instrument of ratification or the receipt of its notification of adherence.
5 The provisions of the Schedule shall not apply prior to 1 July 1948. Amendments to the Schedule adopted pursuant to Article V shall not apply prior to 1 July 1949.

Article XI

Any Contracting Government may withdraw from this Convention on June thirtieth of any year by giving notice on or before January first of the same year to the depositary Government, which upon receipt of such a notice shall at once communicate it to the other Contracting Governments. Any other Contracting Government may, in like manner, within one month of the receipt of a copy of such a notice from the depositary Government, give notice of withdrawal, so that the Convention shall cease to be in force on June thirtieth of the same year with respect to the Government giving such notice of withdrawal.

This Convention shall bear the date on which it is opened for signature and shall remain open for signature for a period of fourteen days thereafter.

IN WITNESS WHEREOF the undersigned, being duly authorized, have signed this Convention.

DONE in Washington this second day of December 1946, in the English language, the original of which shall be deposited in the archives of the Government of the United States of America. The Government of the United States of America shall transmit certified copies thereof to all the other signatory and adhering Governments.

Protocol of Amendment

A Protocol to the International Convention for the Regulation of Whaling was adopted in Washington, D.C. on 19 November 1956. The Protocol provides as follows:

The Contracting Governments to the International Convention for the Regulation of Whaling signed at Washington under date of December 2, 1946 which Convention is hereinafter referred to as the 1946 Whaling Convention, desiring to extend the application of that Convention to helicopters and other aircraft and to include provisions on methods of inspection among those Schedule provisions which may be amended by the Commission, agree as follows:

Article I

Subparagraph 3 of Article II of the 1946 Whaling Convention shall be amended to read as follows:

'3. "whale catcher" means a helicopter, or other aircraft, or a ship, used for the purpose of hunting, taking, killing, towing, holding on to, or scouting for whales.'

Article II

Paragraph 1 of Article V of the 1946 Whaling Convention shall be amended by deleting the word 'and' preceding clause (h), substituting a semicolon for the period at the end of the paragraph, and adding the following language:

'and (i) methods of inspection.'

Article III

1 This Protocol shall be open for signature and ratification or for adherence on behalf of any Contracting Government to the 1946 Whaling Convention.
2 This Protocol shall enter into force on the date upon which instruments of ratification have been deposited with, or written notifications of adherence have been received by, the Government of the United States of

America on behalf of all the Contracting Governments to the 1946 Whaling Convention.

3 The Government of the United States of America shall inform all Governments signatory or adhering to the 1946 Whaling Convention of all ratifications deposited and adherences received.

4 This Protocol shall bear the date on which it is opened for signature and shall remain open for signature for a period of fourteen days thereafter, following which period it shall be open for adherence.

IN WITNESS WHEREOF the undersigned, being duly authorized, have signed this Protocol.

DONE in Washington this nineteenth day of November 1956, in the English language, the original of which shall be deposited in the archives of the Government of the United States of America. The Government of the United States of America shall transmit certified copies thereof to all Governments signatory or adhering to the 1946 Whaling Convention.

[Schedule omitted; the schedule changes according to IWC votes. In 1996, the 'moratorium' remains in effect so that all commercial whaling is officially banned.]

APPENDIX C
Current Aboriginal Whaling Quotas

Restrictions are placed on the number of whales that can be struck, then lost. 'Landed' whales are those successfully brought back to shore. Current quotas from the 1995 IWC Meeting are as follow:

Bering-Chukchi-Beaufort seas stock of bowhead whales taken by Alaskan Eskimos: The total number of landed whales for the years 1995, 1996, 1997, and 1998 shall not exceed 204 whales.

Eastern North Pacific gray whales taken by the Native peoples of Chukotka, Russia: An annual catch of 19 whales is allowed for the years 1995, 1996, and 1997.

West Greenland minke whales taken by Greenlanders: The total number of whales struck for the years 1995, 1996, and 1997 shall not exceed 465, with a maximum number of 165 in any given year.

East Greenland minke whales taken by Greenlanders: An annual catch of 12 whales is allowed for the years 1995, 1996, and 1997.

Humpback whales taken by St. Vincent and the Grenadines, Caribbean: For the seasons 1993-4 to 1995-6, the annual catch shall not exceed two whales.

Notes

Preface

1 The first version of the relevant article was presented at the annual meeting of the Canadian Political Science Association, Prince Edward Island University, June 1992, and was entitled 'International Organization and Normative Transition: The Death of Whaling and the Survival of the Whale.' The published article is entitled 'International Politics and the Protection of Great Whales,' *Environmental Politics* 2 (1993):277-302. Finally, the book is entitled *Atoms, Whales, and Rivers: Global Environmental Security and International Organization* (Commack, NY: Nova Science Publishers 1995).

2 For a recent discussion, see M. Peterson, 'Whalers, Cetologists, Environmentalists, and the International Management of Whaling,' *International Organization* 46 (1992):147-86.

3 Indeed some states, including Canada, no longer belong to the IWC, but we examine their position as well. By maintaining ties to the organization, with a vested interest in cetacean survival for tourism purposes, and by having a very small aboriginal whaling population, Canada is certainly involved in the network.

4 Some activists have even threatened violent responses to a Makah hunt; the celebrity Paul Watson has warned: 'Our Orca Force Could Hit at Any Time.' 'Indian Whaling Ships "Will Be Sunk,"' *Vancouver Sun*, 24 May 1995.

Chapter 1: Ecopolitics

1 L. Kaufman, 'Why the Ark Is Sinking,' in *The Last Extinction*, eds. L. Kaufman and K. Mallory, 2nd ed. (Cambridge, MA: MIT Press 1993), 12.

2 See, among many examples, P. Sands, 'Enforcing Environmental Security: The Challenges of Compliance with International Obligations,' *Journal of International Affairs* 46 (1993):367-90; P.H. Sand, *Lessons Learned in Global Environmental Governance* (Washington, DC: World Resources Institute 1990); A. Hurrell and B. Kingsbury, eds., *The International Politics of the Environment: Actors, Interests, and Institutions* (Oxford: Clarendon 1992); and N. Choucri, ed., *Global Accord: Environmental Challenges and International Responses* (Cambridge, MA: MIT Press 1993).

3 In point of fact, the Schedule was amended so that the catch quotas for all

species were set at zero. Most commentators have taken to calling this quota a moratorium, though some dislike the term.

4 It is an old, if odd, custom to call a whaling operation a fishery. Of course, whales are not fish. However, by the time this fact was common knowledge, the term had widespread use. On occasion, we see the term whalery, but it is awkward.

5 W. Beckerman, 'Global Warming and International Action: An Economic Perspective,' in *International Politics of the Environment*, eds. Hurrell and Kingsbury, 253-89.

6 S. Krasner, 'Sovereignty, Regimes, and Human Rights,' in *Regime Theory and International Relations*, ed. V. Rittberger (Oxford: Clarendon Press 1993), 139-42. See also P.M. Wijkman, 'Managing the Global Commons,' *International Organization* 36 (1982):511-36.

7 M. M'Gonigle and D. Babicki, 'The Turbot's Last Stand?' *Globe and Mail*, 21 July 1995. The authors call for a 'consistency rule' which 'makes sure the same strict [fishing] standards apply on both sides of what is, from an ecological point of view, an artificial 200-mile demarcation on the map.'

8 N. Myers, 'Sharing the Earth with Whales,' in *Last Extinction*, eds. Kaufman and Mallory, 179-80.

9 See for example, J. Loomis and L. Douglas, 'Total Economic Values of Increasing Gray Whale Populations: Results from a Contingent Valuation Survey of Visitors and Households,' *Marine Resource Economics* 9 (1994):275-86; K. Yoshihiro and C. Tisdell, 'Economics of Antarctic Minke Whale Catches: Sustainability and Welfare Considerations,' *Marine Resource Economics* 9 (1994):141-58; and K. Yoshihiro and C. Tisdell, 'Institutional Management of an International Mixed Good: The IWC and Socially Optimal Whale Harvests' *Marine Policy* 17 (1993):235-50.

10 This term is adapted from the important recent collection of essays, *Governance without Government: Order and Change in World Politics*, eds. J. Rosenau and E.-O. Czempiel (Cambridge: Cambridge University Press 1992). In M. Zacher's essay for this volume, he writes: 'This appears to be a time when it is possible to judge that the world is in the process of a fundamental transformation from a system of highly autonomous states to one where states are increasingly enmeshed in a network of interdependencies and regimes.' 'The Decaying Pillars of the Westphalian Temple: Implications for International Order and Governance,' 98.

11 D. Mitrany, who was concerned with the need to establish a 'working peace system,' is generally considered the intellectual founder of this thinking in modern times, though it has links with Kant and others. Mitrany's definitive effort was the book, *A Working Peace System* (Chicago: Quadrangle 1966).

12 General Assembly Resolution 1803 (XVII), 14 December 1962.

13 See R. White, 'Environmental Management and National Security: Some Issues from Senegal,' *International Journal* XLV (1990):106-37; J. Goldemberg and E.R. Durham, 'Amazonia and National Sovereignty,' *International Environmental Affairs* 2 (1990):22-39; and J. Daudelin, 'L'environnement comme Cheval de Troie? Le cas de l'Amazonie brésilienne,' paper presented to the Canadian Political Science Association, Carleton University, ON, June 1993.

14 I base this observation on interviews with members of the Department of

Fisheries and Oceans, Ottawa, 1992-3. See also S. Waters, 'Non-consumptive Utilisation of Marine Mammals in Canada: International and National Regulation,' in *Canadian Ocean Law and Policy,* ed. D. VanderZwaag (Toronto: Butterworths 1992), 141-72.

15 R.E. Benedick, *Ozone Diplomacy: New Directions in Safeguarding the Planet* (Cambridge, MA: Harvard University Press 1991), 207. See also White, 'Environmental Management and National Sovereignty,' 106-37.

16 T. Brenton, *The Greening of Machiavelli: The Evolution of International Environmental Politics* (London: Earthscan 1994), 202.

17 More precisely: 'The developed countries acknowledge the responsibility that they bear in the international pursuit of sustainable development in view of the pressures their societies place on the global environment and of the technologies and financial resources they command.' Rio Declaration.

18 It is to be hoped that we can at last leave the confusing term 'Third World' behind.

19 R. Keohane, 'Multilateralism: An Agenda for Research,' *International Journal* XLV (1990):731-64.

20 D. Puchala, 'The UN and Ecosystem Issues: Institutionalizing the Global Interest,' in *Politics in the United Nations System,* ed. L. Finkelstein (Durham: Duke University Press 1988), 218.

21 H. French, 'After the Earth Summit: The Future of Environmental Governance,' *World Watch Paper* 107 (March 1992):6.

22 J. MacNeill, P. Winsemius, and T. Yakushiji, *Beyond Interdependence: The Meshing of the World's Economy and the Earth's Ecology* (New York: Oxford University 1991), 120.

23 For standard texts, see S. Krasner, 'Structural Causes and Regime Consequences: Regimes as Intervening Variables,' in *International Regimes,* ed. S. Krasner (Ithaca, NY: Cornell University Press 1983), 1-22; R. Keohane, *After Hegemony: Cooperation and Discord in the World Political Economy* (Princeton, NJ: Princeton University Press 1984); M. Zacher, 'Toward a Theory of International Regimes,' *Journal of International Affairs* 44 (1990):139-58; O. Young, 'The Politics of International Regime Formation: Managing Natural Resources and the Environment,' *International Organization* 43 (1989):349-75. For more recent work, see in particular V. Rittberger, ed., *Regime Theory and International Relations* (Oxford: Clarendon Press 1993); and the perceptive review essay by Andreas Behnke, 'Ten Years After: The State of the Art of Regime Theory,' *Cooperation and Conflict* 30 (1995):179-97.

24 For example, see P. Sands, 'EC Environmental Law: The Evolution of a Regional Regime of International Environmental Protection,' *Yale Law Journal* 100 (1991):2,511-23.

25 O. Young, 'Regime Dynamics: The Rise and Fall of International Regimes,' in *International Regimes,* ed. Krasner, 93-113.

26 T. Bernauer, 'The Effect of International Environmental Institutions: How Might We Learn More?' *International Organization* 49 (1995):351.

27 M. Levy, G. Osherenko, and O. Young, 'The Effectiveness of International Regimes: A Design for Large-Scale Collaborative Research,' paper based on a workshop held at Dartmouth College, 31 October-3 November 1991. Instead

of *regime*, the authors prefer the even less precise term *behavioural complex*, a 'system composed of actors, institutions, norms, principles and rules' that operates in a 'specific time as well as geographic and functional area' (p. 10).

28 A. Moravcsik, 'Explaining International Human Rights Regimes: Liberal Theory and Western Europe,' *European Journal of International Relations* 1 (1995):157-89. A similar call for advanced work in this area, which stresses the need to link domestic societies with regimes, is an article by S. Haggard and B. Simmons, 'Theories of International Regimes,' *International Organization* 41 (1987):491-517. This strategy is an avenue of great potential for students of environmental policy.

29 The Scientific Committee is a group of cetologists (those who study whales) and other marine mammal experts, appointed by member-states of the IWC.

30 United Press International, 'Tokyo Agrees to Join Ivory Import Ban,' *Boston Globe*, 21 October 1989; see also A. Chayes and A.H. Chayes, 'On Compliance,' *International Organization* 47 (1993):200-1.

31 Levy, Osherenko, and Young, 'The Effectiveness of International Regimes,' 29. On social learning, see E. Haas, *When Knowledge Is Power: Three Models of Change in International Organization* (Berkeley: University of California 1990).

32 Thomas Donaldson, however, comments on Kant: '[His] seeming optimism, for which he is roundly criticized, was nonetheless limited. His international moralism is tempered by his recognition of the great difficulty that any international confederation that lacks the power of sanction will have protecting a system of moral practises.' Regime theorists need to keep this rather realistic temperament in mind. 'Kant's Global Rationalism,' in *Traditions of International Ethics,* eds. T. Nardin and D. Mapel (Cambridge: Cambridge University Press 1992), 148.

33 R. Mitchell, *Intentional Oil Pollution at Sea: Environmental Policy and Treaty Compliance* (Cambridge, MA: MIT Press 1994). I have reviewed this book in *Illahee: Journal for the Northwest Environment* 11 (1996):218-20. Also see T. Biersteker, 'Constructing Historical Counterfactuals to Assess the Consequences of International Regimes: The Global Debt Regime and the Course of the Debt Crisis of the 1980s,' in *Regime Theory and International Relations,* ed. Rittberger, 282-314.

34 F. Pearce, *Green Warriors: The People and the Politics behind the Environmental Revolution* (London: Bodley Head 1991), 22.

35 R. Payne, *Among Whales* (New York: Scribners 1995), 265.

36 Personal communication with R. Gambell, secretary of the IWC, July 1995.

37 See J. Keeley, 'The Latest Wave: A Critical Review of Regime Literature,' in *World Politics: Power, Interdependence, and Dependence,* eds. D. Haglund and M. Hawes (Toronto: Harcourt Brace Jovanovich 1990), 553-69.

38 E. Nadelmann, 'Global Prohibition Regimes: The Evolution of Norms in International Society,' *International Organization* 44 (1990):481.

39 R. Keohane, 'A Personal Intellectual History,' in *International Institutions and State Power: Essays in International Relations Theory,* ed. R. Keohane (Boulder, CO: Westview 1989), 31. Reflecting his liberal orientations, however, Keohane concludes: 'But I believe international cooperation, though not sufficient, is a necessary

condition of life, liberty and the pursuit of happiness in the twenty-first century,' (p. 31).

40 S. Dalby, 'Security, Modernity, Ecology: The Dilemmas of Post-Cold War Security Discourse,' *Alternatives* 17 (1992):102.

41 See P. Wapner, 'Politics Beyond the State: Environmental Activism and World Civic Politics,' *World Politics* 47 (1995):313. Wapner states: 'Like its domestic counterpart, global civil society consists of structures that define and shape public affairs ... In targeting these processes and institutions, activists use the realms of transnational social, cultural, and economic life to influence world public affairs,' (p. 313).

42 J. Rosenau adopts this term in *Turbulence in World Politics: A Theory of Change and Continuity* (Princeton, NJ: Princeton University Press 1990).

43 See in particular T. Burke, 'Friends of the Earth and the Conservation of Resources,' in *Pressure Groups in the Global System: The Transnational Relations of Issue-Oriented Non-Governmental Organisations,* ed. P. Willetts (London: Francis Pinter 1982), 105-24.

44 See R. Scarce, *Eco-Warriors: Understanding the Radical Environmental Movement* (Chicago: Noble 1990); D. Day, *The Environmental Wars* (New York: Ballantine 1989); R. Hunter, *Warriors of the Rainbow: A Chronicle of the Greenpeace Movement* (New York: Holt, Rinehart and Winston 1979); and Pearce, *Green Warriors*. For a critical perspective on the famous $5 million operation to save two ice-trapped gray whales (a third died) in Alaska in 1989, see T. Rose, *Freeing the Whales: How the Media Created the World's Greatest Non-Event* (New York: Birch Lane 1989); for a questioning look at environmental NGOs, see J. Allen, 'Anti-sealing as an Industry,' *Journal of Political Economy* 87 (April 1979): 423-8.

45 For example, see the collection of essays in J. Brecher, J. Childs, and J. Cutler, *Global Visions: Beyond the New World Order* (Montreal: Black Rose Books 1993).

46 A similar framework has appeared in two of my recent publications: *Atoms, Whales, and Rivers;* and 'Global Environmental Security, Energy Resources and Planning: A Framework and Application,' *Futures: The Journal of Forecasting, Planning and Policy* 26 (1994):741-58.

47 D. Pirages, *Global Ecopolitics: The New Context for International Relations* (North Scituate, MA: Duxbury Press 1978), 30.

48 Letter from P. Hammond, ex-chairman, IWC Scientific Committee, to R. Gambell, secretary of the IWC, 26 May 1993.

49 Keep in mind the Norwegians have consistently opposed the 1982 moratorium on all commercial whaling. S. Andresen, 'Increased Public Attention: Communication and Polarization,' in *International Resource Management: The Role of Science and Politics,* eds. S. Andresen and W. Ostreng (London: Bellhaven 1989), 37. See also Andresen's 'Science and Politics in the International Management of Whales,' *Marine Policy* 13 (1989):99-117; and M. Peterson, 'Whalers, Cetologists, Environmentalists, and the International Management of Whaling,' *International Organization* 46 (1992):147-86.

50 B. Buzan, 'New Patterns of Global Security in the Twenty-First Century,' *International Affairs* 67 (1991):433.

51 The classic text is J.E. Lovelock's *Gaia: A New Look at Life on Earth* (New York: Oxford University Press 1979). Gaia was the Greek goddess of the earth. For those interested in exploring the bond between humans and the biosphere, I highly recommend E.O. Wilson's engaging *Biophilia: The Human Bond With Other Species* (London: Cambridge University Press 1984).

52 L. Caldwell, *International Environmental Policy: Emergence and Dimensions*, 2nd ed. (Durham: Duke University Press 1990), 29.

53 N. Myers, *The Sinking Ark: A New Look at the Problem of Disappearing Species* (New York: Pergamon 1979); Kaufman and Mallory, eds., *Last Extinction*; P. Ehrlich and A. Ehrlich, *Extinction: The Causes and Consequences of the Disappearance of Species* (New York: Random House 1981); J. Swaney and P. Olson, 'The Economics of Biodiversity: Lives and Lifestyles,' *Journal of Economic Issues* XXVI (1992):1-26; and D. Paterson, *The Deluge and the Ark: A Journey into Primate Worlds* (Boston: Houghton Mifflin 1989). For an example of early denial regarding environmental problems, which is in retrospect an entertaining book, see M. Grayson and T. Shepard, Jr., *The Disaster Lobby: Prophets of Ecological Doom and Other Absurdities* (Chicago: Follett 1973).

54 Thus, the subtitle of the excellent (if already outdated) text edited by Hurrell and Kingsbury. (See Chapter 1, n. 2.)

55 For a succinct overview, see O. Holsti, 'Models of International Relations and Foreign Policy,' *Diplomatic History* 13 (1989):15-44.

56 E. Haas, *When Knowledge Is Power*, 8.

57 H. Meclo, 'Issue Networks and the Executive Establishment,' in *The New American Political System*, ed. A. King (Washington, DC: American Enterprise Institute 1978), 87-124.

58 K. Sikkink, 'Human Rights, Principled Issue-Networks, and Sovereignty in Latin America,' *International Organization* 47 (1993):411-41. Sikkink refers to H. Aldrich and D. Whetten, 'Organization-sets, Action-sets, and Networks: Making the Most of Simplicity,' in *Handbook of Organizational Design*, eds. P. Nystrom and W. Starbuck (New York: Oxford University Press 1981), 385-408; C. Jonsson, 'Interorganization Theory and International Organization,' *International Studies Quarterly* 30 (March 1986):39-57; G. Ness and S. Brechin, 'Bridging the Gap: International Organizations as Organizations,' *International Organization* 42 (Spring 1988):245-73.

59 *Oxford Dictionary* gives us the following definition of a *network:* **1** *n.* arrangement with intersecting lines and interstices; complex systems of railways, etc.; chain of interconnected persons or operations or electrical conductors; group of broadcasting stations connected for simultaneous broadcast of same programme. **2** *v.t.* broadcast thus. Today the term is often employed in the latter sense, as a verb. This usage is perhaps helpful as well, for while we might speak of governmental officials and, for example, wildlife conservation lobby groups *networking* at a meeting of the Convention on Trade in Endangered Species, we would be unlikely to speak of them 'regiming' or 'institutionalizing.' R.E. Allen, ed., *The Oxford Dictionary of Current English* (Oxford: Oxford University Press 1969), 493.

60 B. Crane, 'International Population Institutions: Adaptation to a Changing World Order,' in *Institutions for the Earth: Sources of International Environmen-*

tal Protection, eds. P. Haas, R. Keohane, and M. Levy (Cambridge, MA: MIT Press 1993), 357, n. 9. Crane refers to Hugh Meclo (see Chapter 1, n. 57) and R. Keohane and J. Nye, 'Transgovernmental Relations and International Organizations,' *World Politics* 27 (1974):39-62. A policy coalition is similar, but transcends, the concept of the epistemic community, made popular by P. Haas and others. See in particular his 'Epistemic Communities and the Dynamics of International Environmental Co-Operation,' in *Regime Theory and International Relations,* ed. Rittberger, 168-201.

61 This term was employed by William Chittick in *The Analysis of Foreign Policy Outputs* (Columbus: Merrill 1975), 6.

62 For early examples, see L. Leonard, 'The International Protection of Whales,' *American Journal of International Law* 35 (1941):90; S. Hayden, *The International Protection of Wildlife: An Examination of Treaties and Other Agreements for the Preservation of Birds and Mammals* (New York 1942); L. Caldwell, 'International Conservation Efforts: Cooperation to Protect Endangered Species and Environments,' in *In Defense of the Earth: International Protection of the Biosphere,* L. Caldwell, ed. (Bloomington: Indiana University 1972), 53-90; and L. Teclaff and A. Utton, eds., *International Environmental Law* (New York: Praeger 1974).

63 See K. Dorsey, 'Putting a Ceiling on Sealing: Conservation and Cooperation in the International Arena, 1909-1911,' *Environmental History Review* 15 (1991):27-46; and D. Ehrenfeld, *Conserving Life on Earth* (New York: Oxford University Press 1972), 18.

64 R. Boardman, *International Organisation and the Conservation of Nature* (Bloomington: Indiana University Press 1981).

65 See J. Macgregor, 'The Paradoxes of Wildlife Conservation in Africa,' *Africa Insight* 19 (1989):201-12; and M. Trexler, 'The Convention on International Trade in Endangered Species of Wild Fauna and Flora: Political or Conservation Success?' PhD dissertation, University of California, 1990. J.S. Adams and T. McShane stress the vital but often overlooked human dimension of conservation efforts in their recent *The Myth of Wild Africa: Conservation without Illusion* (New York: Norton 1992).

66 See also the chronology in Appendix A of this book.

67 R. Cox, 'Multilateralism and World Order,' *Review of International Studies* 18 (1992):178. See also I.G. Simmons, *Changing the Face of the Earth: Culture, Environment, History* (Oxford: Basil Blackwell 1989); and S. Boyden, *BioHistory: The Interplay between Human Society and the Biosphere, Past and Present* (Paris: UNESCO 1992).

68 Boardman, *International Organisation and the Conservation of Nature,* 184.

69 For an interesting, if perhaps overly hopeful, example of optimistic speculation based on past normative transition, see J. Ray, 'The Abolition of Slavery and the End of International War,' *International Organization* 43 (1989):406-39.

70 W. Catton, *Overshoot: The Ecological Basis of Revolutionary Change* (Chicago: University of Illinois 1982), 3. See also M. Soroos, 'Ecology and the Time Dimension in Human Relationships,' in *The Global Predicament: Ecological Perspectives on World Order,* eds. D. Orr and M. Soroos (Durham, NC: North Carolina University 1979), 337-43; E.B. Weiss, *In Fairness to Future Generations: International Law, Common Patrimony and Intergenerational Equity* (Dobbs Ferry,

NY: Transnational 1989); and A. D'Amato, 'Do We Owe a Duty to Future Generations to Preserve the Global Environment?' *American Journal of International Law* 84 (1990):190-8.

71 For a discussion on related legal norms that appeal to the interests of future generations, or our `temporal neighbours,' see C. Stone, 'The Law as a Force in Shaping Cultural Norms: Relating to War and the Environment,' in *Cultural Norms, War, and the Environment,* ed. A. Westing (Oxford: Oxford University Press 1988), 64-82; and A. Springer, 'International Environmental Law after Rio: The Continuing Search for Equity,' *Ethics and International Affairs* 7 (1993):117.

72 The statement of principles that emerged from the United Conference on Environment and Development (UNCED), Rio de Janeiro, Brazil, 1992. More than 150 nation-states attended, and the Declaration (though it was less strongly worded than advocates of an 'Earth Charter' would have preferred) was adopted by consensus.

73 H. Shue, 'The Unavoidability of Justice,' in *International Politics of the Environment,* eds. Hurrell and Kingsbury, 373-97.

74 See J. McNeely, K. Miller, and N.V. Reid, *Conserving the World's Biological Diversity* (Washington, DC: IUCN 1990); and J. McNeely, *Economics and Biological Diversity: Developing and Using Economic Incentives to Conserve Biological Resources* (Switzerland: IUCN 1988). Two analysts listed the four major threats to species in Europe, in order, as follows: (1) loss of habitat, (2) degeneration of environment, (3) disturbance of biological balance, and (4) pursuit by man. That all four are interrelated is obvious. R. van der Woude and A. Van Wijngaarden, *Animals in Danger: A Study of Certain Mammal Species Threatened with Extinction in Europe* (Brussels: Council of Europe 1969); see also Boardman, *International Organisation and the Conservation of Nature,* 10.

75 All three reports are described in 'Whales and Pollution,' *Globe and Mail,* 3 June 1995.

76 D.M. Johnston, 'Marine Pollution Agreements: Successes and Problems,' in *International Environmental Diplomacy: The Management and Resolution of Transfrontier Environmental Problems,* ed. J.E. Carroll (Cambridge: Cambridge University Press 1988), 205.

Chapter 2: The Whale and the Whaler

1 L. Caldwell, *International Environmental Policy: Emergence and Dimensions,* 2nd ed. (Durham: Duke University Press 1990), 286.

2 T. Foose, 'Riders of the Last Ark: The Role of Captive Breeding in Conservation Strategies,' in *The Last Extinction,* eds. Kaufman and Mallory, 141-65.

3 Measured in terms of brain-size relative to body-size, however, whales are less impressive.

4 See K. Fichtelius and S. Sjolander, *Man's Place: Intelligence in Whales, Dolphins, and Humans* (London: Gollancz 1973); and more recently M. Klinowska, 'How Brainy Are Cetaceans?' *Oceanus* 32 (1989):19-20. Most texts on cetaceans devote some space to the question of intelligence. In an appendix to the Australian government's 1978 *Inquiry into Whales and Whaling,* Myron Jacobs concludes: 'Whales as a group should be thought of as having reached a level of morphological and functional brain development in the aquatic environment

comparable to man's in his environment.' Appendix 16: 'Whale Brain and Its Intelligence Potential,' 324.

5 This point can be taken to rather extreme lengths. For example, an International Symposium on Dolphin Assisted Therapy was planned for 8-10 September 1995 in Cancun, Mexico, hosted by Dolphin Discovery and the AquaThought Foundation. Advertisement posted on the Internet via MARMAM (Marine Mammal Research and Conservation Discussion Group), 28 July 1995.

6 Nonetheless, many cetaceans, such as dolphins (including killer whales) and porpoises, and some of the smaller whales, such as narwhals and belugas, live within the 200-mile exclusive economic zones of coastal states.

7 This being said, it is clearly not a necessary condition: the African elephant, for example, attracts much attention despite being confined to a few sub-Saharan African states.

8 Quoted in D. Francis, *The Great Chase: A History of World Whaling* (Toronto: Penguin 1990), 207. How creatures that have survived quite well on their own for over thirty million years became 'wards' of humanity is not yet scientifically understood.

9 M.B. Fenton, 'Species Impoverishment,' in *Planet Earth: Problems and Prospects,* eds. J. Leith, R. Price, and J. Spencer (Montreal and Kingston: McGill-Queen's University Press 1995), 83-110. See also P. Ehrlich and A. Ehrlich, *Extinction* (New York: Wiley 1986); N. Eldredge, *The Miner's Canary: Unravelling the Mysteries of Extinction* (New York: Prentice-Hall 1991); and P. Colinvaux, *Why Big Fierce Animals Are Rare: An Ecologist's Perspective* (Princeton, NJ: Princeton University Press 1978).

10 See D. Jablonski, 'Mass Extinctions: New Answers, New Questions,' in *Last Extinction,* eds. Kaufman and Mallory, 47-68.

11 Jablonski, 'Mass Extinctions,' 52.

12 L. Kaufman, 'Why the Ark is Sinking,' 43. See also Kaufman's 'Catastrophic Change in Species-Rich Freshwater Ecosystems: The Lessons of Lake Victoria,' *Bioscience* 42 (1992):846-58; and Y. Baskin, 'Africa's Troubled Waters: Fish Introductions and a Changing Physical Profile Muddy Lake Victoria's Future,' *Bioscience* 42 (1992):476-81.

13 T. Foose, 'Raiders of the Last Ark: The Role of Captive Breeding in Conservation Strategies,' in *Last Extinction,* eds. Kaufman and Mallory, 149-78.

14 J. Scarff, 'Ethical Issues in Whale and Small Cetacean Management,' *Environmental Ethics* 2 (1980):244, n. 14.

15 L.H. Matthews, *The Life of Mammals: Volume One* (London: Weidenfield and Nicolson 1969), 67-8.

16 For an extensive survey of whale types, see S.W. Tinker, *Whales of the World* (Honolulu: Bess 1988). A classic text is A.B. Howell's *Aquatic Mammals: Their Adaptations to Life in the Water* (New York: Dover 1930). Several other books on whale anatomy and behaviour have been consulted for this book, and are listed in the bibliography. Used along with Tinker for this survey is N. Bonner's *Whales of the World* (New York: Facts on File 1989).

17 See C.S. Baker and S.R. Palumbi, 'Which Whales Are Hunted? A Molecular Genetic Approach to Monitoring Whaling,' *Science* 265 (9 September 1994): 1,538-9.

18 The following is taken largely from K.R. Allen's *Conservation and Management of Whales* (London: Butterworths 1980). This book remains an essential text from the scientific side of the debate. Allen was in fact one of the 'Committee of Three' commissioned by the IWC to study cetacean management in the early 1960s, and which led to the abolishment of the disastrous Blue Whale Unit, which allowed whalers to take whales according to a rough size equivalence to blue whales.

19 Ibid., 64-81.

20 Ibid., 67.

21 For example, S.W. Tinker reports that in sperm whales 'an occasional ossified thigh bone (femur)' has been found, and one Sperm was found with 'a rudimentary stump of the hind leg ... projecting from the surface of the body.' *Whales of the World*, 18.

22 Ibid., 188.

23 Different communities (groups of pods) can be recognized by their acoustic variations. One group of researchers, working off the west coast of British Columbia, Canada, and Washington State, USA, has concluded that a third type of community exists, which they have provisionally labelled 'offshore.' This type of community is seldom seen near protected coastal waters and is thought to engage in a 'piscivorous lifestyle. However, the possibility that they also take marine mammals cannot be ruled out.' J. Ford, G. Ellis, and K. Balcomb, *Killer Whales: The Natural History and Genealogy of* Orcinus orca *in British Columbia and Washington State* (Vancouver and Seattle: UBC Press and University of Washington Press 1994), 20.

24 H. Marsh and T. Kasuya, 'An Overview of the Changes in the Role of a Female Pilot Whale with Age,' in *Dolphin Societies: Discoveries and Puzzles,* eds. K. Pryor and K. Norris (Berkeley: University of California Press 1991), 281-5; see the accompanying discussion by the editors, 'Some Thoughts on Grandmothers.'

25 At the 1995 Meeting, the IWC called upon the Home Rule government of the Faroe Islands to use alternative methods in the drivery, away from the gaffs.

26 James Fairley, *Irish Whales and Whaling* (Belfast: Blackstaff 1981), 54. We should note that when we speak of a 'rare' species, the reference is to a species that, insofar as is scientifically known, occurs rarely in the natural world. This term is quite different from extinct, or endangered, or threatened – designations that imply that species were once abundant in the natural world, but have been reduced for a variety of reasons. Of course, it is often the case that a rare species, especially when it comes to exotic plants and animals, will be highly desired and therefore become thrreatened by poaching or illegal trade. In these cases, a rare species becomes endangered very quickly.

27 At one point, belugas were killed by fishermen since they were perceived as competitors, but this practice has supposedly stopped.

28 P.A. Weaver, 'The 1987 Beluga *Delphinapterus leucas* Harvest,' Department of Fisheries and Oceans Central and Arctic Region, Winnipeg, 1991, report no. 2,097.

29 *Globe and Mail*, 30 March 1994. See also the 'Interdepartmental Action Plan to Favour the Survival of the St. Lawrence Beluga Whale,' Department of Fisheries and Oceans, Ottawa, 1991.

30 In particular, the great migration of thousands of narwhals on the eastern side of Baffin Island in the second week of August is famous. During spring migrations northwards, the males leave first, followed several days later by the females and calves. See J.T. Strong, 'Reported Harvests of Narwhal, Beluga and Walrus in the Northwest Territories, 1948-1987,' Department of Fisheries and Oceans Central and Arctic Region, Winnipeg, *Canadian Data Report of Fisheries and Aquatic Sciences* 734 (1988).

31 For a lovely photoessay, see F. Bruemmer's *The Narwhal: Unicorn of the Sea* (Toronto: Key Porter 1993).

32 We should note that the sperm whale family (Physeteridae) includes the uncommon pygmy and dwarf sperm whales (*Kogia breviceps, kogia simus*). For a very old text, see T. Beale, *The Natural History of the Sperm Whale* (London: Holland Press 1839); and also P.B. Best, 'The Biology of the Sperm Whale as it Relates to Stock Management,' in *The Whale Problem: A Status Report,* ed. W.E. Schevill (Cambridge, MA: Harvard University Press 1974), 257-93.

33 Amazingly, as Bonner reports, even 'deeper ascents have been deduced from the discovery of fresh specimens of bottom-dwelling sharks in the stomach of a sperm whale which was shot in an area where the depth of water was in excess of 3,200 m' (10,400 feet or almost two miles). Bonner, *Whales of the World,* 89-90.

34 See P. Best, 'Social Organization in Sperm Whales,' in *Behaviour of Marine Mammals, Volume Three: Cetaceans,* eds. H. Winn and B. Olla (New York: Plenum 1979), 273-80.

35 An interesting question surrounds the temporary stoppage of the sperm hunt from the 1860s until after the Second World War. Did the replacement of former sperm products (most importantly, mineral oil – kerosene – replaced sperm oil for lighting) result in a severe drop in demand, or was the species approaching extinction and therefore no longer commercially viable? Evidence exists for both arguments. We also wonder what rate of recovery was in evidence in the intervening non-hunting years. Since early whaling records remain sketchy (despite dedicated work by historians in the field), it is difficult to answer any of these questions.

36 This is in itself an amazing bit of zoology detective work; see Bonner, *Whales of the World,* 89-93. A British biologist, Malcolm Clarke, 'suggested that a mechanism might exist for flushing water through the right nasal passage, which, with its expanded sacs at the front and the back of the spermaceti organ, would be well fitted to act as a useful heat-exchanger. This would cool the spermaceti, increasing its specific gravity and causing the whale to become less buoyant ... Conversely, warming it again will cause it to rise ... By ceasing to circulate water through the nasal passages, and by vaso-constriction at the skin surface, it will cease to lose heat. Any activity of the trunk muscles will cause heat to accumulate and this can be transferred to the spermaceti organ via the blood.' Bonner, *Whales of the World,* 90.

37 A.A. Berzin, *The Sperm Whale (Kashalot),* trans. E.H.Z. Blake (Jerusalem: Israel Program for Scientific Translations/Keter Press 1972), 325. The term 'cachalot' does not refer to the catching abilities of sperm whale hunters; rather, it derives from the latin *quichal* or from the Spanish *quixal,* referring to teeth and jaw.

38 'Indian Band Applies for Grey Whale Hunt,' *Vancouver Sun*, 23 May 1995.
39 Bonner, *Whales of the World*, 75.
40 C.W. Clark, 'Acoustic Behaviour of Mysticete Whales,' in *Sensory Abilities of Cetaceans*, eds. J. Thomas and R. Kastelein (New York: Plenum Press 1990), 571-83. Clark lists an extensive bibliography of related scientific publications.
41 Ibid., 574. See for example, A. Alling and R. Payne, 'Song of the Indian Ocean Blue Whale, *Balaenoptera musculuc*,' in *Special Issue on the Indian Ocean Sanctuary*, ed. S. Leatherwood (Cambridge: International Whaling Commission 1990); D. Ljungblad et al., 'Underwater Sounds Recorded from Migrating Bowhead Whales, *Balaena mysticetus*,' *Journal of the Acoustics Society of America* 71 (1982):477-82; R. Payne and S. McVay, 'Songs of Humpback Whales,' *Science* 173 (1971):583-97; and R. Payne's *Communication and Behaviour of Whales* (Boulder, CO: Westview 1983).
42 Breaching involves flinging the entire body out of the water and crashing down; killers also do this on occasion. Finning involves flapping the fin against the water; in the humpback's case, this movement creates a substantial impact. Lob-tailing involves smacking the tail in a similar manner. There is considerable debate over what these variations imply; despite the wealth of knowledge accumulated about modern whales, we are still unsure whether these activities express joy or hostility. See L. King and H. Wynn, *Wings in the Sea: The Humpback Whale* (Hanover: University Press of New England 1985).
43 See J. Lien and B. Merdsoy, 'The Humpback Is Not Over the Hump,' *Natural History* 88 (1979):46-9.
44 'Singing the Blues for the Blues,' *U.S. News and World Report*, 3 July 1989.
45 Hawes continues: 'As a matter of fact, sperm oil is distinctly superior to any other whale oil, and the bowhead, which is really only a larger right whale, has the longest and finest "bone" there is, but the name "right" was given to the North Atlantic fellow long before either of these other whales were known.' C.B. Hawes, *Whaling* (Garden City, NY: Doubleday, Page and Co. 1924), 2-3; courtesy of the AJT Taylor Arctic Collection, University of British Columbia.
46 In death, the cooling ability is lost. L.H. Matthews has written of what whalers 'term a "burnt whale," for when they cut it up the blackened flesh falls away from the bone like an enormous Irish stew.' *The Life of Mammals*, 132. Beached whales suffer from this heat effect as well.
47 G.P. Donovan, 'The IWC and the Revised Management Procedure,' paper written for the Conference on Responsible Wildlife Resource Management, 29-30 June 1993, European Parliament, Brussels.
48 See C. De Jong, 'The Hunt of the Greenland Whale: A Short History and Statistical Sources,' in *Special Issue on Historical Whaling Records* (Cambridge: International Whaling Commission 1983), 83-106. In the same volume, see also J. Bockstoce and D. Botkin, 'The Historical Status and Reduction of the Western Arctic Bowhead Whale (*Balaena mystocetus*) Population by the Pelagic Whaling Industry,' 107-41; and C.D. Evans and L.S. Underwood, 'How Many Bowheads?' *Oceanus* 21 (1978):17-23.
49 Francis, *The Great Chase*, 40.
50 G. Kent, 'Ocean Fisheries Management,' in *Global Predicament*, eds. Orr and Soroos, 240.

51 R. Webb, *On the Northwest: Commercial Whaling in the Pacific Northwest, 1790-1967* (Vancouver: UBC Press 1988), 83.

52 See K. Watt, *Ecology and Resource Management* (New York: McGraw-Hill 1968); C. Clark, 'The Economics of Overexploitation,' *Science* 181 (1973):630-4; and the classic book by G. Small, *The Blue Whale* (New York: Columbia 1971).

53 They continue: 'Nature is conceived as a mechanism that exists to serve humans, and subject to improvement by them, or as an adversary to be conquered (e.g., Francis Bacon).' F. Sagasti and M. Colby, 'Eco-Development Perspectives on Global Change from Developing Countries,' in *Global Accord: Environmental Challenges and International Responses,* ed. N. Choucri (Cambridge, MA: MIT Press 1993), 181-2.

54 A short list would include Webb, *On the Northwest;* E. Stackpole, *Whales and Destiny: The Rivalry between America, France, and Britain for Control of the Southern Whale Fishery, 1785-1825* (Amherst: University of Massachusetts Press 1972); D. Francis, *Arctic Chase: A History of Whaling in Canada's North* (Toronto: Breakwater 1984); J.R. Bockstoce, *Whales, Ice, and Men: The History of Whaling in the Western Arctic* (Seattle: University of Washington Press 1986); G. Jackson, *The British Whaling Trade* (London: Adam and Charles Nlack 1978); R. Harrison, 'History of Whaling,' in *Whales, Dolphins and Porpoises,* eds. M. Bryden and R. Harrison (London: Merehurst 1988), 182-95; A. Barrow, 'The North-East Coast Whale Fishery, 1750-1850,' PhD dissertation, Council for National Academic Awards (UK), 1989; C. Sanger, 'The Origins of the Scottish Northern Whale Fishery,' PhD dissertation, University of Dundee, 1985; and what is probably the most widely read and authoritative, if outdated, J. Tonnessen and A. Johnsen, *The History of Modern Whaling,* trans. by R. Christophersen (Los Angeles: University of California Press 1982).

55 Hawes, *Whaling,* 17.

56 F.D. Ommanney, *Lost Leviathan* (London: Hutchinson 1971), 82.

57 Hawes, *Whaling,* 16.

58 J. McDevitt, *The House of Rotch: Massachusetts Whaling Merchants, 1734-1828* (New York: Garland 1986), 160-2.

59 Ibid., 172.

60 Hawes, *Whaling,* 22.

61 Hawes, *Whaling,* 24. We must be careful with these figures, of course, since it is unlikely they are in any way exact. Nonetheless, the widespread consensus among whaling historians is that the Dutch were at this time the dominant whalers, just as they were in many respects the dominant maritime nation.

62 De Jong, 'The Hunt of the Greenland Whale.' We should note also that, as a result of the Dutch decline, the British intensified their whaling efforts.

63 Ibid., 83. The 'peace-and-war cycle' common to naval affairs also put stress on the contractual relationship between seamen and their employers. See A. Gifford, 'The Economic Organization of 17th through mid-19th Century Whaling and Shipping,' *Journal of Economic Behaviour and Organization* 20 (1993):137-51.

64 P. Best, 'Sperm Whale Stock Assessments and the Relevance of Historical Whaling Records,' in *Special Issue on Historical Whaling Records* (Cambridge:

International Whaling Commission 1983), 41. This fascinating book not only gives considerable detail about early deep-sea whaling, but also serves as an excellent example of historical methodology-in-the-making. Old whaling ships' logs were examined in a workshop at the Kendall Whaling Museum in Sharon, Massachusetts, and experts from various disciplines offered their opinion of the manuscript's usefulness. In total, an inventory identified 5,018 manuscript logbooks and journals held in eighty-two public collections located throughout the world. Of course, great records of much whaling, including aboriginal whaling in both hemispheres, have been lost.

65 See J. Williams and R. Nowak, 'Vanishing Species in Our Own Backyard: Extinct Fish and Wildlife of the United States and Canada,' in *Last Extinction,* eds. Kaufman and Mallory, 109.

66 See J.-P. Proulx, 'Basque Whaling in Labrador in the Sixteenth Century' (Ottawa: Environment Canada, Parks Service, and National Historic Sites 1993)

67 Webb, *On the Northwest,* 142.

68 The current scientific editor of the IWC, G.P. Donovan, believes the invention of the stern slipway was the most decisive invention leading to modern commercial whaling. Donovan, 'The IWC and the Revised Management Procedure.'

69 C.B. Hawes claims that early 'Norwegians are said to have used poisoned harpoons [against the fin whale], long before the days of the harpoon gun, the poison consisting of the decaying flesh of a dead whale and promptly setting up septicaemia' (blood poisoning). *Whaling,* 6.

70 S. Dribble, *History and General Views of the Sandwich Islands Mission* (New York: Taylor and Didd 1839), 101. In the 1854 *Whalemen's Shipping List and Merchant's Transcript,* published in New Bedford every Tuesday morning, alongside advertisements for harpoons and other supplies, we found an advertisement for 'Vallet's Great remedies – for Safe, Speedy, and permanent cure of Gonorrhoea Strictures, Gleet, Seminal weakness, and all disorders of the Urinary regions.' 1 August 1854.

71 See E. Mitchell, 'Potential of Whaling Logbook Data for Studying Aspects of Social Structure in the Sperm Whale, *Physeter macrocephalus*, with an example: The Ship *Mariner* to the Pacific, 1936-1840,' in *Special Issue on Historical Whaling Records,* 63-80.

72 B.C. Busch, *'Whaling Will Never Do For Me': The American Whaleman in the Nineteenth Century* (Lexington: Kentucky University Press 1994), 22-3.

73 Ibid, 31-3.

74 Ibid, 14-15. Barks were large three-masted vessels, around 100 feet.

75 See P. Chapman, *Trouble on Board: The Plight of International Seafarers* (Ithaca: Cornell University Press 1992). An early assessment was Richard Dana's *Two Years Before the Mast,* originally printed in 1840 but reprinted (New York: P.F. Collier) in 1937.

76 Bonner, *Whales of the World,* 176.

77 Hawes, *Whaling,* 42.

78 Busch, *'Whaling Will Never Do For Me,'* 48.

79 Hawes, *Whaling* 332.

80 Francis, *The Great Chase,* 208.

81 Ibid., 210.
82 G. Jackson, *The British Whaling Trade* (Hamden: Archon 1978).
83 See the official text in Appendix B of this book.
84 R.M. M'Gonigle, 'Economics, Ecology, and the Endangered Whale: Competing Foundations for Environmental Law and Politics,' *Ecology Law Quarterly* 9 (1980):132-3.
85 Using an interesting metaphor, Cherfas writes that 'America pulled the IWC's teeth in the first place, and ... now provides the IWC's only dentition,' by way of the sanctions discussed here. J. Cherfas, *The Hunting of the Whale: A Tragedy that Must End* (London: Bodley Head 1988), 3. To add to the irony, one nation demanding a more tightly binding original convention was Norway, whose whaling lobby would later cry foul when the IWC turned preservationist and which in 1992 unilaterally declared it would disregard the regime. In fact the unilateral Norwegian Whaling Act of 1929 was a precursor of international regulation (Francis, *The Great Chase*, 208).
86 See Peterson, 'Whalers, Cetologists, Environmentalists,' for a discussion of this 'epistemic community.' This may not be an accurate identification, since the broader 'community' of cetologists and marine biologists is large, and includes researchers with different ideological, if not epistemological, orientations towards whales and whaling.
87 When first used by an international whaling cartel in the 1930s, one BWU = 3 humpbacks or 5 sei whales. In 1944, one BWU = 2 fins, 2.5 humpbacks, or 6 sei whales.
88 MSY is now a common term in conservation circles. The MSY is calculated based on a 'model of biological growth that assumes that at any given population level less than a certain level K, a surplus production exists that can be harvested in perpetuity without altering the stock level. If the surplus is not harvested ... this causes a corresponding increase in the stock level, which ultimately approaches the environmental carrying capacity K, where surplus production is reduced to zero.' Colin Clark, *Mathematical Bioeconomics: The Optimal Management of Renewable Resources* (New York: John Wiley 1976), 1. This model makes sense, although in this crude formulation it ignores other variables, such as the effects of a deteriorating environment. The MSY is usually considered to be between 40 and 60 per cent of the environmental carrying capacity. This estimate assumes, of course, that scientists can possess concrete knowledge concerning longevity, population dynamics (pre-exploitation population levels, for example), mating habits, and many other factors. As even those most expert in the field readily admit, little of this knowledge is possessed by anyone in the case of Cetacea. Worse, in the fisheries in general, MSY was criticized for encouraging 'a level of effort that promoted, if not assured, overinvestment.' M.J. Peterson, 'International Fisheries Management,' in *Institutions for the Earth: Sources of Effective International Environmental Protection*, eds. P. Haas, R. Keohane, and M. Levy (Cambridge, MA: MIT Press 1994), 269.
89 Allen, *Conservation and Management of Whales*, 83.
90 S. Frost, *Inquiry into Whales and Whaling* (Canberra: Government of Australia 1978), 30.

91 A similar exercise in conservation/compensation occurred in 1911 after the signing of the Convention for the Preservation and Protection of Fur Seals between Japan, Russia, and the UK (Canada). Pelagic sealing was driving the seals to dangerously low levels. Hunting was allowed only on specific breeding islands, and Japan and Canada received 15 per cent of the seal skins as compensation for giving up the right to hunt whales at sea. The seal population recovered, though whaling became an alternative. FAO, *Marine Fisheries and the Law of the Sea: A Decade of Change* 853 (Rome: FAO Fisheries Circular 1993).

92 Francis, *The Great Chase,* 248-9.

93 Busch, *'Whaling Will Never Do for Me,'* 4-5. Busch obtained these prices from Michael Haines, 'An Economic Analysis and Statistical View of the American Whaling Industry, 1790-1860,' unpublished paper, 1968.

94 Clark, *Mathematical Bioeconomics,* 4.

Chapter 3: Cetapolitics

1 *Globe and Mail,* 15 May 1993.

2 This phrase is common. For example, see Cherfas, *Hunting of the Whale.*

3 Bureau of International Whaling Statistics, *International Whaling Statistics* LXI (Oslo 1968), 8. This kill was achieved with an army of 48 shore stations, 26 'floating factories,' and 444 catcherboats. However, the figure is probably low, given recent revelations concerning under-reporting by the Soviet Union during this time.

4 In fact, it was originally believed that the IWC would become a United Nations agency. Thus Article III:6 of the ICRW: 'Desiring to avoid duplication of functions, the Contracting Governments will consult among themselves within two years after the coming into force of this Convention to decide whether the Commission shall be brought within the framework of a specialized agency related to the United Nations.' For the complete text, see Appendix B of this book.

5 J.L. McHugh, 'The Role and History of the International Whaling Commission,' in *The Whale Problem: A Status Report,* ed. W. Schevill (Cambridge: Harvard University Press 1974), 318.

6 The original text of the convention can also be found in H. Degenhardt, 'Organisations for the Preservation of the Living Resources of the Sea,' *Treaties and Alliances of the World,* 4th ed. (Detroit: Gale 1986), 102.

7 See Y. Hirasawa, 'The Whaling Industry in Japan's Economy,' in *The Whaling Issue in US-Japan Relations,* eds. J. Schmidhauser and G. Totten (Boulder, CO: Westview 1978), 82-114.

8 Quoted in R. McClung, *Hunted Mammals of the Sea* (New York: Morrow 1978), 40. Iceland, by withdrawing from the IWC in 1992, is trying to prove his point.

9 See W. Rowland, *The Plot to Save the World: The Life and Times of the Stockholm Conference on the Human Environment* (Toronto: Clarke 1973).

10 See Caldwell, *International Environmental Policy,* 37 and 286; and D. Day, *The Whale War* (Vancouver: Douglas and McIntyre 1987), 16.

11 Rep. of the UN ConHE, UN Doc. A/Conf.48/14 Rev. 1.

12 Haas, Keohane, and Levy, *Institutions for the Earth,* 6.
13 I have found Dr. Gambell especially helpful while researching this book. He epitomizes the diplomatic skill and discretion needed in the tricky world of international organization. He was engaged in fisheries research from 1957 to 1963 before turning to full-time cetology at the Whale Research Unit, Institute of Oceanographic Sciences, Natural History Museum in London, from 1963 to 1976. He was a scientific adviser and member of the British delegation to the IWC from 1965 to 1975. Among other works, see his 'International Management of Whales and Whaling,' *Arctic* 46 (1993):97-107; and 'Bowhead Whales and Alaskan Eskimos: A Problem of Survival,' *Polar Record* 21 (1983):467-73.
14 See M'Gonigle, 'Economics, Ecology, and the Endangered Whale,' 190, n 2. Seychelles is an island in the western Indian Ocean. It gained independence from Britain in 1976, is governed by a fairly closed political system, and has 65,000 inhabitants. The Americans maintain a large satellite tracking station there. Seychelles withdrew from the IWC in 1994 when funding for IWC activities was cut. According to Director General G. Troian, Ministry of Foreign Affairs, Planning and Environment, Division of Environment, the Seychellian government has satisfied itself 'that most of the major objectives for which it had pugnaciously fought had been achieved [and thus] decided to shift its priorities and withdraw.' Personal correspondence with the author, 6 March 1995.
15 P. Birnie, 'The Role of Developing Countries in Nudging the International Whaling Commission from Regulating Whaling to Encouraging Non-consumptive Uses of Whales,' *Ecology Law Quarterly* 12 (1985):957.
16 Ibid., 962.
17 Kate O'Connell, international conservation director of the British Whale and Dolphin Conservation Society, claims that 'the quickest way to get guaranteed aid from Japan is to say, "I'm interested in the whaling issue."' Quoted in A. Pollack, 'Commission to Save Whales Endangered, Too,' *New York Times,* 18 May 1993.
18 Recommendation One says that, with the 'exception to take, in appropriate circumstances, a limited number of dolphins live for display purposes' whaling should cease; and Recommendation Seven suggests Australia 'seek to achieve a worldwide ban on whaling.' The Inquiry has been reproduced and published by Friends of the Earth (San Francisco) and the Whale Coalition in 1979.
19 Fifteenth Session, Christchurch, New Zealand, 11-23 October 1981; quoted in B. Raster and B. Simma, eds., *International Protection of the Environment: Treaties and Related Documents,* Second Series (New York: Oceana 1989), 20.
20 S. Lyster, *International Wildlife Law: An Analysis of International Treaties Concerned with the Conservation of Wildlife* (Cambridge: Grotius 1985), 39; see also P. Birnie, 'The Development of the International Regulation of Whaling: Its Relation to the Emerging Law of Conservation of Marine Mammals,' PhD dissertation, University of Edinburgh, 1979. Of course, some maritime international organizations serve functionalist roles above or beyond the LOSC, such as the Intergovernmental Maritime Consultative Organization and the International Oceanographic Commission.

21 On the CCAMLR, see J. Barnes, 'Legal Aspects of Environmental Protection in Antarctica,' in *The Antarctic Legal Regime,* eds. C. Joyner and S. Chopra (Dordrecht: Martinus Nijhoff 1988), 241-68; and J. Barnes, 'The Emerging Convention on the Conservation of Antarctic Marine Living Resources: An Attempt to Meet the New Realities of Resource Exploitation in the Southern Ocean,' in *The New Nationalism and the Use of Common Spaces: Issues in Marine Pollution and the Exploitation of Antarctica,* ed. J. Charney (New Jersey: Allanheld 1982), 239-86.

22 Brenton, *Greening of Machiavelli,* 212.

23 J. Adams chronicles the transition of some Caribbean hunters in the Grenadine Islands in 'Last of the Caribbean Whalemen,' *Natural History* 103 (November 1994):64-73.

24 Interview with R. Gambell, 22 April 1992.

25 Day, *Whale War,* 38.

26 Ibid., 73-7.

27 For an argument supporting the right to indigenous whaling, see N. Doubleday, 'Aboriginal Subsistence Whaling: The Right of Inuit to Hunt Whales and Implications for International Environmental Law,' *Denver Journal of International Law and Policy* 17 (1989):373-93; and for a reply, see A. D'Amato and S. Chopra, 'Whales: Their Emerging Right to Life,' *American Journal of International Law* 85 (1991):21-62.

28 The Schedule reads: 'It is forbidden to use a whale catcher attached to a factory ship for the purpose of killing or attempting to kill baleen whales in the waters south of 40 degrees South Latitude from 70 degrees West Longitude westwards as far as 160 degrees West Longitude.' International Whaling Commission, 'Whale Sanctuaries and the IWC,' press release, July 1994.

29 Scarff, 'Ethical Issues in Whale and Small Cetacean Management,' 279, n. 172.

30 Institute of Cetacean Research, 'Sustainable Utilization and Conservation of Minke Whales,' Tokyo, n.d.

31 Press release from the Office of the Minister of Foreign Affairs and Trade, Parliament Buildings, Wellington, New Zealand, 26 May 1994.

32 See the Government of New Zealand, 'Official Report: A Celebration,' First International Conference on the Southern Ocean Whale Sanctuary, Viaduct Basin, Auckland, 15-16 October 1995.

33 Press release from the Office of the Minister of Foreign Affairs and Trade, Parliament Buildings, Wellington, New Zealand, 15 February 1995.

34 Pearce, *Green Warriors,* 227-8.

35 P. Weber, 'Protecting Oceanic Fisheries and Jobs,' in *State of the World 1995,* eds. L. Brown et al. (London: Earthscan 1995), 29.

36 This information is from Josse Truda Palazzo, president of the International Wildlife Coalition of Brasil. Palazzo claims further that the military regime of General Joao Baptista de Figueiredo (1979-85) voted with Japanese interests in order to obtain 'goodwill' in financial aid. Personal communication, 26 July 1995. An attempt to contact the IWC commissioner for Brazil failed; my communication got as far as Rubens Antonio Barbosa, Brazilian ambassador to the United Kingdom, who forwarded my questions to the Environment Department of the Brazilian Ministry of Foreign Affairs, from where they have yet to surface.

37　Bonner, *Whales of the World*, 29-30.
38　Personal communication, 31 July 1995. The JWA was originally established to represent large commercial coastal whalers, as well as the high seas whaling companies, both of which were dissolved in 1988. The JWA has a relatively smaller base of support now, though firm answers to questions about its funding sources remain rather elusive.
39　Weber, 'Protecting Oceanic Fisheries and Jobs,' 35. See also K. Ruddle, 'The Continuity of Traditional Management Practices: The Case of Japanese Coastal Fisheries,' in *The Traditional Knowledge and Management of Coastal Systems in Asia and the Pacific*, eds. R. Johannes and K. Ruddle (Jakarta Pusat, Indonesia: UNESCO 1985).
40　N. Yagi, assistant director, Far Seas Fisheries Division, Fisheries Agency, Government of Japan, personal communication, March 1995.
41　See for example M. Soroos, 'Global Interdependence and the Responsibilities of States: Learning from the Japanese Experience,' *Journal of Peace Research* 25 (1988):17-29.
42　Ronald Reagan quoted in R. Buckley, *US-Japan Alliance Diplomacy 1945-1990* (Cambridge: Cambridge University Press 1992), preface.
43　Bonner, *Whales of the World*, 169.
44　*Chairman's Report of the 44th Annual Meeting of the International Whaling Commission* (Cambridge: International Whaling Commission 1992), 11.
45　See for example: E. Linden, 'Sharpening the Harpoons,' *Time*, 24 May 1993; and then M. Lemonick, 'The Hunt, the Furor,' *Time*, 2 August 1993. Meanwhile an occasionally interesting Usenet discussion can be found at (the unfortunately named) alt.kill.the whales.
46　This argument is specious and we needn't treat it in any depth here.
47　*Times*, 14 May 1990.
48　Information posted on the Marine Mammal Research and Conservation Internet Discussion Group (MARMAM@UVVM!BITNET) by Gene Buck, Congressional Research Service, Library of Congress, Washington, DC, 6 July 1995.
49　'Greenpeace and Minke Whales,' *Globe and Mail*, 8 April 1995.
50　Norway's rejection of membership has caused considerable diplomatic dismay in Europe. See P. Koring, 'Europe Split over Norwegian Rejection,' *Globe and Mail*, 30 November 1994. The plebiscite, which drew an 88.6 per cent turnout, drew 52.2 per cent 'no' votes. The turnout was 'the highest since 1905, when nearly every Norwegian who was able to vote cast a ballot for independence and the end of union with Sweden.' On the whaling issue, see P. Davies, 'Legality of Norwegian Commercial Whaling under the Whaling Convention and Its Compatibility with European Community Law,' *International and Comparative Law Quarterly* 270 (1994):270-95.
51　Cherfas, *Hunting of the Whale*, 183.
52　D. Caron, 'The IWC and the North Atlantic Marine Mammal Commission: The Institutional Risks of Coercion in Consensus Structures,' *American Journal of International Law* 89 (1995):154-74. This excellent article addresses the question of IWC legitimacy given the establishment of NAMMCO and the resumption of Norwegian whaling.
53　Ibid., 165.

54 On an earlier boycott of Icelandic products, see 'Greenpeace Hurting Iceland Canners Most, But Frozen Whitefish Producers Also Hit,' Quick Frozen Foods International, *Global Seafood Magazine*, April 1989.

55 See A. Bryden, 'The Eye of the Guest: Icelandic Nationalist Discourse and the Whaling Issue,' PhD dissertation, McGill University, 1991.

56 See A. Knight, *The KGB: Police and Politics in the Soviet Union* (Boston: Allen and Unwin 1988).

57 This point is of course an Associated Press error, since the commission did not exist in the 1930s; however, the ban on right whale kills did.

58 'Soviets Lied about Size of Whale Catch, Russian Finds' (Associated Press), *Globe and Mail*, 21 February 1994. See also N. Angier, 'DNA Tests Find Meat of Endangered Whales for Sale in Japan,' *New York Times*, 13 September 1994, who reports that from 1948 to 1973, the Soviet Union killed 48,477 humpbacks rather than the 2,710 it officially reported to the IWC.

59 Summary Report of the 1995 IWC Meeting, United States Delegation. I am especially grateful to Kevin Chu of the US Department of Commerce National Oceanic and Atmospheric Administration for making a copy of this document available.

60 R. Paarlberg, 'Ecodiplomacy: US Environmental Policy Goes Abroad,' in *Eagle in a New World: American Grand Strategy in the Post-Cold War Era*, ed. Kenneth Oye (New York: HarperCollins 1992), 212. Paarlberg notes that during the first term of the anti-regulatory presidency of Ronald Reagan, American international environmental policies were not even strong enough to qualify as convenient.

61 See especially M'Gonigle, 'Economics, Ecology, and the Endangered Whale: Competing Foundations for Environmental Law and Politics,' 190.

62 See W. Schevill, ed., *The Whale Problem: A Status Report*.

63 R. Haskell, 'Abandoning Recent Whale Conservation Initiatives in Japan Whaling Association v. American Catacean Society,' *Harvard Environmental Law Review* 11 (1987):558-9.

64 See Cherfas, *Hunting of the Whale*, 128; Haskell, 'Abandoning Recent Whale Conservation Initiatives in Japan Whaling Association v. American Catacean Society,' 561; Lyster, *International Wildlife Law*, 35.

65 See D. Caron, 'International Sanctions, Ocean Management, and the Law of the Sea: A Study of Denial of Access to Fisheries,' *Ecological Law Quarterly*, 16 (1989):311-54; and Day, *Whale War*, 81-3.

66 S. Larson, 'U.S. Whale Policy: The Judiciary Casts Its Vote in Favor of a Moderate Approach,' *Vanderbilt Journal of Transnational Law* 20 (1990):123-59. See also Haskell, 'Abandoning Recent Whale Conservation Initiatives in Japan Whaling Association v. American Catacean Society'; and C.S. Gibson, 'Narrow Grounds for a Complex Decision: The Supreme Court's Review of an Agency's Statutory Construction in JWA vs. American Cetacean Society,' *Ecology Law Quarterly* 14 (1987):485-516.

67 See D. Wilkinson, 'The Use of Domestic Measures to Enforce International Whaling Agreements: A Critical Perspective,' *Denver Journal of International Law and Policy* 77 (1989):271-92.

68 Day, *Whale War*, 35.

69 See the Annual Report of the U.S. Delegation to the Annual IWC Meeting, various years, submitted to the secretary of state. I have listed two of these reports in the bibliography.

70 R. Gambell is not sanguine on this issue; he senses it will be 'almost impossible to get agreement.' Personal communication, 19 July 1995.

71 Bonner, *Whales of the World*, 171.

72 Personal communication with L. Stefanini, Ministere des Affaires Étrangères, Paris, IWC commissioner for France, February 1995. He even suggested that, following the establishment of the Indian and Southern Ocean sanctuaries, another 'sanctuary should be established in the future (in the Northern Hemisphere particularly).' Mr. Stefanini made it clear that his responses to my questions could be quoted as 'official French positions.'

73 Brenton, *Greening of Machiavelli*, 126.

74 H. Fischer, Danish IWC commissioner since 1986, notes the importance of the whaling issue in two of three parts of the Kingdom of Denmark: Greenland and the Faroe Islands. While the former is accepted by the IWC as an instance of aboriginal whaling, the other is condemned, though arguably the IWC has no jurisdiction on this issue. Personal communication, January 1995.

75 'Green Laws Fall Prey to Subsidiarity,' *European*, 17 December 1993.

76 With the obvious exception of the Japanese, who feel that the IWC 'Administration's efficiency has a certain limitation because any person in the administration staff, such as the Chairman of the IWC, may be affected by national policy of his/her country.' N. Yagi, assistant director, Far Seas Fisheries Division, Fisheries Agency, Government of Japan, personal communication, March 1995.

77 The classic text on this topic is R. Barnet and R. Muller's *Global Reach: The Power of the Multinational Corporation* (New York: Simon and Schuster 1974). See also R. Gilpin, *U.S. Power and the Multinational Corporation: The Political Economy of Direct Foreign Investment* (New York: Basic Books 1975).

78 For a related chart, see C. Kegley and E. Wittkopf, *World Politics: Trend and Transformation*, 4th ed. (New York: St. Martin 1993), 194-6.

79 T. Princen, M. Finger, and J. Manno, 'Nongovernmental Organizations in World Environmental Politics,' *International Environmental Affairs* 7 (1995):42-58. See also T. Princen and M. Finger, *Environmental NGOs in World Politics: Linking the Local and the Global* (London: Routledge 1994); and K. Stairs and P. Taylor, 'Non-Governmental Organizations and Legal Protection of the Oceans: A Case Study,' in *International Politics of the Environment*, eds. Hurrell and Kingsbury, 110-41.

80 See S. Morphet, 'NGOs and the Environment,' in *'The Conscience of the World': The Influence of Non-Governmental Organisations in the UN System*, ed. P. Willetts (Washington, DC: Brookings 1996), 116-46.

81 From Pearce, *Green Warriors*, 22-3: 'Greenpeace's love affair with whales began a year after the Stockholm conference in 1973 with a renegade biologist from New Zealand called Paul Spong, who was thrown out of a job at the Vancouver Public Aquarium after publicly proclaiming that a killer whale he had been studying at the aquarium "wanted to be free" ... The Tarot card faction loved him.'

82 Ibid., 24.
83 *New York Times,* 6 June 1974. See also R. Mandel, 'Transnational Resource Conflict: The Politics of Whaling,' *International Studies Quarterly* 24 (1980):99-127; and D. Hill, 'Vanishing Giants,' *Audubon* 77 (1975):56-90. The JWA continues to maintain public relations experts in the United States.
84 P. Watson and W. Rogers, *Sea Shepherd: My Fight for Whales and Seals* (New York: W.W. Norton 1982), 17. Watson left Greenpeace in the late 1970s complaining of its bureaucratic inertia. To put it mildly, he is not well liked in Norwegian circles.
85 Day, *Whale Wars,* 53-9 and 132-3. See C. Manes, *Green Rage: Radical Environmentalism and the Unmaking of Civilization* (Boston: Little, Brown and Company 1990), esp. 107-11; and M. Bookchin, *Defending the Earth* (Montreal: Black Rose Books 1991). Watson, maintaining his celebrity, has recently been involved in overfishing protests off the Canadian Atlantic coast; he has also threatened to stop Makah band members if they do in fact resume hunting for gray whales.
86 See P. Birnie, *Legal Measures for the Prevention of 'Pirate' Whaling* (Switzerland: IUCN 1981); and C. van Note, *Outlaw Whalers: An Exposé of Unregulated Whaling Around the World* (Whale Protection Fund 1979). For American governmental investigation, see *Outlaw Whaling: Hearing Before the Committee on Commerce, Science, and Transportation,* United States Senate, 96th Congress (First Session on Whaling Operations Conducted Outside the Control of the IWC), 22 June (Washington, DC, 1979); *Review of the 34th IWC Meeting, Hearing Before the Subcommittee on Human Rights and International Organizations of the Committee on Foreign Affairs,* House of Representatives, 97th Congress, 16 September (Washington, DC, 1982); and, for a portrait of a notorious outlaw whaler, see P. Evans, *Ari: The Life and Times of Aristotle Socrates Onassis* (London: Jonathan Cape 1986).
87 E.B. Weiss, 'The Planetary Trust: Conservation and Intergenerational Equity,' *Ecology Law Quarterly* 11 (1984):572-4.
88 L. Spencer, 'The Not So Peaceful World of Greenpeace,' *Forbes,* 11 November 1991.
89 This type of media blitz has occurred, with similar success, rarely: examples related to FOE (UK) include the Windscale inquiry (June 1977), an anti-nuclear rally one year after the Harrisburg accident, and sympathizers' mailing of empty beverage cans to the prime minister (May 1981). On FOE (UK), see P. Lowe and J. Goyder, 'Friends of the Earth,' in *Environmental Groups in Politics* (London: Allen and Unwin 1983), 124-37.
90 Interview with R. Gambell, secretary of the IWC, 22 April 1992. A list published by the commission of attendees of the 41st Annual Meeting (June 1989 in San Diego) included many diverse organizations: the African Wildlife Foundation, Assembly of Rabbis (disguised 'eco-detectives' according to Day (*Whale Wars,* 21-2), Fundacao Brasileira para a Conservacao da Natureza, Save the Children, and the Women's International League for Peace and Freedom. See Table 3 for further examples.
91 C. Plowden and S. Shoup, 'Whaling,' *Greenpeace,* January/February 1990. See also R. Hunter, *Warriors of the Rainbow: A Chronicle of the Greenpeace Movement*

(New York: Holt, Rinehart and Winston 1979); and R. Hunter and R. Weyler, *To Save a Whale: The Voyages of Greenpeace* (Vancouver: Douglas and McIntyre 1978). This issue-dependency has been criticized, for example by D. Buzzelli of Dow Chemical: 'Each environmental issue group has mastered the technique of attracting and locking-in media and public attention for its single cause. As a result, the public hears a loud, mixed, emotional overload. No wonder eyes glaze over during the nightly news broadcasts.' 'Key Environmental Issues for the 1990s and Beyond in Canada and the United States,' *Canada-United States Law Journal* 18 (1992):11.

92 'Greenpeace's Corporate Blueprint,' *Globe and Mail* (originally in the *Economist*), 23 August 1995.

93 Meanwhile, M. Takeuchi was the representative of the Japanese group Riches of the Sea.

94 Lowe and Goyder, 'Friends of the Earth,' 164. The authors are referring primarily to the EEC context.

95 'IWC Supervision and Control Arrangement: New Zealand Views' (Wellington, NZ: Ministry of Foreign Affairs and Trade). I am grateful to New Zealand's commissioner for the IWC, J.K. McLay, for this and other relevant documentation regarding New Zealand policy.

96 Information supplied by A. Macnow, consultant to the Japan Whaling Association.

97 R. Barstow, 'Non-consumptive Utilization of Whales,' *Ambio* 15 (1986):155-60.

98 In a personal communication of July 1995, R. Gambell referred to the Caribbean members as having a particular concern about the implications of expanding the mandate of the IWC to include small cetaceans on their sovereignty.

99 S. Weisman, 'Whale: Food for Deep Thought, or Just Food?' *New York Times*, 4 April 1992.

Chapter 4: Whale Ethics

Another version of this chapter is forthcoming in the British journal *Environmental Values*. I am especially indebted to Ellen Chu, University of Washington, for helpful suggestions on an earlier draft.

1 B. Lopez, *Arctic Dreams* (New York: Scribners 1986); quoted from the chapter 'Lancaster Sound: *Monodon monoceros*' reprinted in F. Stewart, ed., *In the Presence of Whales: Contemporary Writings on the Whale* (Vancouver: Whitecap 1995), 156-77.

2 K.R. Allen suggests the North American gray whale population is the only whale population that can be estimated with any degree of accuracy by a direct count. *Conservation and Management of Whales*, 48; see also A. Wolman and D. Rice, 'Current Status of the Gray Whale,' *Report to the International Whaling Commission* 29 (1979):275-9.

3 H. Matthews, *The Natural History of the Whale* (London: Weidenfeld and Nicolson 1978), 126.

4 There are some variations to this route. The southward migration 'splits opposite Santa Barbara, with some whales taking the island route on to Guadeloupe and Socorro and the rest hugging the coast.' Lyall Watson, *Sea Guide to Whales of the World* (New York: E.P. Dutton 1981), 80.

5 'Indian Band Applies for Grey Whale Hunt,' *Vancouver Sun*, 23 May 1995. According to R. Gambell, both the US and the Russian Federation 'foreshadowed increased aboriginal catches' at the 1995 meeting. A formal request involves the submission of a statement of need, which explains why it is essential for affected aboriginals to whale.

6 See the Boreal Institute for Northern Studies, *Small-Type Coastal Whaling in Japan: Report of an International Workshop*, Occasional Publication 27 (Edmonton: University of Alberta 1988); and A. Kalland and B. Moeran, *Japanese Whaling: End of an Era?* (London: Scandinavian Institute of Asian Studies/Curzan Press 1992).

7 Kalland and Moeran, *Japanese Whaling*, 194.

8 Fenton, 'Species Impoverishment,' 102. He refers to J.A. Lee, 'Seals, Wolves and Words: Loaded language in Environmental Controversy,' *Alternatives* 15 (1988):20-9. For a new and fascinating treatment of the subject of the symbolic meanings of nature, see W. Cronon, ed., *Uncommon Ground: Toward Reinventing Nature* (New York: Norton 1995).

9 M. Tobias, *World War III: Population and the Biosphere at the End of the Millennium* (Sante Fe: Bear and Company 1994), 316. Tobias does not give a source for this figure.

10 F. Stewart, ed., *In the Presence of Whales*, 15.

11 Y. Kuronuma and C. Tisdell, 'Institutional Management of an International Mixed Good: The IWC and Socially Optimal Whale Harvests,' *Marine Policy* 17 (1993):235-50. Existence value is akin to non-consumptive value.

12 For example, in 1961-2, almost 70,000 large whales were killed, and this statistic does not reflect recent revelations about intentional Soviet underreporting. Bureau of International Whaling Statistics, *International Whaling Statistics*, LXI (Oslo 1968), 8.

13 Bonner, *Whales of the World*, 29.

14 Myers, 'Sharing the Earth with Whales,' 93.

15 J.E. Scarff, 'Ethical Issues in Whale and Small Cetacean Management,' *Environmental Ethics* 2 (1980):241-80.

16 P. Slurink, 'Paradox and Tragedy in Human Morality,' *International Political Science Review* 15 (1994):369. In the same interesting issue, see Mary Maxwell, 'Fact and Value in International Relations,' 379-416.

17 D. Sarokin and J. Schulkin, 'Environmental Justice: Co-evolution of Environmental Concerns and Social Justice,' *Environmentalist* 14 (1994):121-9.

18 T. Hobbes, *Leviathan*, 1651; this quote from the edition edited by C.B. MacPherson (New York: Penguin 1968), 197.

19 See P. Taylor, *Respect for Nature: A Theory of Environmental Ethics* (Princeton, NJ: Princeton University Press 1986); Arne Naess, *Ecology, Community and Lifestyle: Outline of an Ecosophy*, trans. D. Rothenberg (Cambridge: Cambridge University Press 1989); and more generally, B. Devall and G. Sessions, *Deep Ecology: Living as if Nature Mattered* (Salt Lake City: Peregrine Smith 1985).

20 Payne, *Among Whales*, 266. Payne was partially responsible for the first recordings of humpback singing, and his career has included groundbreaking studies of southern right whales in an out-of-the-way research station at Peninsula Valdes in Patagonia.

21 For a succinct discussion based on her earlier work, see E.B. Weiss, 'Intergenerational Equity: Toward an International Legal Framework,' in *Global Accord: Environmental Challenges and International Responses*, ed. N. Choucri (Cambridge, MA: MIT Press 1993), 333-54.

22 W.C. French, 'Against Biological Egalitarianism,' *Environmental Ethics* 17 (1995):56. See also D. Cooper, 'Other Species and Moral Reason,' in *Just Environments: Intergenerational, International, and Interspecies Issues*, eds. D. Cooper and J. Palmer (London: Routledge 1995), 137-48; and S. Baker, *Picturing the Beast: Animals, Identity, and Representation* (Manchester: Manchester University Press 1993).

23 For an engaging and wide discussion, see Foose, 'Raiders of the Last Ark.' S. and J. Heimlich-Boran write on killer whale captives:

> The survival rate in captivity is less than in the wild, and the mortality of captive-born calves has been high. Factors range from possible complications at birth and general poor health (even adults are susceptible to infection and disease in artificial confines), to parental inexperience. In the wild, killer whale females may gain training in calf-rearing from older females ... Females used in breeding programmes collected before maturation might simply not know how to be mothers ... Behavioral problems also arise, usually in response to undue stress caused by restraint, strained relations between tank-mates, or poor rapport with trainers ... In 1991, a trainer was hauled around a tank and drowned by an aggravated captive. In 1989, a long-standing conflict between a killer whale from the Pacific Ocean and one from Iceland ended in death, when one rammed the other ... Stress also arises from boredom and living in an artificial environment. It is difficult, if not impossible, to design a tank large enough to suit a 4 ton animal that can travel over 80 km (49.7 miles) per day in the wild. The complexity of the ocean environment can never be fully reproduced in a concrete tank, no matter how well designed. Most importantly, the social environment of the extended killer whale family is missing in captivity. *Killer Whales* (Stillwater, MN: Voyageur 1994), 62.

At any rate, larger cetaceans are clearly inappropriate for captivity.

24 The British government's report to CITES in 1979 states that a gray whale calf was kept in semi-captivity for 'a few months,' though it is unclear as to the fate of the mammal or, for that matter, what 'semi-captivity' means. Government of the United Kingdom, *Proposals Concerning the Cetacea: Second Meeting of the Conference of the Parties to CITES*, San Jose, Costa Rica, 1979.

25 I have a copy of this letter in my possession.

26 Payne: 'Unless there is a very basic change of heart among ... whaling nations, I'm betting that minke whales will simply go the way of all their relatives.' *Among Whales*, 271.

27 Letter from P. Hammond, ex-chairman, IWC Scientific Committee, to R. Gambell, secretary, IWC, 26 May 1993.

28 See F. Lynge, *Arctic Wars, Animal Rights, Endangered Peoples*, trans. M. Stenbaek (Hanover: University Press of New England 1992). Lynge focuses on what he terms the 'seal war,' the 'whale war,' and the 'trap War,' arguing all have harmed the lifestyles of Native peoples. Similarly, a recent Inuit Circumpolar Conference (Alaska, Greenland, and Canada) urged Inuits to work towards an

'overall strategy to counter the anti-harvest lobby.' *Principles and Elements for a Comprehensive Arctic Policy* (Montreal: Centre for Northern Studies and Research, McGill University 1992).

29 See in particular A. Kalland, 'Management by Totemization: Whale Symbolism and the Anti-Whaling Campaign' *Arctic: Journal of the Arctic Institute of North America* 46 (1993):124-33.

30 D. Esty, *Greening the GATT: Trade, Environment, and the Future* (Washington, DC: Institute for International Economics 1994), 188.

31 Scarff, 'Ethical Issues in Whale and Small Cetacean Management,' 248. Of course, film footage of African elephant culls is hardly an easy watch either.

32 *Chairman's Report of the 44th Annual Meeting of the International Whaling Commission*, 6-7.

33 In a recent communication, R. Gambell told me the IWC would look into whale-watching in greater detail if there were any evidence it is harming the mammals, July 1995. Meanwhile a standardized approach to whalewatching has been developing for some time now, though of course it is hardly institutionalized. See E. Hogt, *The Whale Watcher's Handbook* (Markham: Penguin 1984).

34 Press release from the National Oceanic and Atmospheric Administration Public Affairs. *U.S. Department of Commerce: News,* 14 May 1993.

35 'Historically, numerous different subsistence-based societies have traded in various commodities over long distances. The idea that true subsistence users do not think of the products they obtain from hunting, fishing and gathering as commodities is a romantic and unsubstantiated myth and serves only to confuse efforts to regulate subsistence practises.' O. Young et al., 'Subsistence, Sustainability, and Sea Mammals: Reconstructing the International Whaling Regime,' *Ocean and Coastal Management* 23 (1994):117-27.

36 *Report of the U.S. Delegation to the 45th Annual Meeting of the IWC*, Kyoto, Japan, 10-14 May 1993. Submitted to the secretary of state by Michael Tillman, acting commissioner for the US, prepared by Kevin Chu, 7. Again, note that Canada is not an IWC member, having withdrawn in 1982 when the moratorium became imminent.

37 On regimes, see our discussion in Chapter 1, and in particular, S. Krasner, *International Regimes* (Ithaca, NY: Cornell University Press 1983); and V. Rittberger, *Regime Theory and International Relations.*

38 *Report of the U.S. Delegation to the 45th Annual Meeting*, 9.

39 In Canada, the Inuit Tapirisat of Canada is an important related group. For the Tapirisat perspective, which denounces the IWC for its preservationist perspective and quite clearly insists Canada not rejoin the IWC as a full-fledged member, see the article by its president, Rosemarie Kuptana, *Globe and Mail*, 27 May 1993.

40 *Globe and Mail*, 26 September 1994.

41 Interview with K. Blankenbekar, foreign affairs specialist, Office of International Affairs, National Marine Fisheries Service, National Oceanic and Atmospheric Administration, United States Department of Commerce, Washington, DC, 23 May 1995.

42 We should note however that Norwegian scientists have admitted to overestimating northeast Atlantic populations to justify the 1994 spring hunt.

Greenpeace insists the Norwegians had originally estimated there were almost 87,000; a more realistic figure would be around 60,000. 'Greenpeace and Minke Whales,' *Globe and Mail*, 8 April 1995.

43 *Chairman's Report of the 46th Annual Meeting of the International Whaling Commission*, Puerto Vallarta, Mexico, 23-27 May; published in Cambridge, UK, October 1994. I am grateful to R. Gambell for related material.

44 'Meat from Endangered Whales Sold, Study Claims,' *Vancouver Sun*, 13 September 1994.

45 Marvin Soroos, 'Global Interdependence and the Responsibilities of States: Learning from the Japanese Experience,' *Journal of Peace Research* 25 (1988):17-29.

46 Young et al., 'Subsistence, Sustainability, and Sea Mammals,' *Ocean and Coastal Management* 23 (1994):117-27, have recommended three categories be in place: aboriginal subsistence whaling; other subsistence whaling (e.g., the pilot whale fishery in the Faroe Islands); and artisanal whaling (e.g., small-type coastal whaling in Norway, Japan, and Iceland).

47 Lyster, *International Wildlife Law*, 22.

48 These arrangements are often strengthened by bilateral agreements, such as the 'Exchange of Notes Constituting an Arrangement Relating to an International Observer Scheme For the Whaling Station at Cheynes Beach in Western Australia,' UN Doc. 17495, UN Treaty Series Vol. 1124 (1979), 43-8; or the 'Agreement Between the USA and Japan Concerning an International Observer Scheme For Whaling Operations From Land Stations in the North Pacific Ocean,' UN Doc. 14640, UN Treaty Series Vol. 1148 (1979), 444-95.

49 Interview with John Knaus, IWC commissioner for the United States, 22 April 1992.

50 Interviews, 23 April 1992 and 22 September 1992.

51 Hawes, *Whaling*, 10.

52 The original UN Resolution, 44/225, was adopted by consensus on 22 December 1989; subsequently, Resolution 45/197, of 21 December 1990, further encouraged states to stop all driftnet fishing. The latter resolution noted that the IWC's 42nd Annual Meeting (July 1990) 'referred to the use large-scale pelagic driftnets in many areas of the high seas, including important habitats for cetaceans encompassing feeding and breeding grounds and migratory pathways.'

53 *Globe and Mail*, 27 November 1992; see D.M. Johnston, 'The Driftnetting Problem in the Pacific Ocean: Legal Considerations and Diplomatic Options,' *Ocean Development and International Law* 21 (1990):5-40.

54 P. Weber, 'Facing Limits in Oceanic Fisheries,' *Natural Resources Forum* 18 (1994):292-303. Fisheries experts generally use 100 million tons per year (20 million tons more than the 1993 catch) as an estimate of the potential catch for commercially viable species which, at present does not include whales but does include crustaceans (crabs, lobsters, shrimp) and molluscs (snails, oysters).

55 Ibid., 297; FAO, *Marine Fisheries and the Law of the Sea: A Decade of Change*, FAO Fisheries Circular No. 853, Rome, 1993.

56 Weber, 'Facing Limits,' 292.

57 W. Broad, 'Delicate Ecology of the Deep Threatened,' *Globe and Mail*, 27 December 1995.

58 G. Knox, 'The Key Role of Krill in the Ecosystem of the Southern Ocean with Special Reference to the Convention on the Conservation of Antarctic Marine Living Resources,' *Ocean Management* 9 (1984):143.
59 O. Young, *International Cooperation: Building Regimes for Natural Resources and the Environment* (Ithaca: Cornell 1989), 100.
60 D. McAllister, 'Offshore and Deep-sea Marine Reserves and Parks: A Major Gap in Protected Area Networks,' *Sea Wind: Bulletin of Ocean Voice International* 9 (1995):11-12.
61 Fenton, 'Species Impoverishment,' 100.
62 Myers, 'Sharing the Earth with Whales,' 188.
63 Bonner, *Whales of the World,* 179.
64 J. Geraci, 'Physiologic and Toxic Effects on Cetaceans,' in *Sea Mammals and Oil: Confronting the Risks,* eds. J. Geraci and D. St. Aubin (San Diego: Academic Press 1990), 167-97.
65 J. Geraci et al., 'Bottlenose Dolphins, *Tursiops truncatus,* Can Detect Oil,' *Canadian Journal of Fisheries and Aquatic Science* 40 (1983):1,515-22.
66 W.R. Koski, G. Miller, and R. Davis, 'The Potential Effects of Tanker Traffic on the Bowhead Whale in the Beaufort Sea,' Environmental Studies/Northern Affairs Program no. 58, Department of Indian Affairs, Canada, 1989; see also 'Oil Companies, Whalers Agree on Activity Limit in Chukchi, Beaufort,' *Platt's Oilgram News,* 30 November 1990.
67 M. Glassner, *Neptune's Domain: A Political Geography of the Sea* (Boston: Unwin Hyman 1990), 72.
68 A. Gunn, 'Why Should We Care about Rare Species?' *Environmental Ethics* 2 (1980):37. Gunn continues: 'Environmentalism is likely to meet the same stares of blank incomprehension as did the ideas of Thomas Paine when presented to the aristocracy of the eighteenth century. Unfortunately, rare species cannot wait for environmentalism to spread as slowly as democracy.'
69 Myers, 'Sharing the Earth with Whales,' 181.
70 Personal communication, N. Yagi, assistant director, Far Seas Fisheries Division, Fisheries Agency, Government of Japan, March 1995.
71 The usual estimate given for total human catch is 100 million tons. See Weber, 'Protecting Oceanic Fisheries and Jobs,' 21-37.

Chapter 5: Conclusion
1 Rosenau, *Turbulence in World Politics,* 422.
2 E. Haas, M. Williams, and D. Babai, *Scientists and World Order: The Uses of Technical Knowledge in International Organizations* (Berkeley: University of California Press 1977), 184. In light of the recent regime literature on the role played by 'epistemic (knowledge-based) communities,' this is a pioneering book. See P. Haas, ed., 'Epistemic Communities and International Policy Coordination' [special issue], *International Organization* 46 (1992).
3 E. Haas, *When Knowledge is Power,* 11.
4 Birnie, *Legal Measures for the Prevention of 'Pirate' Whaling,* 76; see also J. Wettestad and S. Andresen, 'Science and North Sea Policy-Making: Organization and Communication,' *International Journal of Estuarine and Coastal Law* 5 (1990):111-22. For a Foucaldian analysis of the intersection between science

and global environmental politics, see the new book by K. Litfin, *Ozone Discourses: Science and Politics in Global Environmental Cooperation* (New York: Columbia University Press 1994).

5 Personal communication with R. Conde de Saro, ministerio de agricultura, Madrid, March 1995. Mr. Conde de Saro was also the chairman of the IWC Subcommittee on Aboriginal Subsistence Whaling in 1994, and of the Subcommittee of Small Cetaceans in 1993.

6 Personal communication, 6 February 1995.

7 M. Ignatieff, 'Science and Politics on Planet Earth,' in *Planet Earth: Problems and Prospects,* eds. Leith, Price, and Spencer, 174. See also various chapters in N. Choucri, ed., *Global Accord: Environmental Challenges and International Responses* and K. Litfin, *Ozone Discourses.*

8 Brenton, *Greening of Machiavelli,* 154.

9 J.G. Ruggie, 'Collective Goods and Future International Collaboration,' *American Political Science Review* LXVI (1972):892-3.

10 From Keohane's essay in *International Institutions and State Power,* 30.

11 Personal communication, 19 July 1995.

12 Chayes and Chayes, 'On Compliance,' 204.

13 M. Freeman, 'Is the U.S. Whaling Policy What the Public Wants?' Paper presented at the Symposium on Scientific Management of Fisheries and Marine Mammals, Washington, April 1994.

14 See R. Benedick, *Ozone Diplomacy* (Cambridge, MA: Harvard University Press 1991), 76-116.

15 K. Ramakrishna, 'North-South Issues, the Common Heritage of Mankind and Global Environmental Change,' in *Global Environmental Change and International Relations,* eds. I. Rowlands and M. Greene (London: Macmillan and *Millennium* 1992), 145-68; L. Lunde, 'North/South and Global Warming – Conflict or Cooperation?' *Bulletin of Peace Proposals* 22 (1991):199-210.

16 Esty mentions also the American ban on Japanese pearl imports to encourage Japan to adopt the moratorium. *Greening the GATT,* 140-1.

17 It is obvious that intransigence characterizes both sides of the debate, despite protestations. Given the ethical question of lethal cetacean utilization, there is no real room for compromise without a significant shift in position.

18 Personal communication with J.K. McLay, 28 February 1995.

19 Birnie, 'International Environmental Law,' 51-84. See also C.M. Chinkin, 'The Challenge of Soft Law: Development and Change in International Law,' *International and Comparative Law Quarterly* 38 (1989):850-66.

20 Birnie, 'International Environmental Law,' 57.

21 Keohane, 'Multilateralism,' 739.

22 *Report of the U.S. Delegation to the 46th Annual Meeting of the IWC,* Puerto Vallarta, Mexico, 23-7 May 1994, Submitted to the Secretary of State by James Baker, Commissioner for the US, prepared by Kevin Chu, p. 16.

23 Ibid.,18.

24 Incidentally, the idea that the IWC could become a UN agency is still discussed on occasion. It is unlikely the pro-whalers would agree, since they would probably be in an even smaller minority if all UN members automatically belonged. On the other hand, official connections to the UN could lessen the financial

strain on the institution and facilitate closer ties with other agencies involved in implementing the Agenda 21, Chapter 17 programme.

25 Appendix 19: Amendments to the Financial Regulations, *Chairman's Report of the 46th Annual Meeting of the International Whaling Commission*, 23-27 May 1994, 67.

26 This practice has been widely reported; see for example Day, *Whale War*, 5-6; and J. and S. Heimlich-Boran, *Killer Whales* (Stillwater, MN: Voyageur Press 1994), 65. The latter write: 'In 1956, Icelandic fishermen in the Greenland halibut fisheries became so alarmed that the US Navy was requested to rid the coastal waters of killer whales.'

27 E. Flaherty, 'Forces Go Whale Watching as Explosions Used to Test Toughness of New Frigates,' *Vancouver Sun*, 18 November 1994.

28 M. Watts, 'On the Poverty of Theory: Natural Hazards Research in Context,' in *Interpretations of Calamity from the Viewpoint of Human Ecology*, ed. K. Hewitt (Boston: Allen and Unwin 1983), 231-62.

29 See P. Knudtson and D. Suzuki, *Wisdom of the Elders* (Toronto: Stoddart 1992).

30 D. Freestone, 'The Precautionary Principle,' in *International Law and Global Climate Change*, eds. R. Churchill and D. Freestone (London: Graham and Trotham 1991), 21-39; A. Moiseev, 'The GEF: Aspects of Purpose, Formation, and Change,' MA thesis, University of Guelph, 1996, 49-53.

31 On the general theme of the 'integrated management' of the oceans, see H.D. Smith, 'The Development and Management of the World Ocean,' *Ocean and Coastal Management* 24 (1994):3-16; on UNCED in particular, see L. Kimball, 'UNCED and the Oceans Agenda: The Process Forward,' *Marine Policy* 17 (1993):491-500. This special issue of *Marine Policy* ('UNCED's Marine Agenda: The Challenges of Implementation,' Lee Kimball, guest editor), includes P. Birnie's highly relevant 'UNCED and Marine Mammals,' 501-14.

32 See P. Tyler, 'Soviets' Secret Nuclear Dumping Raises Fears for Arctic Waters,' *New York Times*, 4 May 1992.

33 Pirages, *New Context for International Relations*, 200.

34 Foose, 'Raiders of the Last Ark.'

35 J. Darling quoted in B. Obee and G. Ellis, *Guardians of the Whales: The Quest to Study Whales in the Wild* (Vancouver: Whitecap 1992).

36 We should note that, as ugly as poaching is, the biggest long-term threat to elephants and rhinos is habitat destruction.

37 Personal communication with Dr. Y. Gong, director of the Department of Oceanography and Marine Resources, Korean National Fisheries Research and Development Agency. Korea favours the establishment of regional organizations to deal with small cetaceans.

38 A.H. Hoel, 'Regionalization of International Whales Management: The Case of the North Atlantic Marine Mammals Commission,' *Arctic* 46 (1993):116-23. Hoel is, of course, explicitly anti-preservationist. So is B. Floistad, who echoes his thoughts: 'A single-species approach giving insufficient ecological knowledge, combined with the protectionist objective that today characterizes the IWC, can very well lead to management based on ... a moral conclusion rather than scientific knowledge.' 'Scientific Knowledge in the Management of Fish and Whale: Global or Regional Organizations, Single and

Multi-Species Approach,' in *International Resource Management: The Role of Science and Politics,* eds. S. Andresen and W. Ostreng (London: Belhaven Press 1989), 232-50.

39 Hoel, 'Regionalization of International Whales Management,' 121.

40 Personal communication with M.A. Al-Barwan, fisheries adviser and IWC Commissioner for Oman, March 1995.

41 J. Loomis and D. Larson, 'Total Economic Values of Increasing Gray Whale Populations: Results from a Contingent Valuation Survey of Visitors and Households,' *Marine Resource Economics* 9 (1994):275-6. Meanwhile, Y. Kuronuma and C. Tisdell, who favour a return to commercial whaling based on economic calculations, consider minke whales 'international private good[s] from a bioeconomic perspective.' The decision to impose a moratorium on 'whale harvesting,' according to these analysts, 'can be considered to be an extreme means of eliminating a negative externality.' See their 'Economics of Antarctic Minke Whale Catches: Sustainability and Welfare Considerations,' *Marine Resource Economics* 9 (1994):141-58; and 'Institutional Management of an International Mixed Good: The IWC and Socially Optimal Whale Harvests,' *Marine Policy* 17 (1993):235-50.

42 Ford, Ellis, and Balcomb, *Killer Whales,* 57.

43 See for example K.J. Finley, 'Cross-Cultural Exchange of Ecological Knowledge: Toward a Community-Based Conservation Strategy for the Bowhead Whale,' Canadian Environmental Assessment Research Council Microlog MR8-92, Hull, Quebec, 1988.

44 Appendix 16, 'Approved Budget 1994/95: Forecast 1995/96,' *Chairman's Report of the 46th Annual Meeting of the International Whaling Commission* (October 1994). Of this, 648,900 is devoted to secretariat costs, 179,000 to the annual meeting held in Dublin earlier this year, and only 180,000 to research.

Appendix A
Compiled by the author, this chronology also borrows from the chronology in Francis, *The Great Chase,* 9-14.

1 We now know that even these figures are low, since the Soviet Union deliberately under-reported. See Chapter 3.

Bibliography

Publications of Governments and Organizations

Academic Council on the United Nations System. Halpern, S. 'The UNCED: Process and Documentation.' *ACUNS Reports and Papers* 1993

Australia. The Hon. Sir Sydney Frost, *Inquiry Into Whales and Whaling.* Presented to the Rt. Hon. Malcolm Fraser, prime minister. Canberra 1 December 1978

Boreal Institute for Northern Studies. *Small-Type Coastal Whaling in Japan: Report of an International Workshop.* Calgary 1988. Co-published with Japan Social Sciences Association of Canada

Bureau of International Whaling Statistics. *International Whaling Statistics.* Oslo: Various years

Canada. Arima, E.Y. 'A Report on a West Coast Whaling Canoe Reconstructed at Port Renfrew, B.C.' Department of Indian and Northern Affairs, Parks Canada, National Historic Sites Branch 1975

–. Berstad, G.A. 'Water Colour and Temperature in the Southern Beaufort Sea: Remote Sensing in Support of Ecological Studies of the Bowhead Whale.' Department of Fisheries and Oceans, Technical Report of Fisheries and Aquatic Sciences no. 1,350. Winnipeg 1985

–. Department of Fisheries and Oceans. 'Interdepartmental Action Plan to Favour the Survival of the St. Lawrence Beluga Whale: Annual Report.' Ottawa 1991

–. Finley, K.J. 'Cross-Cultural Exchange of Ecological Knowledge: Toward a Community-Based Conservation Strategy for the Bowhead Whale,' Canadian Environmental Assessment Research Council Microlog MR8-92. Hull, PQ, 1988

–. Joensen, J.S., and P. Zachariassen. 'Statistics for Pilot Whale Killing in the Faroe Islands, 1548-1640 and 1709-1978.' Department of Fisheries and Oceans no. 5,233, Natural Research Council, Canadian Institute for Scientific and Technical Information. Ottawa 1988

–. Koski, W.R., G. Miller, and R. Davis. 'The Potential Effects of Tanker Traffic on the Bowhead Whale in the Beaufort Sea.' Environmental Studies/Northern Affairs Program no. 58, Department of Indian Affairs. Ottawa 1989

–. Lankester, K. 'The Scientific Justification of Management of Whale Populations in the IWC,' trans. from Dutch. Department of Fisheries and Oceans no. 5,408. Natural Research Council, Canadian Institute for Scientific and Technical Information. Ottawa 1988

–. Proulx, J.-P. 'Basque Whaling in Labrador in the Sixteenth Century.' Environment Canada, Parks Service, and National Historic Sites. Ottawa 1993

–. Strong, J.T. 'Reported Harvests of Narwhal, Beluga and Walrus in the Northwest Territories, 1948-1987.' Department of Fisheries and Oceans Central and Arctic Region, *Canadian Data Report of Fisheries and Aquatic Sciences* no. 734. Winnipeg 1990

–. Weaver, P.A. 'The 1987 Beluga *Delphinapterus leucas* Harvest.' Department of Fisheries and Oceans Central and Arctic Region, report no. 2,097. Winnipeg 1991

–. 'Whaling in the North Atlantic: From Earliest Times to the mid-19th Century.' Parks Canada, Studies in Archaeology, Architecture and History. Ottawa 1986

Global Environment Facility. *Operational Strategy of the GEF*. Washington, DC, 1996

International Union for the Conservation of Nature and Natural Resources. Mitchell, E. *Porpoise, Dolphin, and Small Whale Fisheries of the World*. Morges, Switzerland, 1975

International Whaling Commission. *Aboriginal/Subsistence Whaling (with Special Reference to the Alaska and Greenland Fisheries)*. IWC Special Issue 4. Cambridge 1982

–. *Behaviour of Whales in Relation to Management*. IWC Special Issue 8. Cambridge 1986

–. Brownell, R.L., P.B. Best, and J. Prescott. *Right Whales: Past and Present Status*. IWC Special Issue 10. Cambridge 1986

–. *Chairman's Report of IWC Annual Meeting*. Cambridge: Various years

–. Donovan, G.P., ed. *The Comprehensive Assessment of Whale Stocks: The Early Years*. IWC Special Issue 11. Cambridge 1989

–. Hammond, P., S. Mizroch, and G.P. Donovan. *Individual Recognition of Cetaceans: Use of Photo-Identification and Other Techniques to Estimate Population Parameters*. IWC Special Issue 12. Cambridge 1990

–. Hoelzel, A.R. *Genetic Ecology of Whales and Dolphins: Incorporating the Proceedings of the Workshop on the Genetic Analysis of Cetacean Populations*. IWC Special Issue 13. Cambridge 1991

–. Mitchell, E.D., R.R. Reeves, and A. Evely. *Bibliography of Whale Killing Techniques*. IWC Special Issue 7. Cambridge 1986

–. Perrin, W., R. Brownell, and D. DeMaster. *Reproduction of Whales, Dolphins, and Porpoises*. IWC Special Issue 6, Cambridge 1984

–. *Report of the Panel to Consider Cultural Aspects of Aboriginal Whaling in North Alaska*. Seattle, February 1979

–. *Report of the Technical Committee Working Group on Aboriginal/Subsistence Whaling*. Washington, DC, 4-6 April 1979

–. Tillman, M.F., and G.P. Donovan, eds. *Special Issue on Historical Whaling*

Records, Including the Proceedings of the International Workshop of Historical Whaling Records. IWC Special Issue 5. Cambridge 1983
Institute of Cetacean Research. 'Antarctic Whale Sanctuary.' Tokyo n.d.
–. 'Sustainable Utilization and Conservation of Minke Whales.' Tokyo n.d.
Inuit Circumpolar Conference. *Principles and Elements for a Comprehensive Arctic Policy.* Montreal 1992
Japan. Environment Agency. *The Quality of the Environment in Japan (White Paper on the Environment).* Tokyo 1980
–. Ministry of Foreign Affairs. *Diplomatic Bluebook: Japan's Diplomatic Activities.* Tokyo: Various years
Japan Whaling Association. Various promotional brochures. Tokyo: Various years
–. *Whale Stock: Research and Management.* Tokyo 1980
New Zealand. 'IWC Supervision and Control Arrangement: New Zealand Views.' Ministry of Foreign Affairs and Trade, Parliament Buildings. Wellington, NZ, 1994
–. Official Report: 'A Celebration: First International Conference on the Southern Ocean Whale Sanctuary.' Viaduct Basin, Auckland, 15 and 16 October 1994
Norway. Committee for Whaling Statistics. *International Whaling Statistics.* Nos. 1-49. Norwegian Whaling Council. Oslo 1930-63
Old Dartmouth Historical Society. Downey, J. and V. Adams. *Whaling Logbooks and Journals 1613-1927: An Inventory of Manuscript Records in Public Collections.* New York 1986
Smithsonian Institution. True, F. *The Whalebone Whales of the Western North Atlantic.* Contributions to Knowledge Series. Volume 33. Washington, DC, 1904
United Kingdom of Great Britain and Northern Ireland. *Proposals Concerning the Cetacea: Second Meeting of the Conference of the Parties to the Convention on International Trade in Endangered Species of Wild Fauna and Flora.* Published by the Nature Conservancy Council for the Department of the Environment of Her Britannic Majesty's Government. San Jose, Costa Rica, 1979
United Nations. *Earth Summit, Agenda 21: The UN Programme of Action From Rio.* Final Texts of Agreements Negotiated by Governments at the United Nations Conference on Environment and Development, 3-14 June 1992, Rio de Janeiro, Brazil. New York 1993
–. *Global Outlook 2000: An Economic, Social, and Environmental Perspective.* ST/ESA/215/Rev 1, 1990
–. *Marine Fisheries and the Law of the Sea: A Decade of Change.* FAO Fisheries Circular No. 853, Rome 1993
–. *Our Common Future.* World Commission on Environment and Development. Oxford 1987
–. *Register of International Treaties and Other Agreements in the Field of the Environment.* UNEP. Nairobi 1989
–. 'Report of the UN Stockholm Declaration on the Human Environment.' *UN Doc. A/Conf.* 48/14, 1972

–. *Selected Multilateral Treaties in the Field of the Environment.* UNEP. Eds. I. Rummel-Balska and S. Osofo. Cambridge 1991
–. *World Review of High Seas and Highly Migratory Fish Species and Straddling Stocks.* FAO Fisheries Circular 858, Rome 1993
United States of America. *Global 2000 Report to the President.* Three Volumes. U.S. Gov't Printing Office 1980
–. National Oceanic and Atmospheric Administration Public Affairs. *U.S. Department of Commerce: News.* Washington, DC, various editions
–. *Report of the U.S. Delegation to the 45th Annual Meeting of the IWC*, Kyoto, Japan, May 10-14, 1993.' Submitted to the Secretary of State by Michael Tillman, acting commissioner for the US. Prepared by Kevin Chu
–. *Report of the U.S. Delegation to the 46th Annual Meeting of the IWC*, Puerto Vallarta, Mexico, May 23-27, 1994. Submitted to the secretary of state by James Baker, commissioner for the US. Prepared by Kevin Chu
–. *Summary Report of the 1995 IWC Meeting, US Delegation to the IWC.* Prepared by Kevin Chu

Books, Articles, Dissertations, and Papers Presented at Conferences
Adams, J. 'Last of the Caribbean Whalemen.' *Natural History* 103 (November 1994):64-73
Adams, J.S., and T. McShane. *The Myth of Wild Africa: Conservation Without Illusion.* New York: Norton 1992
Adler, E., and B. Crawford. *Progress in Postwar International Relations.* New York: Columbia University Press 1991
Allen, J. 'Anti-sealing as an Industry.' *Journal of Political Economy* 87 (April 1979):423-8
Allen, K.R. *Conservation and Management of Whales.* London: Butterworths 1980
Anderson, K. *Economic Growth, Environmental Issues and Trade.* Centre for Economic Policy Research Discussion Paper 830. London: CEPR 1993
Andreson, S. 'The Effectiveness of the International Whaling Commission.' *Arctic: Journal of the Arctic Institute of North America* 46, 2 (1993):108-15
–. 'Increased Public Attention: Communication and Polarization.' In *International Resource Management: The Role of Science and Politics*, eds. S. Andreson and W. Ostreng, 25-44. London: Belhaven Press 1989
–. 'Science and Politics in the International Management of Whales.' *Marine Policy* 13, 2 (1989):99-117
Angier, N. 'DNA Tests Find Meat of Endangered Whales for Sale in Japan.' *New York Times,* 13 September 1994
Asgrimsson, H. 'Developments Leading to the 1982 Decision of the International Whaling Commission for a Zero Catch Quota 1986-90.' In *International Resource Management: The Role of Science and Politics*, eds. S. Andresen and W. Ostreng, 221-31. London: Belhaven Press 1989
Attfield, R. 'Attitudes to Wildlife in the History of Ideas.' *Environmental History Review* 15, 2 (1991):71-8
Axelrod, R. *The Evolution of Cooperation.* New York: Basic Books 1984
Baker, C.S., and S.R. Palumbi. 'Which Whales Are Hunted? A Molecular

Genetic Approach to Monitoring Whaling.' *Science* 265 (9 September 1994):1,538-9

Baker, S. *Picturing the Beast: Animals, Identity, and Representation.* Manchester: Manchester University Press 1993

Barcena, A. 'Marine Agenda of UNCED: Role of the Earth Council.' *Marine Policy: The International Journal of Ocean Affairs* 18, 2 (1994)

Barkham, M. 'French Basque "New Found Land" Entrepreneurs and the Import of Codfish and Whale Oil to Northern Spain, c. 1580 to c. 1620: The Case of Adam de Chibau, Burgess of Saint-Jean-de-Luz and "Sieur de St. Julien."' *Newfoundland Studies* 10, 1 (1994):1-43

Barnes, J. 'The Emerging Convention on the Conservation of Antarctic Marine Living Resources: An Attempt to Meet the New Realities of Resource Exploitation in the Southern Ocean.' In *The New Nationalism and the Use of Common Spaces: Issues in Marine Pollution and the Exploitation of Antarctica,* ed. J. Charney, 239-86. New Jersey: Allanheld 1982

Barstow, R. 'Non-consumptive Utilization of Whales.' *Ambio* 15 (1986):155-60

Baskin, Y. 'Africa's Troubled Waters: Fish Introductions and a Changing Physical Profile Muddy Lake Victoria's Future.' *Bioscience* 42, 7 (1992):476-81

Beckerman, W. 'Global Warming and International Action: An Economic Perspective.' In *The International Politics of the Environment: Actors, Interests, and Institutions,* eds. A. Hurrell and B. Kingsbury. Oxford: Clarendon 1992

Behnke, A. 'Ten Years After: The State of the Art of Regime Theory.' *Cooperation and Conflict* 30, 2 (1995):179-97

Bell, F.W. *Food from the Sea: The Economics and Politics of Ocean Fisheries.* Boulder, CO: Westview Press 1978

Benedick, R. *Ozone Diplomacy.* Cambridge, MA: Harvard University Press 1991

Bennett, A.L. *International Organizations: Principles and Issues.* 6th ed. Englewood Cliffs, NJ: Prentice Hall 1995

Bermingham, John. 'Laying Their Claim.' *Province,* 23 May 1995

Bernauer, T. 'The Effect of International Environmental Institutions: How Might We Learn More?' *International Organization* 49, 2 (1995):351-77

Berzin, A.A. *The Sperm Whale (Kashalot).* Trans. E.H.Z. Blake. Jerusalem: Israel Program for Scientific Translations, Kater Press 1972

Best, P. 'Social Organization in Sperm Whales.' In *Behaviour of Marine Mammals, Volume Three: Cetaceans,* eds. H. Winn and B. Olla, 273-80. New York: Pelnum 1979

Bilderbeek, S., ed. *Biodiversity and International Law: The Effectiveness of International Environmental Law.* Amsterdam: IOS 1992

Birnie, P. 'International Environmental Law: Its Adequacy for Present and Future Needs.' In *The International Politics of the Environment: Actors, Interests, and Institutions,* eds. A. Hurrell and B. Kingsbury, 51-84. Oxford: Clarendon Press 1992

–. 'International Legal Issues in the Management and Protection of the Whale: A Review of Four Decades of Experience.' *Natural Resources Journal* 29 (1989):903-34

–. *The International Regulation of Whaling: From Conservation of Whaling to Conservation of Whales and Regulation of Whale-Watching.* New York: Oceana 1985

–. *Legal Measures for the Prevention of 'Pirate' Whaling.* Switzerland: IUCN 1981
–. 'The Role of Developing Countries in Nudging the International Whaling Commission from Regulating Whaling to Encouraging Non-consumptive Uses of Whales.' *Ecology Law Quarterly* 12 (1985):937-75
–. 'The United Nations and the Environment.' In *United Nations, Divided World: The U.N.'s Roles in International Relations,* eds. A. Roberts and B. Kingsbury, 327-84. Oxford: Clarendon Press 1993
–. 'UNCED and Marine Mammals.' *Marine Policy* 17, 6 (1993):501-14
–, and A. Boyle. *International Law and the Environment.* Oxford: Oxford University Press 1992
Boardman, R. *International Organisation and the Conservation of Nature.* Bloomington, IN: Indiana University 1981
Bockstoce, J.R. *Whales, Ice, and Men: The History of Whaling in the Western Arctic.* Seattle: University of Washington Press 1986
Bonner, N. *Whales of the World.* New York: Facts on File 1989
Bonner, R. 'Crying Wolf Over Elephants.' *New York Times Magazine,* 7 February 1993
Boulding, K. 'Commons and Community: The Idea of a Public.' In *Managing the Commons,* eds. G. Hardin and J. Baden, 280-94. San Francisco: W.H. Freeman and Company 1977
Boyden, S. *BioHistory: The Interplay Between Human Society and the Biosphere, Past and Present.* Paris: UNESCO 1992
Bradsher, K. 'Japan Won't Hunt Whales, Miyazawa Says.' *New York Times,* 3 July 1992
Bramble, B., and G. Porter. 'Non-Governmental Organizations and the Making of US International Environmental Policy.' In *The International Politics of the Environment: Actors, Interests, and Institutions,* eds. A. Hurrell and B. Kingsbury, 313-54. Oxford: Clarendon Press 1992
Brecher, J., J. Childs, and J. Cutler. *Global Visions: Beyond the New World Order.* Montreal: Black Rose Books 1993
Breitmeier, H., and K.D. Wolf. 'Analysing Regime Consequences: Conceptual Outlines and Environmental Explorations.' In *Regime Theory and International Relations,* ed. V. Rittberger, 339-60. Oxford: Clarendon Press 1993
Brenton, T. *The Greening of Machiavelli: The Evolution of International Environmental Politics.* London: Earthscan 1994
Bright, M. *Masters of the Oceans: Whales, Dolphins, Sharks.* London: Prion 1991
Broad, W. 'Delicate Ecology of the Deep Threatened.' *Globe and Mail,* 27 December 1995
Bromley, D.W., ed. *Making the Commons Work: Theory, Practice, and Policy.* San Francisco: Institute for Contemporary Studies Press 1992
Brooke, J. 'UN Chief Closes Summit with an Appeal for Action.' *New York Times,* 15 June 1992
Brooks, B., ed. *The Whole Whale Catalog.* Waukegan, IL: Greatlakes Living Press 1978
Brown, L., ed. *State of the World.* New York: Norton, various years

Brown, S. 'Explaining the Transformation of World Politics.' *International Journal* XLVI, 2 (1991):207-19

Bruemmer, F. *The Narwhal: Unicorn of the Sea.* Toronto: Key Porter 1993

Bryden, A. 'The Eye of the Guest: Icelandic Nationalist Discourse and the Whaling Issue.' Phd dissertation, McGill University 1991

Buckley, R. *US-Japan Alliance Diplomacy 1945-1990.* Cambridge: Cambridge University Press 1992

Burke, T. 'Friends of the Earth and the Conservation of Resources.' In *Pressure Groups in the Global System: The Transnational Relations of Issue-Oriented Non-Governmental Organisations,* ed. P. Willetts, 105-24. London: Francis Pinter 1982

Busch, B.C. *'Whaling Will Never Do For Me': The American Whaleman in the Nineteenth Century.* Lexington, KY: University Press of Kentucky 1994

Buzan, B. 'From International System to International Society: Structural Realism and Regime Theory Meet the English School.' *International Organization* 47, 3 (1993):327-52

Byers, B. 'Ecoregions, State Sovereignty and Conflict.' *Bulletin of Peace Proposals* 22, 1 (1991):65-76

Caldwell, L. 'International Conservation Efforts: Cooperation to Protect Endangered Species and Environments.' In *In Defense of the Earth: International Protection of the Biosphere,* ed. L. Caldwell, 53-90. Bloomington, IN: Indiana University Press 1972

–. *International Environmental Policy: Emergence and Dimensions.* 2nd ed. Durham, NC: Duke University Press 1990

–. 'U.S. Interests and the Global Environment.' *Occasional Paper No. 35* Muscatine, IA: Stanley Foundation 1985

Caron, D. 'International Sanctions, Ocean Management, and the Law of the Sea: A Study of Denial of Access to Fisheries.' *Ecological Law Quarterly* 16, 1 (1989):311-54

–. 'The IWC and the North Atlantic Marine Mammal Commission: The Institutional Risks of Coercion in Consensual Structures.' *American Journal of International Law* 98, 1 (1995):154-73

Carpenter, B. 'The Expanding Human Threat.' *U.S. News and World Report,* 13 July 1992

Carroll, J.E., ed. *International Environmental Diplomacy: The Management and Resolution of Transfrontier Environmental Problems.* Cambridge: Cambridge University Press 1988

Catton, W. *Overshoot: The Ecological Basis of Revolutionary Change.* Chicago: University of Illinois 1982

Chapman, P. *Trouble on Board: The Plight of International Seafarers.* Ithaca, NY: Cornell University Press 1992

Charney, J., ed. *The New Nationalism and the Use of Common Spaces: Issues in Marine Pollution and the Exploitation of Antarctica.* New Jersey: Allanheld 1982

Chayes, A., and A.H. Chayes. 'On Compliance.' *International Organization* 47, 2 (1993):175-205

Cherfas, J. *The Hunting of the Whale: A Tragedy that Must End.* London: Bodley Head 1988

Chisholm, P. 'Prince of the Tides.' *Maclean's*, 14 June 1993

Choucri, N., ed. *Global Accord: Environmental Challenges and International Responses*. Cambridge, MA: MIT Press 1993

Ciriacy-Wantrup, S.V. *Resource Conservation: Economics and Policies*. Berkeley: University of California Press 1952

Clark, C. *Bioeconomic Modelling and Fisheries Management*. New York: John Wiley 1985

–. 'The Dynamics of Commercially Exploited Animal Populations.' *Mathematical Biosciences* 13 (1972):149-64

–. 'The Economics of Overexploitation.' *Science* 181, 4,100 (1974):630-4

–. *Mathematical Bioeconomics: The Optimal Management of Renewable Resources*. New York: John Wiley 1976

Colinvaux, P. *Why Big Fierce Animals Are Rare: An Ecologist's Perspective*. Princeton, NJ: Princeton University Press 1978

Cook, J. *Pursuing the Whale: A Quarter-Century of Whaling in the Arctic*. London: John Murray 1926

Cooper, D. 'Other Species and Moral Reason.' In *Just Environments: Intergenerational, International, and Interspecies Issues*, eds. D. Cooper and J. Palmer, 137-48. London: Routledge 1995

Cooper, R. 'United States Policy Toward the Global Environment.' In *The International Politics of the Environment: Actors, Interests, and Institutions*, eds. A. Hurrell and B. Kingsbury, 290-312. Oxford: Clarendon Press 1992

Cousteau, J., and P. Diole. *The Whale: Mighty Monarch of the Sea*. New York: Doubleday 1972

Cox, R. 'The Crisis in World Order and the Challenge to International Organization.' *Cooperation and Conflict* 29, 2 (1994):99-113

Crane, B. 'International Population Institutions: Adaptation to a Changing World Order.' In *Institutions for the Earth: Sources of International Environmental Protection*, eds. P. Haas, R. Keohane, and M. Levy, 351-96. Cambridge, MA: MIT Press 1993

Cronon, W., ed. *Uncommon Ground: Toward Reinventing Nature*. New York: Norton 1995

D'Amato, A. 'Do We Owe a Duty to Future Generations to Preserve the Global Environment?' *American Journal of International Law* 84 (1990):190-8

–, and S. Chopra. 'Whales: Their Emerging Right to Life.' *American Journal of International Law* 85, 1 (1991):21-62

Dana, R. *Two Years Before the Mast*. New York: P.F. Collier 1937

Davies, P. 'Legality of Norwegian Commercial Whaling under the Whaling Convention and Its Compatibility with European Community Law.' *International and Comparative Law Quarterly* 270 (1994):270-95

Day, D. *The Environmental Wars*. New York: Ballantine 1989

–. *The Whale War*. Vancouver: Douglas and McIntyre 1987

De Jong, C. 'The Hunt of the Greenland Whale: A Short History and Statistical Sources.' In *Special Issue on Historical Whaling Records*, 83-106. Cambridge: International Whaling Commission 1983

Devall, B., and G. Sessions. *Deep Ecology: Living as if Nature Matters*. Salt Lake City: Peregrine Smith 1985

Doak, W. *Encounters with Whales and Dolphins*. London: Hodder and Stoughton 1988

Donovan, G.P. 'The IWC and the Revised Management Procedure.' Paper written for the Conference on Responsible Wildlife Resource Management held in the European Parliament, Brussels, 29-30 June 1993

–. 'The IWC: Given Its Past, Does It Have a Future?' In *Symposium Whales: Biology – Threats – Conservation,* ed. N. Symoens, 23-44. Brussels 1992

Dornan, C. 'A Whale of an Insight Into Unsolved Mysteries.' *Globe and Mail,* 1 July 1995

Dornbusch, R., and J. Poterba, eds. *Global Warming: Economic Policy Responses*. Cambridge, MA: MIT Press 1991

Dorsey, K. 'Putting a Ceiling on Sealing: Conservation and Cooperation in the International Arena, 1909-1911.' *Environmental History Review* 15, 3 (1991):27-46

Doubleday, N. 'Aboriginal Subsistence Whaling: The Right of Inuit to Hunt Whales and Implications for International Environmental Law.' *Denver Journal of International Law and Policy* 17, 2 (1989):373-93

Druett, J. *Petticoat Whalers: Whaling Wives at Sea, 1820-1920*. Auckland: Collins 1991

D'Vincent, Cynthia et al. *Voyaging With the Whales*. Chicago: Oakwell Boulton 1989

Ehrenfeld, D. *Conserving Life on Earth*. New York: Oxford University Press 1972

Ehrlich P., and A. Ehrlich. *Extinction: The Causes and Consequences of the Disappearance of Species*. New York: Random House 1981

Eldredge, N. *The Miner's Canary: Unravelling the Mysteries of Extinction*. New York: Prentice Hall 1991

Engel, J.R., and J.G. Engel. *Ethics of Environment and Development: Global Challenge, International Response*. Tucson: University of Arizona Press 1990

Erwin, J., T. Maple, and G. Mitchell, eds. *Captivity and Behaviour: Primates in Breeding Colonies, Laboratories, and Zoos*. New York: Van Nostrand Reinhold 1979

Esty, D. *Greening the GATT: Trade, Environment, and the Future*. Washington, DC: Institute for International Economics 1994

Evans, P.G.H. *The Natural History of Whales and Dolphins*. London: Christopher Helm 1987

Fairley, J. *Irish Whales and Whaling*. Belfast: Blackstaff 1981

Falk, R., ed. *The Promise of World Order: Essays in Normative International Relations*. Brighton, Sussex, 1987

Fenton, M.B. 'Species Impoverishment.' In *Planet Earth: Problems and Prospects,* eds. J. Leith, R. Price, and J. Spencer, 83-110. Kingston and Montreal: McGill-Queen's University Press 1995

Fichtelius, K., and S. Sjolander. *Man's Place: Intelligence in Whales, Dolphins, and Humans*. London: Gollancz 1973

Floistad, B. 'Scientific Knowledge in the Management of Fish and Whale: Global or Regional Organizations, Single and Multi-Species Approach.' In *International Resource Management: The Role of Science and Politics,* eds. S. Andresen and W. Ostreng, 232-50. London: Belhaven Press 1989

Foose, T. 'Raiders of the Last Ark: The Role of Captive Breeding in Conservation Strategies.' In *The Last Extinction*, eds. L. Kaufman and K. Mallory, 149-78. 2nd ed. Cambridge, MA: MIT Press 1993

Ford, J., G. Ellis, and K. Balcomb. *Killer Whales: The Natural History and Genealogy of Orcinus orca in British Columbia and Washington State.* Vancouver and Seattle: UBC Press and University of Washington Press 1984

Forster, M. 'IWC: Trying Hard?' *Environmental Policy and Law* 15 (1985):8-9

Francis, D. *Arctic Chase: A History of Whaling in Canada's North.* Toronto: Breakwater 1984

–. *The Great Chase: A History of World Whaling.* Toronto: Penguin 1990

Franck, T.M. *The Power of Legitimacy among Nations.* New York: Oxford University Press 1990

Freeman, M. 'A Commentary on Political Issues with Regard to Contemporary Whaling.' *North Atlantic Studies* 2 (1990):106-16

–. 'Community-Based Whaling in the North.' *Arctic: Journal of the Arctic Institute of North America* 46, 2 (1993):iii-iv

–. 'Is the U.S. Whaling Policy What the Public Wants?' Paper presented at the Symposium on Scientific Management of Fisheries and Marine Mammals. Washington, DC, April 1994

Freestone, D. 'The Precautionary Principle.' In *International Law and Global Climate Change,* eds. R. Churchill and D. Freestone, 21-39. London: Graham and Trotham 1989

French, H. *After the Earth Summit: The Future of Environmental Governance.* Worldwatch Paper 107. Washington, DC: Worldwatch Institute 1992

French, W.C. 'Against Biological Egalitarianism.' *Environmental Ethics* 17, 1 (1995):39-57

Friends of the Earth. *Whale Manual.* London: FOE 1978

Fukai, S. 'Japanese Policy-Making on Issues of North-South Relations.' In *Japan and the World: Essays on Japanese History and Politics in Honour of Ishida Takeshi,* eds. G. Bernstein and H. Fukui, 197-219. Basingstoke, UK: Oxford University Press 1988

Gambell, R. 'International Management of Whales and Whaling: An Historical Review of the Regulation of Commercial and Aboriginal Subsistence Whaling.' *Arctic: Journal of the Arctic Institute of North America* 46, 2 (1993):97-107

George, S. 'Managing the Global House: Redefining Economics.' In *Paradigms Lost: The Post Cold War Era,* eds. C. Hartman and P. Vilanova. London: Pluto 1992

Geraci, J. 'Physiologic and Toxic Effects on Cetaceans.' In *Sea Mammals and Oil: Confronting the Risks,* eds. J. Geraci and D. St. Aubin, 167-97. San Diego: Academic Press 1990

– et al. 'Bottlenose Dolphins, *Tursiops truncatus,* Can Detect Oil.' *Canadian Journal of Fisheries and Aquatic Science* 40, 9 (1983):1,515-22

Gifford, A. 'The Economic Organization of 17th through mid-19th Century Whaling and Shipping.' *Journal of Economic Behaviour and Organization* 20 (1993):137-51

Gilpin, R. *U.S. Power and the Multinational Corporation: The Political Economy of Direct Foreign Investment.* New York: Cambridge University Press 1975
–. *War and Change in World Politics.* Cambridge: Cambridge University Press 1981
Glassner, M. *Neptune's Domain: A Political Geography of the Sea.* Boston: Unwin Hyman 1990
Haas, E. *When Knowledge Is Power: Three Models of Change in International Organisation.* Berkeley: University of California Press 1990
–, with M. Williams and D. Babai. *Scientists and World Order: The Uses of Technical Knowledge in International Organizations.* Berkeley: Univeristy of California Press 1977
Haas, P. 'Do Regimes Matter? Epistemic Communities and Mediterranean Pollution Control.' *International Organization* 43, 3 (1989):377-403
–. 'Epistemic Communities and the Dynamics of International Environmental Co-Operation.' In *Regime Theory and International Relations,* ed. V. Rittberger, 168-201. Oxford: Clarendon Press 1993
–. 'Making Progress in International Environmental Protection.' In *Progress in Postwar International Relations,* eds. E. Adler and B. Crawford, 273-311. New York: Columbia University Press 1991
–. *Saving the Mediterranean: The Politics of International Environmental Cooperation.* New York: Columbia University Press 1990
–, R. Keohane, and M. Levy. *Institutions for the Earth: Sources of International Environmental Protection.* Cambridge, MA: MIT Press 1993
Hahn, R., and K. Richards. 'The Internationalization of Environmental Regulation.' *Harvard International Law Journal* 30, 2 (1989):421-46
Hall, Neal. 'Indian Whaling Ships "Will Be Sunk."' *Vancouver Sun,* 24 May 1995
Hampson, F.O. 'Peace, Security, and New Forms of International Governance.' In *Planet Under Stress: The Challenge of Global Change,* eds. C. Mungall and D. McLaren, 301-17. Toronto: Oxford University Press 1990
Hardin, G. 'The Tragedy of the Commons.' *Science* 162 (1968):1,243-47
–. and J. Baden, ed. *Managing the Commons.* San Francisco: W.H. Freeman 1977
Harrison, R. 'History of Whaling.' In *Whales, Dolphins and Porpoises,* eds. M. Bryden and R. Harrison, 182-95. London: Merehurst 1988
Haskell, R. 'Abandoning Recent Whale Conservation Initiatives in Japan Whaling Association v. American Cetacean Society.' *Harvard Environmental Law Review* 11, 2 (1987):551-91
Hawes, C.B. *Whaling.* Garden City, NY: Doubleday, Page and Company 1924
Hayden, S. *The International Protection of Wildlife: An Examination of Treaties and Other Agreements for the Preservation of Birds and Mammals.* New York: 1942
Heazle, M. 'A Community on Edge: Ban on Whaling Threatens Future of Ayukawa.' *Far Eastern Economic Review,* 10 June 1993
Heimlich-Boran, J., 'Behavioral Ecology of Killer Whales.' *Canadian Journal of Zoology* 66 (1988):565-78

–, and S. Heimlich-Boran. *Killer Whales*. Stillwater, MN: Voyageur Press 1994

Hjorth, R. 'Baltic Sea Environmental Cooperation: The Role of Epistemic Communities and the Politics of Regime Change.' *Cooperation and Conflict: Nordic Journal of International Studies* 29, 1 (1994):11-32

Hoel, A.H. 'Regionalization of International Whales Management: The Case of the North Atlantic Marine Mammals Commission.' *Arctic: Journal of the Arctic Institute of North America* 46, 2 (1993):116-23

Hoffman, S. 'The Role of International Organization: Limits and Possibilities.' In *The United Nations Political System*, ed. D. Kay, 400-19. New York: John Wiley and Sons 1967

Holsti, O. 'Models of International Relations and Foreign Policy.' *Diplomatic History* 13, 1 (1989):15-44

Hossie, L. 'Slipping Environment onto the Agenda.' *Globe and Mail*, 26 May 1993

Hoyt, Erich. *Orca: The Whale Called Killer*. New York: E.P. Dutton 1981

Hunter, R. *Warriors of the Rainbow: A Chronicle of the Greenpeace Movement*. New York: Holt, Rinehart and Winston 1979

–, and R. Weyler. *To Save a Whale: The Voyages of Greenpeace*. Vancouver: Douglas and McIntyre 1978

Hurrell, A., and B. Kingsbury, eds. *The International Politics of the Environment*. Oxford: Clarendon Press 1992

Ignatieff, M. 'Science and Politics on Planet Earth.' In *Planet Earth: Problems and Prospects*, eds. J. Leith, R. Price, and J. Spencer, 172-7. Montreal and Kingston: McGill-Queen's University Press 1995

Jablonski, D. 'Mass Extinctions: New Answers, New Questions.' In *The Last Extinction*, eds. L. Kaufman and K. Mallory. 2nd ed. Cambridge, MA: MIT Press 1993

Jackson, G. *The British Whaling Trade*. London: Adam and Charles Nlack 1978

Johnston, D.M. 'The Driftnetting Problem in the Pacific Ocean: Legal Considerations and Diplomatic Options.' *Ocean Development and International Law* 21, 1 (1990):5-40

–. 'Marine Pollution Agreements: Successes and Problems.' In *International Environmental Diplomacy: The Management and Resolution of Transfrontier Environmental Problems*, ed. J. Carroll, 199-206. New York: Cambridge University Press 1988

Kalland, A. 'Management by Totemization: Whale Symbolism and the Anti-Whaling Campaign.' *Arctic: Journal of the Arctic Institute of North America* 46, 2 (1993): 124-33

–, and B. Moeran. *Japanese Whaling: End of an Era?* London: Curzon 1992

Kaufman, L. 'Catastrophic Change in Species-Rich Freshwater Ecosystems: The Lessons of Lake Victoria.' *Bioscience* 42, 11 (1992):846-58

–. 'Why the Ark is Sinking.' In *The Last Extinction*, eds. L. Kaufman and K. Mallory, 1-46. 2nd ed. Cambridge, MA: MIT Press 1993

–, and K. Mallory, eds. *The Last Extinction*. 2nd ed. Cambridge, MA: MIT Press 1993

Kay, D.A., and H. Jacobsen, eds. *Environmental Protection: The International Dimension*. Totawa, NJ: Allanheld, Osmun 1983

Kegley, C., and E. Wittkopf. *The Global Agenda: Issues and Perspectives.* Englewood Cliffs, NJ: Prentice Hall 1988

–. *World Politics: Trend and Transformation.* 4th ed. New York: St. Martin 1993

Kenchington, R.A. *Managing Marine Environments.* New York: Taylor and Francis 1990

Kennan, G. 'To Prevent a World Wasteland: A Proposal.' *Foreign Affairs* 48 (April 1970):401-13

Kennedy, Paul. *Preparing for the Twenty-first Century.* New York: Random House 1993

Kent, G. 'Ocean Fisheries Management.' In *Ecological Perspectives on World Order,* eds. D. Orr and M. Soroos, 223-48. Durham, NC: University of North Carolina 1979

Keohane, R. 'Multilateralism: An Agenda for Research.' *International Journal* XLV, 4 (1990):731-64

–, and J. Nye. 'Transgovernmental Relations and International Organizations.' *World Politics* 27 (1974):39-62

Kimball, L. *Forging International Agreement: Strengthening Inter-Governmental Institutions for Environment and Development.* Washington, DC: World Resources Institute 1992

–. 'UNCED and the Oceans Agenda: The Process Forward.' *Marine Policy* 17, 6 (1993):491-500

Klinowska, M. 'How Brainy Are Cetaceans?' *Oceanus* 32 (1989):19-20

Knox, G. 'The Key Role of Krill in the Ecosystem of the Southern Ocean with Special Reference to the Convention on the Conservation of Antarctic Marine Living Resources.' *Ocean Management* 9 (1984):113-56

Krasner, S. *International Regimes.* Ithaca, NY: Cornell University Press 1983

–. 'Sovereignty, Regimes, and Human Rights.' In *Regime Theory and International Relations,* ed. V. Rittberger, 139-67. Oxford: Clarendon Press 1993

Kuronuma. Y., and C. Tisdell. 'Economics of Antarctic Minke Whale Catches: Sustainability and Welfare Considerations.' *Marine Resource Economics* 9, 2 (1994):141-58

–. 'Institutional Management of an International Mixed Good: The IWC and Socially Optimal Whale Harvests.' *Marine Policy* 17, 4 (1993):235-50

Lal, D. 'Trade Blocs and Multilateral Free Trade.' *Journal of Common Market Studies* 31, 3 (1993):349-58

Larson, S. 'U.S. Whale Policy: The Judiciary Casts Its Vote in Favor of a Moderate Approach.' *Vanderbilt Journal of Transnational Law* 20 (1):123-59

Lemonick, M. 'The Hunt, the Furor.' *Time,* 2 August 1993

Leonard, L. 'The International Protection of Whales.' *American Journal of International Law* 35 (1941):90

Levy, M., G. Osherenko, and O. Young. 'The Effectiveness of International Regimes: A Design for Large-Scale Collaborative Research.' Paper based on a workshop held at Dartmouth College, 31 Oct-3 Nov 1991

Lindblom, C. *Inquiry and Change: The Troubled Attempt to Understand and Shape Society.* New Haven, CT: Yale University Press 1990

Linden, E. 'Sharpening the Harpoons.' *Time*, 24 May 1993

List, M., and V. Rittberger. 'Regime Theory and International Environmental Management.' In *The International Politics of the Environment: Actors, Interests, and Institutions*, eds. A. Hurrell and B. Kingsbury, 85-109. Oxford: Clarendon Press 1992

Litfin, K. *Ozone Discourses: Science and Politics in Global Environmental Cooperation*. New York: Columbia University Press 1994

Loomis, J., and L. Douglas. 'Total Economic Values of Increasing Gray Whale Populations: Results from a Contingent Valuation Survey of Visitors and Households.' *Marine Resource Economics* 9, 3 (1994):275-86

Lowe, P. and J. Goyder, 'Friends of the Earth.' In *Environmental Groups in Politics*. London: Allen and Unwin 1983

Lynge, F. *Arctic Wars, Animal Rights, Endangered Peoples*. Trans. Marianne Stenbaek. Hanover: University Press of New England 1992

Lyster, S. *International Wildlife Law: An Analysis of International Treaties Concerned with the Conservation of Wildlife*. Cambridge: Grotius 1985

McAllister, D. 'Offshore and Deep-sea Marine Reserves and Parks: A Major Gap in Protected Area Networks.' *Sea Wind: Bulletin of Ocean Voice International* 9, 3 (1995):4-14

McDevitt, J. *The House of Rotch: Massachusetts Whaling Merchants, 1734-1828*. New York 1986

McGoodwin, J.R. *Crisis in the World's Fisheries*. Stanford: Stanford University Press 1990

Macgregor, J. 'The Paradoxes of Wildlife Conservation in Africa.' *Africa Insight* 19, 4 (1989):201-12

McHugh, J.L. 'The Role and History of the International Whaling Commission.' In *The Whale Problem: A Status Report*, ed. W. Schevill, 305-35. Cambridge: Harvard University Press 1974

McIntyre, J. *The Delicate Art of Whale Watching*. San Francisco: Sierra 1982

McNeely, J., K. Miller, and M. Reid. *Conserving the World's Biological Diversity*. Washington, DC, 1990

–. *Economics and Biological Diversity: Developing and Using Economic Incentives to Conserve Biological Resources*. Switzerland 1988

MacNeill, J., P. Winsemius, and T. Yakushiji. *Beyond Interdependence: The Meshing of the World's Economy and the Earth's Ecology*. New York: Oxford University Press 1991

Mahan, A.T. *The Influence of Sea Power Upon History, 1660-1783*. New York: Dover 1987 (originally printed 1890)

Makiko, S. 'Scientists Clash Over Whaling.' *Christian Science Monitor*, 27 February 1992

Mandel, R. *Conflict Over the World's Resources*. New York: Greenwood 1988

–. 'Transnational Resource Conflict: The Politics of Whaling.' *International Studies Quarterly* 24, 1 (1980):99-127

Manes, C. *Green Rage: Radical Environmentalism and the Unmaking of Civilization*. Boston: Little and Brown 1990

Mansbach, R. *The Global Puzzle: Issues and Actors in World Politics*. Boston: Houghton Mifflin 1994

–. 'The World Turned Upside Down.' *Journal of East Asian Affairs* 7, 2 (1993):451-97
–, Y. Ferguson, and D. Lampert. *The Web of World Politics: Non State Actors in the Global System.* Englewood Cliffs, NJ: Prentice Hall 1976
Martin, G., and J. Brennan. 'Enforcing the International Convention for the Regulation of Whaling: The Pelly and Packwood-Magnuson Amendments.' *Denver Journal of International Law and Policy* 17, 2 (1989)
Martin, M. 'Ecosabotage and Civil Disobedience.' *Environmental Ethics* 12 (Winter 1990)
Matthews, H. *The Natural History of the Whale.* London: Weidenfeld and Nicolson 1978
Matthews, L.H. *The Life of Mammals: Volume One.* London: Weidenfeld and Nicolson 1969
Maull, H.W. 'Japan's Global Environmental Policies.' In *The International Politics of the Environment: Actors, Interests, and Institution,* eds. A. Hurrell and B. Kingsbury, 354-7. Oxford: Clarendon Press 1992
Maynard, F., and A. Dumas. *The Whalers.* London: Hutchinson 1937
Maxwell, M. 'Fact and Value in International Relations.' *International Political Science Review* 15, 4 (1994):379-416
Meadows, D. et al. *Beyond the Limits: Confronting Global Collapse, Envisioning a Sustainable Future.* Post Mills, VT: Chelsea Green 1992
–. *The Limits to Growth.* New York: Times Mirror 1972
Melville, H. *Moby Dick.* New York: Harper and Brothers 1851
M'Gonigle, R.M. 'Economics, Ecology, and the Endangered Whale: Competing Foundations for Environmental Law and Politics.' *Ecology Law Quarterly* 9, 1 (1980):120-237
–, and D. Babicki. 'The Turbot's Last Stand?' *Globe and Mail,* 21 July 1995
–, and M. Zacher. *Pollution, Politics, and International Law: Tankers at Sea.* Berkeley: University of California Press 1979
Mitchell, R.B. *Intentional Oil Pollution at Sea: Environmental Policy and Treaty Compliance.* Cambridge, MA: MIT Press 1994
Mitrany, D. *A Working Peace System: An Argument for the Functional Development of International Organization.* London: Oxford University Press 1943
Moiseev, A. 'The GEF: Aspects of Purpose, Formation, and Change.' MA thesis, University of Guelph, 1996
Moravcsik, A. 'Explaining International Human Rights Regimes: Liberal Theory and Western Europe.' *European Journal of International Relations* 1, 2 (1995):157-89
Morgenthau, H. *Politics Among Nations: The Struggle for Power and Peace.* New York: Knopf 1949
Morley, F.V., and J.S. Hodgson. *Whaling North and South.* New York: Century 1926
Morphet, S. 'NGOs and the Environment.' In *'The Conscience of the World': The Influence of Non-Governmental Organisations in the UN System,* ed. P. Willetts, 116-46. Washington, DC, 1996
Morrisette, P. 'The Evolution of Policy Responses to Stratospheric Ozone Depletion.' *Natural Resources Journal* 29, 3 (1989):793-820

Morse, E.L. 'Managing International Commons.' *Journal of International Affairs* 31, 1 (1977):1-21

Morton, H. *The Whale's Wake.* Honolulu: University of Hawaii Press 1982

Mowat, F. *A Whale for the Killing.* Toronto: McClelland and Stewart 1972

Myers, N. 'Sharing the Earth with Whales.' In *The Last Extinction*, eds. L. Kaufman and K. Mallory, 179-94. 2nd ed. Cambridge, MA: MIT Press 1993

–. *The Sinking Ark: A New Look at the Problem of Disappearing Species.* New York: Pergamon Press 1979

–. 'The Whaling Controversy.' *American Scientist* 63 (1975):448-55

Naess, A. *Ecology, Community and Lifestyle: Outline of an Ecosophy.* Trans. D. Rothenberg. Cambridge: Cambridge University Press 1989

Nye, Joseph. *Peace in Parts: Integration and Conflict in Regional Organization.* Boston: Little, Brown and Company 1971

Obee, B., and G, Ellis. *Guardians of the Whales: The Quest to Study Whales in the Wild.* Vancouver: Whitecap 1992

Olson, M. *The Logic of Collective Action: Public Goods and the Theory of Groups.* New York: Schocken Books 1965

Ommanney, F.D. *Lost Leviathan.* London: Hutchinson 1971

Orr, D. and M. Soroos, eds. *The Global Predicament: Ecological Perspectives on World Order.* Durham NC: North Carolina University 1979

Paarlberg, Robert. 'Ecodiplomacy: U.S. Environmental Policy Goes Abroad.' In *Eagle in a New World: American Grand Strategy in the Post-Cold War Era*, eds. Kenneth Oye et al., 207-32. New York: HarperCollins 1992

Paterson, D. *The Deluge and the Ark: A Journey into Primate Worlds.* Boston: Houghton Mifflin 1989

Payne, R. *Among Whales.* New York: Scribners 1995

Pearce, F. *Green Warriors: The People and the Politics Behind the Environmental Revolution.* London: Bodley Head 1991

Pentland, Charles. *International Theory and European Integration.* New York: Free Press 1973

Peterson, M. 'International Fisheries Management.' In *Institutions for the Earth: Sources of Effective International Environmental Protection*, eds. P. Haas, R. Keohane, and M. Levy, 249-308. Cambridge, MA: MIT Press 1994

–. 'Whalers, Cetologists, Environmentalists, and the International Management of Whaling.' *International Organization* 46, 1 (1992):147-86

Pirages, D. *Global Ecopolitics: The New Context for International Relations.* North Scituate, MA: Duxbury Press 1978

–. *Global Technopolitics: The International Politics of Technology and Resources.* Pacific Grove, CA: Brooks/Cole 1989

Plant, G. 'Institutional and Legal Responses to Global Environmental Change.' In *Global Environmental Change and International Relations*, eds. I. Rowlands and M. Greene, 122-44. London: Macmillan and Millenium 1992

Pollack, A. 'Commission to Save Whales Endangered, Too.' *New York Times*, 18 May 1993

Porter, G., and J.W. Brown. *Global Environmental Politics*. Boulder, CO: Westview Press 1991

Princen, T., M. Finger, and J. Manno. 'Nongovernmental Organizations in World Environmental Politics.' *International Environmental Affairs: A Journal for Research and Policy* 7, 1 (1995):42-58

Prins, G. 'Politics and the Environment.' *International Affairs* 66, 4 (1990):711-30

Pryor, K. and K. Norris, eds. *Dolphin Societies: Discoveries and Puzzles*. Berkeley: University of California Press 1991

Ray, J. 'The Abolition of Slavery and the End of International War,' *International Organization* 43, 4 (1989):406-39

–. *Global Politics*. 6th ed. Boston: Houghton Mifflin 1995

Rickard, L.S. *The Whaling Trade in Old New Zealand*. Auckland: Minerva 1965

Rittberger, V., ed. *Regime Theory and International Relations*. Oxford: Clarendon Press 1993

Rose, T. *Freeing the Whales: How the Media Created the World's Greatest Non-Event*. New York: Birch Lane 1989

Rosenau, J. *Turbulence in World Politics: A Theory of Change and Continuity*. Princeton, NJ: Princeton University Press 1990

–, and E.-O. Czempiel, eds. *Governance Without Government: Order and Change in World Politics*. Cambridge: Cambridge University Press 1992

Ross, G. *Arctic Whalers, Icy Seas: Narratives of the Davis Strait Whale Fishery*. Toronto: Irwin 1985

Rowlands, I. 'Environmental Issues in World Politics.' In *Dilemmas of World Politics: International Issues in a Changing World*, eds. J. Boylis and N. Rengger, 287-309. Oxford: Clarendon Press 1992

Ruggie, J.G. 'Collective Goods and Future International Collaboration.' *American Political Science Review*, LXVI, 3 (1972):874-93

–. 'International Responses to Technology: Concepts and Trends.' *International Organization* 29 (1975):557-84

Sagasti, F., and M. Colby. 'Eco-Development Perspectives on Global Change from Developing Countries.' In *Global Accord: Environmental Challenges and International Responses*, ed. N. Choucri, 175-204. Cambridge, MA: MIT Press 1993

Sager, E. *Seafaring Labour: The Merchant Marine of Atlantic Canada, 1820-1914*. Montreal and Kingston: McGill-Queen's University Press 1989

Sagoff, M. 'On Preserving the Natural Environment.' *Yale Law Journal* 81 (1974):205-67

Said, A.A., C. Lerche, and C. Lerche, Jr. *Concepts of International Politics in Global Perspective*. 4th ed. Englewood Cliffs, NJ: Prentice Hall 1995

Sand, P.H. 'International Cooperation: The Environmental Experience.' In *Preserving the Global Environment: The Challenge of Shared Leadership*, ed. J. Tuchman Mathews, 236-79. New York: W.W. Norton 1991

–. *Lessons Learned in Global Environmental Governance*. Washington, DC: World Resources Institute 1990

–. *Marine Environment Law in the United Nations Environment Programme: An Emergent Eco-regime*. London: Tycooly 1988

Sands, P. 'Enforcing Environmental Security: The Challenges of Compliance with International Obligations.' *Journal of International Affairs* 46, 2 (1993):367-90

Sanger, C. *Ordering the Oceans: The Making of the Law of the Sea.* Toronto: University of Toronto Press 1987

Scarce, R. *Eco-Warriors: Understanding the Radical Environmental Movement.* Chicago: Noble 1990

Scarff, J.E. 'Ethical Issues in Whale and Small Cetacean Management.' *Environmental Ethics* 2 (1980):241-79

–. 'The International Management of Whales, Dolphins and Porpoises: An Interdisciplinary Assessment.' *Ecology Law Quarterly* 6 (1977):323-638

Scheffer, V.B. 'How Much is a Whale's Life Worth Anyway?' *Oceanus* 32 (1989):241-79

Schell, J. *The Fate of the Earth.* New York: Knopf 1982

Schevill, W., ed. *The Whale Problem: A Status Report.* Cambridge, MA: Harvard University Press 1974

Schmidtz, D. 'When is Original Appropriation Required?' *Monist* 73, 4 (1990):504-18

Schmitter, P. 'Change in Regime Type and Progress in International Relations.' In *Progress in Postwar International Relations,* eds. E. Adler and B. Crawford, 89-127. New York: Columbia University Press 1991

Schneider, J. *World Public Order of the Environment: Towards an International Ecological Law and Organization.* Toronto: University of Toronto Press 1970

Schriver, N. 'International Organization for Environmental Security.' *Bulletin of Peace Proposals* 20, 2 (1989):113-22

Sebenius, J. 'Designing Negotiations Toward a New Regime: The Case of Global Warming.' *International Security* 15, 4 (1991):110-48

–. *Negotiating the Law of the Sea.* Cambridge, MA: Harvard University Press 1984

Sewell, James. *Functionalism and World Politics.* Princeton, NJ: Princeton University Press 1966

Shue, H. 'The Unavoidability of Justice.' In *The International Politics of the Environment: Actors, Interests, and Institutions,* eds. A. Hurrell and B. Kingsbury, 373-97. Oxford: Clarendon Press 1992

Sikkink, K. 'Human Rights, Principled Issue-Networks, and Sovereignty in Latin America.' *International Organization* 47, 3 (1993):411-41

Simmons, I.G. *Changing the Face of the Earth: Culture, Environment, History.* Oxford: Basil Blackwell 1989

Singer, Peter. *Animal Liberation.* New York: New York Review 1973

Slurink, P. 'Paradox and Tragedy in Human Morality.' *International Political Science Review* 15, 4 (1994):347-78

Small, G. *The Blue Whale.* New York: Columbia University Press 1971

Smith, H.D. 'The Development and Management of the World Ocean.' *Ocean and Coastal Management* 24 (1994):3-16

Soroos, M. 'Ecology and the Time Dimension in Human Relationships.' In *The Global Predicament: Ecological Perspectives on World Order,* eds. D. Orr

and M. Soroos, 337-43. Chapel Hill, NC: North Carolina University Press
1979

–. 'Global Interdependence and the Responsibilities of States: Learning from
the Japanese Experience.' *Journal of Peace Research* 25, 1 (1988):17-29

Spencer, L. 'The Not-so Peaceful World of Greenpeace.' *Forbes* 148 (11
November 1991):174-81

Springer, A. 'International Environmental Law After Rio: The Continuing
Search for Equity.' *Ethics and International Affairs* 7 (1993):115-30

Stackpole, E. *Whales and Destiny: The Rivalry Between America, France, and
Britain for Control of the Southern Whale Fishery, 1785-1825.* Amherst, MA:
University of Massachusetts 1972

–. *The Sea-Hunters: The New England Whalemen During Two Centuries, 1635-
1835.* Philadelphia: Lippincott 1953

Stairs, K., and P. Taylor. 'Non-Governmental Organizations and the Legal
Protection of the Oceans: A Case Study.' In *The International Politics of the
Environment: Actors, Interests, and Institutions,* eds. A. Hurrell and B. Kings-
bury, 110-41. Oxford: Clarendon Press 1992

Starbuck, A. *History of the American Whale Fishery, From Its Earliest Inception
to the Year 1876.* 2 vols. New York: Argosy-Antiquarian 1964

Stein, A. *Why Nations Cooperate: Circumstance and Choice in International
Relations.* Ithaca, NY: Cornell University Press 1990

Stewart, F., ed. *In the Presence of Whales: Contemporary Writings on the Whale.*
Vancouver: Whitecap 1995

Stoett, P. *Atoms, Whales, and Rivers: Global Environmental Security and International Organization.* Commack, NY: Nova Science Publishers 1995

–. 'Global Environmental Security, Energy Resources and Planning: A Framework and Application.' *Futures: The Journal of Forecasting, Planning and
Policy* 26, 7 (1994):741-58

–. 'International Politics and the Protection of Great Whales.' *Environmental
Politics* 2, 2 (1993):277-302

Strange, S. '*Cave! hic dragones:* A Critique of Regime Analysis.' *International
Organization* 36, 2 (1982):479-96

Strong, A.E. 'Greater Global Warming Revealed by Satellite-Derived Sea-Sur-
face-Temperature Trends.' *Nature* 338 (1989):642-5

Swaney, J., and P. Olson. 'The Economics of Biodiversity: Lives and
Lifestyles.' *Journal of Economic Issues* XXVI, 1 (1992):1-26

Taylor, P. *Respect for Nature: A Theory of Environmental Ethics.* Princeton, NJ:
Princeton University Press 1986

Teclaff, L., and A. Utton, eds. *International Environmental Law.* New York:
Praeger 1974

Thomas, J., and R. Kastelein, eds. *Sensory Abilities of Cetaceans: Laboratory
and Field Evidence.* New York: Plenum 1990

Tinker, S.W. *Whales of the World.* Honolulu: Bess 1988

Tobias, M. *World War III: Population and the Biosphere at the End of the Millennium.* Sante Fe, NM: Bear and Company 1994

Tolba, M.K., ed. *Evolving Environmental Perceptions: From Stockholm to Nairobi.*
Toronto: Butterworths 1988

Tonnessen, J., and A. Johnsen. *The History of Modern Whaling.* Trans. R. Christophersen. Los Angeles: University of California Press 1982

Vaahtoranta, T. 'Atmospheric Pollution as a Global Policy Problem.' *Journal of Peace Research* 27, 2 (1990):169-76

van der Woude, R., and A. Van Wijngaarden. *Animals in Danger: A Study of Certain Mammal Species Threatened with Extinction in Europe.* Brussels: Council of Europe 1969

VanderZwaag, D. *Canada and Marine Environmental Protection: Charting a Legal Course Towards Sustainable Development.* London: Kluwer 1995

von Moltke, K. 'International Commissions and Implementation of International Law.' In *International Environmental Diplomacy: The Management and Resolution of Transfrontier Environmental Problems,* ed. J. Carroll, 87-93. New York: Cambridge University Press 1988

Wapner, P. 'Politics Beyond the State: Environmental Activism and World Civic Politics.' *World Politics* 47 (1995):311-40

Ward, H. 'Game Theory and the Politics of the Global Commons.' *Journal of Conflict Resolution* 37 (1993):203-35

Waters, S. 'Non-consumptive Utilisation of Marine Mammals in Canada: International and National Regulation.' In *Canadian Ocean Law and Policy,* ed. D. VanderZwagg, 141-72. Toronto: Butterworths 1992

Watson, Lyall. *Sea Guide to Whales of the World.* New York: E.P. Dutton 1981

Watson, P., and W. Rogers. *Sea Shepherd: My Fight for Whales and Seals.* New York: W.W. Norton 1982

Watt, K. *Ecology and Resource Management.* New York: McGraw-Hill 1968

Webb, R.L. *On the Northwest: Commercial Whaling in the Pacific Northwest, 1790-1967.* Vancouver: UBC Press 1988

Weber, P. *Abandoned Seas: Reversing the Decline of the Oceans.* Worldwatch Paper 116. Washington, DC: Worldwatch Institute 1993

–. 'Facing Limits in Oceanic Fisheries.' *Natural Resources Forum* 18, 4 (1994):292-303

–. 'Protecting Oceanic Fisheries and Jobs.' In *State of the World 1995,* ed. L. Brown, 21-37. London: Earthscan 1995

Weisman, S. 'Whale: Food For Deep Thought, or Just Food?' *New York Times,* 4 April 1992

Weiss, E.B. *In Fairness to Future Generations: International Law, Common Patrimony and Intergenerational Equity.* Dobbs Ferry, NY: Transnational 1989

–. 'The Planetary Trust: Conservation and Intergenerational Equity.' *Ecology Law Quarterly* 11, 4 (1984):495-581

–, D.B. Magraw, and P.C. Szasz. *International Environmental Law: Basic Instruments and References.* Dobbs Ferry, NY: Transnational 1992

Westing, A. 'Biodiversity and the Challenge of National Borders.' *Environmental Conservation* 20, 1 (1993):5-6

Whalemen's Shipping List and Merchant's Transcript. Various issues. New Bedford, MA, 1854

Wilkinson, D. 'The Use of Domestic Measures to Enforce International Whaling Agreements.' In *Managing the Commons,* ed. J. Baden, 96-111. San Francisco: W.H. Freeman 1977

Willetts, P., ed. *'The Conscience of the World': The Influence of Non-Govern-mental Organisations in the UN System.* Washington, DC: Brookings 1996

Winn, H.E., and B.L. Olla, eds. *Behaviour of Marine Mammals: Current Per-spectives in Research. Volume Three: Cetaceans.* New York: Plenum 1979

Winner, L. 'Kill the Whales?' *Technology Review* 97 (November-December 1994):74

Young, O. *Compliance and Public Authority: A Theory with International Appli-cations.* Baltimore: Cambridge University Press 1979

–. 'The Effectiveness of International Institutions: Hard Cases and Critical Variables.' In *Governance Without Government: Change and Order in World Politics,* eds. J. Rosenau and O. Czempiel, 160-92. New York: Cambridge University Press 1992

–. *International Cooperation: Building Regimes for Natural Resources and the Environment.* Ithaca, NY: Cornell University Press 1989

–, and G. Osherenko, eds. *Polar Politics: Creating International Environmental Regimes.* Ithaca, NY: Cornell University Press 1993

–, et al. 'Subsistence, Sustainability, and Sea Mammals' *Ocean and Coastal Management* 23 (1994):117-27

Yutaka, H. 'The Whaling Industry in Japan's Economy.' In *The Whaling Issue in U.S.-Japan Relations,* eds. J. Schmidhauser and G. Totten, 82-114. Boulder, CO: Westview Press 1978

Zacher, M. 'The Decaying Pillars of the Westphalian Temple: Implications for International Order and Governance.' In *Governance Without Government: Order and Change in World Politics,* eds. J. Rosenau and E.-O. Czempiel, 58-101. Cambridge, MA: Cambridge University Press 1992

Personal Correspondence

This work has benefited greatly from the generosity of many interviewees and recipients of my mail, faxes, and e-mail who managed to find the time to reply to me. Below is a partial list of those who provided assistance in my inquiry; I apologize to those whose names I have missed. I am espe-cially grateful to Dr. Ray Gambell, secretary of the IWC, for taking the time to respond to my many questions.

Mohammed Amour Al-Barwani, Fisheries Adviser, IWC Commissioner for Oman, Oman

Rubens Antonio Barbosa, Brazilian Ambassador to the United Kingdom, London, England

Jim Beckett, Director, Fisheries Research, Government of Canada, Ottawa, Ontario, Canada

John Bermingham, Staff Reporter, *Province,* Vancouver, British Columbia, Canada

Nathalie Billens, Secretary, Social Policy Service, International Union for the Conservation of Nature and Natural Resources, Switzerland

Kim Blankenbekar, Foreign Affairs Specialist, Office of International Affairs, National Marine Fisheries Service, National Oceanic and Atmospheric

Administration, United States Department of Commerce, Silver Spring, Maryland, United States

Robert Boardman, Professor of Political Science, Dalhousie University, Halifax, Nova Scotia, Canada

Ellen Chu, Marine Biologist, University of Washington, Washington State, United States

Kevin Chu, Fisheries Biologist and Foreign Affairs Specialist, Office of International Affairs, National Marine Fisheries Service, National Oceanic and Atmospheric Administration, United States Department of Commerce, Silver Spring, Maryland, United States

John Collie, Senior Conservation Officer, Division of Environment, Mahe, Seychelles

Rafael Conde de Saro, Director General de Recursos Pesqueros, Madrid, Spain, and IWC Commissioner for Spain

Ariel Delouya, Foreign Service Officer, Environment Division, Department of External Affairs, Government of Canada, Ottawa, Ontario, Canada

Joseph Edmunds, Ambassador to the United States, Embassy of St. Lucia, Washington, DC, United States

Hennk Fischer, IWC Commissioner for Denmark since 1986, Ministry for Greenland, Prime Minister's Office, Ministry of Foreign Affairs, Denmark

Rachel Fleishman, International Affairs Officer, Office of the Deputy Under-Secretary of Defense for Environmental Security, United States Government, Washington, DC, United States

John Eli Fuller, IWC Commissioner for Antigua and Barbados

Ray Gambell, Secretary, International Whaling Commission, Histon, Cambridge, United Kingdom

Dan Goodman, Canadian delegate to the IWC, Oceans and Fisheries, Government of Canada, Ottawa, Ontario, Canada

Yeong Gong, Director, Department of Oceanography and Marine Living Resources, National Fisheries Research and Development Agency, Korea, and IWC Commissioner for Republic of Korea

Martin Harvey, Executive Officer, IWC, Cambridge, United Kingdom

N. Kleeschulte, Bundesmisterium fur Ernaehrung, Landwirtschaft und Forsten, Bonn, Germany, and IWC Commissioner for Germany

John Knaus, IWC Commmissioner for the US, US Secretary of Commerce, Washington, DC, United States

Fred Knelman, Environmental Studies Program, University of Victoria, Victoria, British Columbia, Canada

Stellan Kronvall, IWC Commissioner for Sweden since 1992, Ministry of the Environment, Sweden

Eric Lafierrere, Department of Political Science, McGill University, Montreal, Quebec, Canada

Alan Macnow, Consultant to the Japan Whaling Association, Tele-Press Associates, Inc., New York, New York, United States

Hon. J.K. McLay, IWC Commission for New Zealand, New Zealand

Charles Pentland, Department of Political Studies, Queen's University, Kingston, Ontario, Canada

Josse Truda Palazzo, President of the International Wildlife Coalition of Brazil, Brazil

Daniel Reifsnyder, Director, Office of Global Change, Bureau of Oceans and International Environmental and Scientific Affairs, Government of the United States, Washington, DC, United States

Philippe Sands, Director, Foundation for International Environmental Law and Development, London, United Kingdom

Rafael Conde de Saro, Director general de Recursor Pesquero, Ministry of Agriculture, Spain; Chairman of IWC Subcommittee on Aboriginal Subsistence Whaling 1994; same, Committee on Small Cetaceans 1993

Rolland Schmitten, United States Department of Commerce, Silver Spring, Maryland, United States

Mari Skare, Royal Ministry of Foreign Affairs, Oslo, Norway

Laurent Stefanini, Conseiller des Affaires Étrangères, Sous-Directeur de l'Environnement et des Cooperations Sectorielles, Ministere des Affaires Étrangères, Paris, France; IWC Commissioner for France

G. Troian, Director General, Ministry of Foreign Affairs, Planning and Environment, Division of Environment, Republic of Seychelles

Nobuyuki Yagi, Assistant Director, Far Seas Fisheries Division, Fisheries Agency, Government of Japan, Japan

Oran Young, Professor, Institute on International Environmental Governance, Dartmouth College, Hanover, New Hampshire, United States

Stephen Young, Professor, Department of Government, University of Manchester, United Kingdom

Mark Zacher, Professor of Political Science, University of British Columbia, Vancouver, Canada

Index

Index

A.A.U., 3, 60
Advanced swimmer—DEF, 1
Age group swimming, 3, 60
American Red Cross, 3, 31, 60, 61
Arm stroke, 6, 13
  back crawl, 6-7, 9-10, 40, 52
  breast stroke, 12-13, 40, 51
  butterfly, 10-11, 40, 52, 56
  crawl, 6-9, 40
  catch, 7, 9, 57
  elementary back stroke, 57
  finish, 57
  pull, 58
  recovery, 7, 58
  stroke count, 40-41

Back crawl
  arm stroke, 6-7, 9-10, 40, 52
  kick turning, 25, 31, 57
Basic skills, 4
  relaxation, 4
  streamlining, 5, 11
Body surfing, 35-36
Breast stroke
  arm stroke, 12-13, 40, 51
  kick, 12, 15-16, 51, 55, 59
Broken distance training, 47-48, 56
Buddy system, 53, 56
Butterfly
  arm stroke, 10-11, 40, 52, 56
  dolphin kick, 17-18, 52, 56

Catch, 7, 9, 57
Certified scuba diver, 33, 57
Cold water swimming, 55
Competition, 3, 60
Cramp, 55, 57
Crawl stroke
  arm stroke, 6-9, 40
  kick, 13-15, 57
  turns, 24

Diving
  approach, 22, 23
  racing starts, 27-29

springboard, 22-23, 32
standing dive, 21-22
Dolphin kick, 17-18, 52, 56
Distance training, 41-44
Drown proofing, 57

Ear infection, 55, 59
Ear pain, 19, 57
Elementary back stroke, 57
Endurance, 26
Eustachian tubes, 19
Eye irritation, 55

Flexibility in kicking, 14, 16, 17
Flip turns, 29-31
Flutter kick, 13-15, 57
Freestyle, 58

Goals, 37
  distance, 41
  speed, 44
  stroke perfection, 40
Grab start, 28-29, 58

Hyperventilation, 19-29, 55-56, 58

Individual medley, 52
Interval training, 37-50, 58
  defined, 37-38

Jumping into water, 23

Knee pain, 55

Life saving, 3, 31-32, 53

Mouth to mouth resuscitation, 32, 59

N.A.U.I, 58, 60

Ocean swimming, 33-36
"Olympic" size pool, 58